Psychoanalytic Perspectives on Knowing and Being Known

The importance of knowing and being known is at the heart of the human experience and has always been the core of the psychoanalytic enterprise. Freud named his central Oedipal construct after Sophocles' great play that dramatically encapsulated the desire, difficulty, and dangers involved in knowing and being known. Psychoanalysis' founder developed a methodology to facilitate unconscious material becoming conscious, that is, making the unknown known to help us better understand ourselves and our relational lives, including psychic trauma, and multigenerational histories.

This book will stimulate readers to contemplate knowing and being known from multiple perspectives. It bursts with thought-provoking ideas and intriguing cases illuminated by penetrating reflections from diverse theoretical perspectives. It will sensitize readers to this theme's omnipresent, varied importance in the clinical setting and throughout life. Accomplished contributors discuss a wide variety of fascinating topics, illustrated by rich clinical material. Their contributions are grouped under these headings: Knowing through dreams; Knowing through appearances; Dreading and longing to be known; The analyst's ways of knowing and communicating; Knowing in the contemporary sociocultural context; The known analyst; and No longer known. Readers will find each section deeply informative, stimulating thought, insights, and ideas for clinical practice.

Psychoanalytic Explorations in Knowing and Being Known will appeal to psychoanalysts, psychotherapists, psychologists, psychiatrists, clinical social workers, counselors, students in these disciplines, and members of related scholarly communities.

Brent Willock, PhD, Founding President, Toronto Institute for Contemporary Psychoanalysis. Board Member, Canadian Institute for Child and Adolescent Psychoanalytic Psychotherapy; Faculty, Institute for the Advancement of Self Psychology; Advisory Board, International Association for Relational Psychoanalysis and Psychotherapy.

Ionas Sapountzis, PhD, Director of the School Psychology program and faculty member and supervisor in the Psychoanalytic Psychotherapy and Child, Adolescent and Family Psychotherapy programs, and Associate Professor at the Derner Institute, Adelphi University.

Rebecca Coleman Curtis, PhD, Supervisor of Psychotherapy with the Chinese-American Psychoanalytic Alliance and author of *Desire, Self, Mind and the Psychotherapies: Unifying Psychological Science and Psychoanalysis.*

Psychoanalytic Perspectives on Knowing and Being Known

In Theory and Clinical Practice

Edited by Brent Willock,
Ionas Sapountzis and
Rebecca Coleman Curtis

LONDON AND NEW YORK

First published 2019
by Routledge
2 Park Square, Milton Park, Abingdon, Oxon OX14 4RN

and by Routledge
52 Vanderbilt Avenue, New York, NY 10017

Routledge is an imprint of the Taylor & Francis Group, an informa business

© 2019 selection and editorial matter, Brent Willock, Ionas Sapountzis and Rebecca Coleman Curtis; individual chapters, the contributors

The right of the editor to be identified as the author of the editorial material, and of the authors for their individual chapters, has been asserted in accordance with sections 77 and 78 of the Copyright, Designs and Patents Act 1988.

All rights reserved. No part of this book may be reprinted or reproduced or utilized in any form or by any electronic, mechanical, or other means, now known or hereafter invented, including photocopying and recording, or in any information storage or retrieval system, without permission in writing from the publishers.

Trademark notice: Product or corporate names may be trademarks or registered trademarks, and are used only for identification and explanation without intent to infringe.

British Library Cataloguing in Publication Data
A catalogue record for this book is available from the British Library

Library of Congress Cataloging in Publication Data
Names: Willock, Brent, editor. | Sapountzis, Ionas, editor. | Coleman Curtis, Rebecca, editor.
Title: Psychoanalytic perspectives on knowing and being known : in theory and clinical practice / edited by Brent Willock, Ionas Sapountzis and Rebecca Coleman Curtis.
Description: Abingdon, Oxon ; New York, NY : Routledge, 2019. | Includes bibliographical references and index.
Identifiers: LCCN 2018046639 (print) | LCCN 2018049147 (ebook) | ISBN 9780429454295 (e-Book) | ISBN 9780429845284 (Pdf) | ISBN 9780429845277 (ePub 3) | ISBN 9780429845260 (Mobipocket) | ISBN 9781138318793 (hardback : alk. paper) | ISBN 9781138318816 (pbk. : alk. paper)
Subjects: LCSH: Recognition (Psychology) | Psychoanalysis. | Psychotherapy.
Classification: LCC BF378.R4 (ebook) | LCC BF378.R4 P79 2019 (print) | DDC 153.1/24–dc23
LC record available at https://lccn.loc.gov/2018046639

ISBN: 978-1-138-31879-3 (hbk)
ISBN: 978-1-138-31881-6 (pbk)
ISBN: 978-0-429-45429-5 (ebk)

Typeset in Times New Roman
by Newgen Publishing UK

Printed and bound in Great Britain by
TJ International Ltd, Padstow, Cornwall

Contents

About the cover		viii
List of contributors		ix
Acknowledgments		xii

Introduction	1
IONAS SAPOUNTZIS AND REBECCA COLEMAN CURTIS	

Knowing through dreams   13

1   Dreams: the known, unknown, being known, and
learning to know   15
ROBERT I. WATSON, JR.

2   The escape from alligator mom   22
ROBERT U. AKERET

3   Failure to launch: waiting to be known/dreading being known   28
STEPHEN HYMAN

4   On knowing the future   40
BRENT WILLOCK

Knowing through appearances   49

5   Secrets of eating and eating of secrets: daring to be known   51
JEAN PETRUCELLI

6   The analytic dialogue: looking at and listening to each other   59
ANITA WEINREB KATZ

vi Contents

Dreading and longing to be known   67

7 The little girl and Detective Monk   69
IONAS SAPOUNTZIS

8 I won't know you if you won't know me: irrelationship
and the benefits of bad relationships   80
MARK B. BORG, JR., GRANT H. BRENNER, AND DANIEL BERRY

The analyst's ways of knowing and communicating   87

9 Knowing and being known: the effect of the analyst's affection   89
DAN PERLITZ

10 Winnicott's true self/false self concept: using
countertransference to uncover the true self   101
MARYBETH CRESCI

11 Knowing him, knowing me   110
HARRIETTE KALEY

12 Spiritual knowing, not knowing, and being known   117
NINA E. CERFOLIO

Knowing in the contemporary sociocultural context   129

13 Income inequality and psychoanalytic practice: an unexamined
juxtaposition   131
JOHN O'LEARY

14 Invisible immigration: family building across borders and bodies   142
ANNE MALAVÉ

15 If the sons didn't know: Madoff's family business and
financial fraud   154
CLAUDIA DIEZ

16 Catfishing: the new impostor   161
DANIELLE KNAFO

Contents vii

The known analyst   175

17   The therapist revealed: who knows what, when?   177
BRUCE HAMMER

18   Dialectics of desire: longing and fear of being "known" in
the injured analyst   187
MARSHA AILEEN HEWITT

No longer known   199

19   The altered brain and the illusion of knowing   201
J. GAIL WHITE AND MICHELLE FLAX

20   The unrecognized analyst   209
JEFFREY SACKS

Concluding thoughts   218
IONAS SAPOUNTZIS

Subject index   223
Author index   225

About the cover

Photograph of the ancient temple at Hampi, Karnataka, India, featuring a bodhisattva figure (in Mahayana Buddhism, a person who is able to reach nirvana but delays doing so out of compassion in order to save suffering beings) making the Namaste gesture by which a person communicates to another: "My soul acknowledges your soul, the place where we are identical as souls." This communication creates a loop of knowing and being known between sender and receiver, connecting each with the divine.

Contributors

Robert U. Akeret, PhD, Past President, Association of Psychoanalytic Psychologists. Formerly held positions with counseling services at Columbia University and City College of New York. Psychoanalytic training, William Alanson White Psychoanalytic Institute.

Daniel Berry, RN, MHA, Assistant Director, Nursing for Risk Management at a New York City facility serving homeless and undocumented victims of street violence, addiction, and traumatic injuries.

Mark B. Borg, Jr., PhD, is a community psychologist and psychoanalyst; founding partner, The Community Consulting Group and Irrelationship Group; Supervisor of psychotherapy at the William Alanson White Institute and Pace University; Private practice, New York City.

Grant H. Brenner, MD, Faculty, Mount Sinai Beth Israel Hospital. Director, Trauma Service, William Alanson White Institute. Board member, not-for-profit Disaster Psychiatry Outreach. Private practice, New York City.

Nina E. Cerfolio, MD, Assistant Clinical Professor, Icahn School of Medicine at Mount Sinai. Board certified psychiatrist and psychoanalyst practicing in New York City. Former Chief of the Psychiatric Emergency Room and Walk-in-Clinic at St Vincent's Hospital, New York.

MaryBeth Cresci, PhD, ABPP, has been Director of Postgraduate Programs in Psychoanalysis and Psychotherapy, Gordon F. Derner School of Psychology, Adelphi University, Garden City, NY. Former President, Division 39 (Psychoanalysis), American Psychological Association, and Division of Psychoanalysis, New York State Psychological Association. Private practice, Brooklyn, NY.

Rebecca Coleman Curtis, PhD, Professor of Psychology and Director of Research, Adelphi University. Supervisor of Psychotherapy, W.A. White Institute, and National Institute for the Psychotherapies. Faculty and Director of Research, W.A. White Institute.

x Contributors

Claudia Diez, PhD, Assistant Professor (Psychiatry), Icahn School of Medicine at Mount Sinai, New York.

Michelle Flax, PhD, Supervising analyst and faculty, Toronto Institute for Contemporary Psychoanalysis. Executive and faculty member, Advanced Training Program in Psychoanalytic Psychotherapy, Toronto Psychoanalytic Society. Private Practice.

Bruce Hammer, PhD, Adelphi Society for Psychotherapy and Psychoanalysis. Founding faculty, Suffolk Institute for Psychotherapy and Psychoanalysis. Adjunct Assistant Professor, Clinical Psychology Doctoral Program, Long Island University Post.

Marsha Aileen Hewitt, PhD, Professor of Religion, Faculty of Divinity, Trinity College, and Department for the Study of Religion, University of Toronto. Her books include: *Critical Theory of Religion: A Feminist Analysis*; *Freud on Religion; Legacies of the Occult: Unconscious Communication at the Interface of Religion and Psychoanalysis*. Private practice, Toronto.

Stephen Hyman, PhD, Director, Postgraduate Program in Psychodynamic School Psychology for School Psychologists and School Social Workers, Adelphi University. Private Practice, Roslyn Heights, New York.

Harriette Kaley, PhD, Clinical Consultant, New York University Postdoctoral Program; Professor Emerita, City University of New York/Brooklyn College; Faculty, China American Psychoanalytic Alliance; Private practice, New York City.

Anita Weinreb Katz, PhD, Training and Supervising Analyst at New York University's Postdoctoral Program in Psychoanalysis and Psychotherapy, the Metropolitan Institute of Psychoanalytic Psychotherapy, and the Chinese American Psychoanalytic Alliance. Member, Institute for Psychoanalytic Training and Research. Clinical Supervisor, City University of New York.

Danielle Knafo, PhD, Professor, Clinical Psychology Doctoral Program, Long Island University Post. Faculty and Supervisor, NYU Postdoctoral Program in Psychotherapy and Psychoanalysis. Author: *The Age of Perversion: Desire and Technology in Psychoanalysis and Culture.*

Anne Malavé, PhD, Faculty and Supervisor, William Alanson White Institute of Psychiatry, Psychoanalysis, and Psychology. Executive Committee Member, Mental Health Professional Group, American Society for Reproductive Medicine.

John O'Leary, PhD, Faculty and Supervisor, William Alanson White Institute.

Dan Perlitz, MD, Supervising Psychoanalyst, Institute for Advancement of Self-Psychology, Toronto, Canada. Adjunct Lecturer, University of Toronto (psychotherapy supervision of psychiatry residents).

Jean Petrucelli, PhD, Supervising Analyst, Faculty, Director & Co-Founder of the Eating Disorders, Compulsions and Addictions Service, William Alanson White Institute. Faculty, NYU Postdoctoral Program in Psychotherapy and Psychoanalysis and Institute for Contemporary Psychology. Winner, American Board and Academy of Psychoanalysis 2016 Edited Book Award for *Body-States: Interpersonal and Relational Perspectives on the Treatment of Eating Disorders*. Private practice, NYC.

Jeffrey Sacks, DO, Assistant Clinical Professor, Psychiatry and Child Psychiatry, Mount Sinai School of Medicine. Chief Psychiatrist, supervisor of Psychoanalysis and Psychotherapy, teaching faculty, The William Alanson White Psychoanalytic Institute. Member, Paul Ricoeur Society.

Ionas Sapountzis, PhD, Associate Professor, Director of the School Psychology program, and faculty member/supervisor in the Psychoanalytic Psychotherapy and Child, Adolescent and Family Psychotherapy programs, Derner Institute, Adelphi University.

Robert I. Watson, Jr., PhD, Supervising Psychoanalyst, William Alanson White Institute; Faculty, Institute for Contemporary Psychotherapy; Clinical Associate Psychologist, Department of Psychiatry, Columbia University.

J. Gail White, PhD, Supervising Psychoanalyst and Faculty, Toronto Institute For Contemporary Psychoanalysis.

Brent Willock, PhD, Founding President, Toronto Institute & Society for Contemporary Psychoanalysis. Board Member, Canadian Institute for Child and Adolescent Psychoanalytic Psychotherapy; Faculty, Institute for the Advancement of Self Psychology; Advisory Board, International Association for Relational Psychoanalysis and Psychotherapy.

Acknowledgments

This book's inspiration emerged from some very creative brainstorming and passionate, hard work by Dr. Michael Stern (The Psychoanalytic Society of the New York University Postdoctoral Program in Psychoanalysis and Psychotherapy); Dr. Lori C. Bohm (William Alanson White Psychoanalytic Society); Professor Ionas Sapountzis (Adelphi Society for Psychoanalysis and Psychotherapy); Dr. Rhonda Sternberg (Psychoanalytic Society of the New York University Postdoctoral Program); Professor Rebecca Coleman Curtis (William Alanson White Psychoanalytic Society); Björg Sveinsdóttir (The Icelandic Association of Psychoanalytic Psychotherapy); and Dr. Brent Willock (Toronto Institute for Contemporary Psychoanalysis). Onto the thematic tree that evolved, our esteemed authors placed magnificent leaves related to the topic of *Knowing and Being Known*. Kate Hawes, Charles Bath, and the rest of the wonderful team at Routledge Press then worked diligently with us to turn this vision into a reality.

Introduction

Ionas Sapountzis and Rebecca Coleman Curtis

Knowing and being known to oneself and others has been a central theme in psychoanalysis since its inception. Freud thought that curiosity about how babies were conceived was a forerunner of curiosity later on. Knowing and not knowing were, of course, central to his theories of conscious and unconscious processes. To Freud's two fundamental instincts, Melanie Klein added the epistemophilic instinct. "Knowing" in psychoanalysis has always had emotional and non-verbal elements and is not limited to academic knowing.

But hand in hand with the desire to know and be known, to make links and feel understood and recognized, is also the fear of knowing and of being known. The former has to do with the fear of finding out and coming face to face with realities and experiences that are too threatening and destabilizing. Patients who have experienced trauma or had to go on despite repeated failures, individuals who feel disliked and avoided, and those who feel trapped in the margins of social life but are—deep down—troubled by their acts and what has happened to them, tend to avoid knowing. They do not seek to connect past and present, what was and what is, what they did or what was done to them, and where they find themselves as a result. This tendency to avoid knowing and to eschew curiosity is also seen in individuals who feel very uncertain about themselves and feel deeply threatened by the prospect of being found and reminded of their weaknesses or deficits. This is a pattern that one can see in adolescents too, for whom, as Winnicott (1963) observed, the prospect of being found "before anything is there to be found" (p. 189) is deeply threatening. And yet, seeking to know what happened and to understand experiences and reactions, enables one to develop a sense of ownership over one's behavior and to feel, as Bleiberg (2001) pointed out, that their particular reaction did not "just happen" (p. 60) to him or her.

Analysts understand that the quest to know is fraught with limitations and uncertainties. There is the infiniteness of what can be known and, therefore, the infiniteness of what will remain unknown. Side by side with the growth that comes from the effort to know and understand are the limitations that can be created by what becomes known and the different frames various types of knowing can create. Knowledge, of course, is not a static entity, nor is it the mere compilation of facts and skills. The accumulation of knowledge can contribute to experiences of feeling effective and to having access to institutions and positions that would not have been possible without achieving a high level of academic or specialized development. Knowledge, as Mitchell (1993) remarked, is contextual and constructed and always shifting and evolving. Knowing, in other words, is not about knowledge per se but about the willingness to know, the openness to know, and the desire to know and find.

Stern (2004) asked, can the "eye see itself?," pointing to the limitations of what one can see and realize about oneself. Given that one's perception of the other and what is happening is based on one's subjectivity, Stern's question can be expanded to "can one ever fully see the other?" The answer is an obvious one. The seeing eye can only see what is in front of it, and even then, what it sees and what is made out of what is being seen is affected by expectations and previous experiences, emotional states and levels of anticipation. And yet, the effort to know, the wish to know and *see* are not futile endeavors. Present in these efforts is the desire to broaden one's perspective and to feel engaged in the mystery of things. Present in such efforts is also the desire to own one's experience and reflect on what is happening to oneself and the world. The quest and desire to know are therefore based not on a narcissistic or defensive need, although these can be present, but on a desire that is based on the need to feel alive, creative and engaged, a need that is as vital as breathing, to use Bion's (1962) analogy.

This volume explores experiences of knowing and being known as they occur in psychoanalytic and psychoanalytically-based treatments. It is not an exhaustive compilation of chapters on the subject of knowing. It is an attempt to map some of the many facets of knowing and to reflect on how knowledge is affected by personal histories, relational patterns, and sociocultural contexts, what one sees and feels, and of course, what one does not know but assumes one knows. The chapters are organized into seven different sections. Although there are many differences between them, there is a similar thread running through all of them: the willingness and commitment to know and the openness to be known and to come to terms with what one does not know.

Knowing through dreams

The first section examines the role of dreams in knowing. Since ancient times, people have thought that dreams offered a way to know something about the future or something more about themselves. From its inception, psychoanalytic thinking has put a lot of emphasis on dreams and what they reveal about one's unconscious and one's experience of self and others. As Watson states in his chapter, dreams can help an analyst to explore the known, the unknown, and also "being known" and "learning to know." Dreams not only enable an analyst to explore the known, "kind of known," and unknown, but they also offer a great indication of how the analyst is experienced by the patient and the impact the analyst has on the patient. They are, as Watson puts it, spaces in the treatment where the analyst and patient meet and play with the material.

Some dreams are lengthy and turn a page (Quinodoz, 1999) and some, as Akeret states in his chapter, are dreams that individuals have dreamt at a point in their lives when they "need all the help they can get." Akeret calls these "life crisis dreams." He argues that they offer the dreamer a new way to understand and resolve the crisis he or she is facing. He presents the case of a young man whose progress over the course of treatment can be seen in four life crisis dreams. The symbols and insights the young man generated through his dreams aided the process of knowing and being known. Because dreams are not seen as real, they enable an individual to reflect on their possible meaning in the transitional, that is, in the space between the real and the imagined. Although the young man was aware of how disturbed his mother was, it was through his dreams that he was able to contemplate, share, and explore fantasies and conflicts that he had been frightened of and avoided for many years in his life.

Like Akeret, Hyman provides a moving account of how a young man's ability to present and analyze dreams helped him to confront conflicts and begin to explore his difficulty with separation, individuation, and moving into adulthood. Hyman calls the difficulty young men and women experience in moving on "failure to launch." He reviews the sociocultural dynamics that have contributed to an ever-growing trend in our times of postponing or delaying adulthood. Working with these young clients can be difficult because they are dependent on others and often effectively mask their self-defeating patterns under a blasé, dissociative attitude. Confronting them with the consequences of their acts is not helpful. What is helpful is finding the space to offer them a fresh perspective on their mental functioning. That space can be created through the narration of dreams. For the young man in Hyman's chapter, dreams became his pathway to knowing himself and coming to terms with what was crippling him. They tapped into his creativity and his ability to articulate in the transitional and make sense of himself and his struggles.

Willock explores a different kind of knowing through dreams. He presents a lengthy dream of his own in which he dreamt that he discussed two cases at length with a group of colleagues. Willock's dream feels quite real. Only his later comments make it clear how lengthy and evolving the dream was. This speaks to how enlivening and absorbing dreams can be. It is a dream that makes Willock more aware of his patients' needs and difficulties and also of his own experiences and longings in working with them. His patients in the dream all yearn to be reassured that they will be "alright." It is a wish for a future when they will feel less persecuted and more connected to and received by others. The latter, as the dream indicates, is a wish analysts are likely to have as well.

These chapters convey how dreams can make one more attentive to aspects of experience that were previously not in awareness. They can offer a perspective as to how treatment unfolds and the ways the two participants experience themselves and each other. Dreams have the capacity to reveal what was experienced but has remained unthought or dissociated. They have the capacity to surprise us and remind us and invite us to pay attention. They also have the capacity to help us develop a better understanding of ourselves and others.

Knowing through appearances

The issue of what can be known and what is or remains hidden by the way one presents oneself is explored in the next two chapters. Petrucelli focuses on eating disorders. Persons with these disorders often keep their problem secret. This makes them prone to live "a double life of sorts." Underneath eating rituals and behaviors that are kept secret, underneath the starving, binging, and purging are "unlinked," dissociative states of mind. Petrucelli believes that what is dissociated is the knowledge of the secret that is being kept. Bodily symptoms are used to mask emotions and compensate for the difficulty in mentalizing. Symptoms maintain a state of mind full of fantasies and possibilities without acknowledging or facing "what feels unbearable." Paradoxically, the void created by what feels unbearable and is thus excised from knowing becomes an experience. Eating nothing and feeling nothing become, in such cases, a form of feeling something, but it is a form of feeling something by numbing oneself and by keeping oneself from feeling the lack of close relationships. Petrucelli maintains that in allowing the therapist to know their secret, clients allow for change. For that to happen, however, therapists need to tolerate ambiguity and uncertainty and remain keyed to their own experiences of being "in and out of sync." They need to be attentive to shifts in their self- and body-states and the collision of their "dissociative lapses" with those of their patients.

Katz tackles how one views oneself and what one finds in oneself by addressing a client's appearance and what her style of presentation revealed about her internal world. She focuses on what appearances convey about one's psychic state and way of being. She presents the case of a young female patient with an unkempt appearance that conveyed, according to Katz, her discomfort and ambivalence related to being looked at. The young woman had felt unattractive since a facial injury at the age of two and a half had left her lip "hanging" until adolescence when cosmetic surgery was possible. Even though her face was restored, the emotional scar of feeling repulsive and unlikable to others and, perhaps, to her own mother, remained present underneath her unkempt, messy appearance. Gradually, under the maternal gaze of her "fashionista analyst," as the young woman called Katz, and with the growing realization that she was seen and liked, her comfort with herself and her body improved and she began to attend to her own appearance.

Common to these two chapters is the role of the analyst. In both cases, they did not simply comfort and support their young clients but were able to see how fearful they were at the prospect of being seen by others and also how dismissive they were of themselves. Both analysts looked at what felt unbearable to these young women and noticed not just what was missing and what they could not fathom and own, but also how they strove to preserve something through their acts of self-negation. It was their attunement and sensibility to the agony of these two young women that made it possible for their clients to feel less threatened and invaded by their gaze. To paraphrase Winnicott (1967), the two young women looked at their analysts and in their encouraging, facilitating gaze, they began to see a reflection of what they could evoke and how likable they were.

Dreading and longing to be known

Two chapters address the conflict between longing to be known and the dread of being known and even of knowing. Conflict between the wish and the dread of being known is addressed by Sapountzis. He tells the story of a nine-year-old female patient who says very little but comes into his office and makes an enormous mess that requires fifteen minutes to clean up. Sapountzis experiences her as a girl who is very troubled by her perception of herself and convinced that she is unlikable and not good enough. Creating chaos and eliciting bewilderment in others offered her a refuge from the prospect of being seen and understood. Underneath the fear and rebellion that fueled her confusing acts, there was also a wish to have her gestures acknowledged. Reversing perspectives and looking for the longing underneath the acts of such children can enable therapists to tolerate the chaos they create and to form a relationship with them. Acting as if the sessions did not mean much to her and trying not to reveal much about her thoughts and emotions, the young girl did communicate that she found her sessions valuable by coming on time, never missing a session, and being very attentive to her therapist's well-being. She moved away before the end of high school but called years later to resume treatment. This act of acknowledgment on her part was tempered by the reality of the ongoing struggles she had had in life that had resulted in several hospitalizations. Sapountzis questions the value of the treatment that was offered and the meaning the young girl found in her sessions with him.

Borg, Brenner, and Berry focus on the difficulty adults have in being intimate in relationships. These patients are involved in "irrelationships." This term, the authors explain, refers to relationships in which the way partners relate to each other is based not only on each other's needs and the reactions each one elicits in the other, but also on the way they related to their caretakers when they were young. This type of relationship tends to occur when individuals feel overwhelmed by the anxiety they experience in intimate relationships. This is not simply a case of transference. Rather, it is a case of enacting with each other what felt "safe," what helped to lessen their anxiety and sense of responsibility. The authors present the case of a couple who enacted in their relationship the roles they had played in their families of origin. According to Borg et al., what the two clients transferred to their relationship was not merely a pattern of relating to each other but a defense against feeling and, one could add, a defense against knowing.

The analyst's ways of knowing and communicating

The analyst's ways of knowing and communicating are addressed in four chapters. Perlitz looks at the central role of the therapist's affection in treatment. He stresses the importance of the therapist's capacity for "affectionate understanding." This stance involves more than empathic understanding. Perlitz states that the analyst's capacity to acknowledge his or her affection toward the patient "enhances the psychoanalytic process" and broadens the analyst's range of experiences. He describes the deepening of the analytic process that occurred when a patient trusted him enough to tell him that she had erotic feelings for him, and his failure to deepen the analytic process when he found that he had never developed feelings of affection for a suicidal patient.

Cresci reviews Winnicott's ideas of the true and false self and states that they enabled her to see potential self-states of her patients. She describes a patient whose false self focused on his failings and the need to take care of others. She advocates that therapists need to look for the better inner qualities of the person that are obscured by an outer layer of defensiveness. To Cresci, pairing the true/false self-paradigm with countertransferential reactions provides a therapist with a good explanation for his or her negative counter-transference. That countertransference is often a reaction to the patient's false self. Being mindful of that dynamic can help analysts make better sense of their reactions and to realize that they may be primarily reacting to the patient's defensive negative self.

In her description of her work with an elegant, sexually active man, Kaley offers a lively account of how she came to know a lot about herself through her effort to understand him. In listening and reacting to his provocative stories, Kaley came to realize aspects about herself she had not been aware of before. To her surprise, she realized that her reactions to practices and acts that felt repugnant to her revealed an "unexpected self-righteous prejudice." She came to realize that her recurring thought that the patient would be better off with a gay male analyst served simply to mask her anxiety.

Cerfolio explores spiritual knowing. She was shaken and awed when a humpback whale poked its head out of the water without creating a single ripple fifteen feet away from her paddleboard to get a better look at what Cerfolio was doing. This "otherworldly experience" of seeing the humpback looking at her and being so gentle and graceful left Cerfolio transformed. She sensed a great power, a protective embrace, as if from an attuned mother. The encounter moved Cerfolio from submitting "to a defensive illusion of being superwoman" who goes to Chechnya as a humanitarian worker, to surrendering to a new sense of profound interconnectedness with something larger than herself. Her patient commented on her spiritual transformation and pointed out that she seemed more serene and peaceful. Unlike in earlier sessions when Cerfolio's calmness seemed to irritate him, her newly found "equanimity" was "comforting" to him and he became less reactive in his sessions.

Knowing in the contemporary sociocultural context

Four chapters focus on the growing emphasis within the psychoanalytic literature on contemporary sociocultural contexts. O'Leary explores the income inequality. With the exception of those working in clinics and hospitals, the profession rarely draws patients who are not in the top 20 percent of income in the United States. Furthermore, it is difficult for those not in this group, who are often minorities, to get psychoanalytic training. This is a fact about which many psychoanalysts tend to not think. Also rarely acknowledged is how economic considerations can influence treatment and predispose therapists to tolerate or not tolerate some client behaviors. O'Leary provides examples of how knowledge of extreme wealth and poverty can affect a therapist's feelings in treatment. It is an issue most analysts rarely acknowledge, but one that has implications for treatment, including the analyst's capacity to confront enactments and maintain boundaries.

Related to the issues of wealth and the skewed perceptions it can create is Diez's chapter on what Bernie Madoff's sons knew about his fraudulent Ponzi scheme. Although they worked in the family business for years, both sons claimed they did not know what was happening. But as Diez points out, both were known to have had access to information that might have stimulated their curiosity. The failure to know and the failure to seek to know were acts of denial and self-protection that extended to the entire family and helped them to avoid confronting the fraud they were involved in and benefitting from. Faced with the prospect of a truth that was too terrible to entertain, both sons opted to go on denying whatever doubts and uneasiness they experienced. Their determination to not know kept their uncertainties in check for years but had tragic consequences, leading to one son's suicide and perhaps precipitating the death of the second son from a cancer recurrence.

Daniel Knafo also tackles the issue of deceit in contemporary Western culture by reviewing the recent phenomenon of "catfishing"—the misrepresentation of oneself on Internet dating sites. Most people who post online profiles do a little lying, Knafo states. Catfishing goes beyond this kind of misrepresentation in which men lie about their income and height and women about their age and weight. It involves trying to trick another person into desiring them by adopting or creating a different identity. According to Knafo, the degree to which catfishing is conscious and manipulative or unconscious and defensive can only be determined on a case-by-case study. Catfishing takes place along a continuum of self-deception from loneliness and is related to narcissistic vulnerability. The longing that propels one to engage in this practice can take the form of "psychopathic and callous trickery" in extreme cases. Therapists working with clients engaged in catfishing need to be mindful of the "painful gap" between the real and ideal self and work to help patients to accept and recognize the rejected, inferior parts of themselves.

The fourth chapter in this section deals with the issue of adoption and third-party reproduction. In the ever-evolving world of family building, knowing and being known are associated with open and closed adoptions as well as with arrangements of sperm, egg and embryo donation and gestational surrogates that may be known and open to allow for self-disclosure of origins or that are not known and remain secret. The drive to have a child is so profound that it propels people with fertility difficulties to "build families in territory dominated by issues of not knowing or being known." Malave calls this trend *invisible immigration*: invisible because personal identity may not be apparent and origins may be hidden and inaccessible, and immigration because of the impact of "this local and global movement of people and parts of people." In these new family types, therapists must deal with stresses, fears, and feelings of inferiority. The family may be hyper-vigilant about secrets. Learning to tolerate uncertainty and knowing that we are all similar and different and need to be known in this way are useful concepts in these treatments.

The known analyst

Self-disclosure has long been a topic of controversy in psychoanalysis. What patients know about analysts, how analysts come to be experienced and known by their patients and how analysts experience themselves through the reactions of patients are addressed in two chapters. Hammer explores the impasse that occurs when therapists are not mindful of their own transference and their difficulty in tolerating aspects of patients. This is the classical view of countertransference, but Hammer looks at this phenomenon from the perspective of clients' reactions to therapists' omissions, and how the *therapists' reactions to their clients' reactions* can facilitate or hinder treatment. He points to the possibilities that unfold when patients recognize therapists' self-serving, defensive reactions and the latter are able to acknowledge what patients have noticed. In such moments, patients and therapists can experience each other and themselves through the other, a process that can be transformative for both participants.

Hewitt looks at the challenge of self-disclosure when a therapist's illness interrupts treatment. She makes the case that contrary to the more traditional view, patients find this information reassuring and affirming. Disclosing to patients the cause for the interruption is a step that helps prevent the mystification of analysis and the privileging of theory over actual experience. Hewitt reviews the arguments for and against disclosure. She takes the position that one needs to make this decision based not on theories or even on a case-by-case analysis, but on "basic humanity." Having her husband call her clients to inform them about the reasons for the treatment interruption was an act that could make one pause at the possible ramifications of the unexpected introduction of her spouse into the client–therapist relationship. But without a single exception, all patients appreciated receiving the call and being treated with the "respect and courtesy" and, one can add, care they deserved. The patient–therapist relationship is not that one-sided after all. It is a personal relationship built on trust and growing recognition of the other. These are elements that need to be protected and treated with respect.

No longer known

Two chapters address the illusion of knowing, especially when dealing with clients who no longer know the people they once knew and no longer remember what once was. White and Flax describe the difficulty of holding onto the person we knew when catastrophic brain illnesses change the way the person knows and relates to us. Being "present with the absent other" enables us to face the discontinuity we experience and at the same time hold on to the constancy we shared. These continuities can take many forms, from drinking tea with a 96-year-old patient at the same time and place to the thoughtfulness of a male patient who, prior to taking his wife who is in the advanced stages of Alzheimer to their granddaughter's birthday party, makes sure to arrange for a hairdresser to visit the house because his wife was always mindful of her appearance. These gestures reflect a wish to honor and be attentive to the essence of the person who is not the same anymore even though that person may have no memory of what once was. They also reflect a wish to acknowledge the relationship, what the person brought to one's life and what was made possible because of him or her.

Sacks describes the fascinating case of a dissociative patient with a history of self-harming who did not come for her appointment. On his telephoning, she claimed she had no idea who he was and said that she had never been in analysis with him. She eventually came back to treatment with the help of her husband, but remembered nothing of it. Sacks explores this obliteration of the treatment and of knowing from a dialectical perspective on the ongoing struggle for recognition and the inevitable misrecognition that is present in our efforts to see and recognize the other. He uses Ricoeur's work to process the experience of asymmetry in his relationship with this patient and warns analysts to be mindful of it in their treatments. For Sacks, the potential for misrepresentation is present in any encounter. When it occurs, it may signal an opportunity to reconceptualize one's understanding of the patient. Although it is easy to look at the situation as involving a woman in a deteriorating condition, the issue of how visible or invisible, or known and not known one is, is present in every case. One only has to ask: what do clients do after sessions end? What do they remember and what do they know? What do they recognize as shared? We do not like to dwell on these questions, partly because of the narcissistic threat they present and partly because we usually assume we know our patients. That, according to Sacks, may well be a fallacy.

Concluding remarks

The chapters in this book build on a century of thought and experience about knowing and being known in psychoanalysis. They bring refreshing insights into these processes. They point to the infiniteness and the limitations of knowing. They offer a glimpse of the multiple meanings, different forms, and levels of knowing that can emerge and become topics for exploration in a psychoanalytic or psychodynamic treatment. As the numerous case illustrations attest, the experience of knowing and the limitations of what can be known, the interplay between the known and the unknown, what is and what becomes, are present in every treatment.

It only takes reading a few chapters to realize that the experience of knowing can come through dreams, statements, or acts. Knowing can manifest through something that emerges unbidden when least expected, or in the form of a sensation of something that is not shared and yet is felt through the absence or silence it creates. The experiences of knowing and of realizing can come in the form of an event that makes one pause and reflect, or in the form of an accidental encounter or a drifting thought. It can come from a moment of awe and surrender as Cerfolio experienced, a moment of realization such as Hammer, Kaley, and Sacks had, or a moment of seeking and remembering, as described by White and Flax. It can come through an internal dialogue that takes place in a dream, as happened to Willock, or through the experiences dreams can create, as in the chapters of Akeret and Watson. It can emerge through the conflicts of adolescents and their need to be held as described by Hyman and Sapountzis, or as an experience of being seen and feeling liked, as Katz and Petrucelli conveyed to their young patients. It can come in the form of feeling affectionate toward one's patient, as Perlitz realized or, in the form of recognizing as Knafo did, the longing one feels for what one cannot be and who one tries to pretend to be. It can come in the form of becoming aware of one's reaction to the falsity of a client's presentation, as Cresci did or, in the case of Borg and his colleagues, of recognizing individuals' fear to allow themselves to be intimate and vulnerable. It can come in the form of exploring the hopes and fears that are present in the invisible immigration Malave describes, and in the form of realizing the impossible and tragic predicament of Madoff's sons, as Diez demonstrates. It can also come from the realization of how fragile one is, as Hewitt conveyed so well, and also how one needs to convey to clients the respect and sensitivity they deserve. And as O'Leary reminds us, it can come any time one is willing to look at the inequalities in the sociocultural context and realize how limited and self-centered, but also how uplifting and transformative the work one does can be.

These chapters, each and every one, attest to the value of searching to know and wanting to know. They attest to the value of the work we do and how we seek to broaden through our inquiries and dialogues our horizons and our *basic humanity*. In that sense, this collection of chapters is a continuation of the vast number of books and papers that have preceded it and have contributed to the growth of all the authors as clinicians. One hopes that it will be a source of inspiration to others who might come across it. After all, the quest to know is not to achieve a final type of knowledge, a final O, to use Bion's (1965) symbol, but to become in O by being immersed and involved in what the journey brings to all and to appreciate the vistas it can open up.

References

Bion, W.R. (1962). A theory of thinking. In W.R. Bion, *Second Thoughts: Selected Papers on Psychoanalysis* (1967), pp. 110–119. Northvale, NJ: Jason Aronson.

Bion, W.R. (1965). *Transformations*. London: Heineman.

Bleiberg, E. (2001). *Treating Personality Disorders in Children and Adolescents: A Relational Approach*. New York: Guilford.

Mitchell, S. (1993). *Hope and Dread in Psychoanalysis*. New York: Basic Books.

Quinodoz, J.M. (1999). Dreams that turn over a page: Integration dreams with a paradoxical regressive content. *International Journal of Psychoanalysis*, 80: 225–238.

Stern, D.B. (2004). The eye sees itself: Dissociation, enactment and the achievement of conflict. *Contemporary Psychoanalysis*, 40: 197–237.

Winnicott, D.W. (1963). Communicating and not communicating leading to a study of certain opposites. In D.W. Winnicott, *The Maturational Process and the Facilitating Environment* (1965), pp. 179–192. Madison, CT: International Universities Press.

Winnicott, D.W. (1967). Mirror role of mother and child in child development. In D.W. Winnicott, *Playing and Reality* (1971), pp. 111–118. London: Routledge.

Knowing through dreams

Chapter 1

Dreams

The known, unknown, being known, and learning to know

Robert I. Watson, Jr.

One of the most important therapeutic acts in psychoanalysis is changing the "unknown" into the "known," and the relational process that enables this change (Petrucelli, 2010). Working with dreams is an excellent method for discovering the "unknown" and establishing a mutual working dyad essential to this process.

Dreams also aid greatly in exploring the known, being known, and learning to know. Working with patients' dreams can help them become more curious and interested in their self and to think analytically about themselves.

The following example illustrates how exploring a dream assists with a variety of these "knowing" issues, thereby deepening the therapeutic process. The patient was 35, married, a professional, living in New York City. She grew up as an only child in the United States and France. After being in treatment for three years, she told me this dream:

> It is in Paris … I'm living there and about to leave. The apartment has doubled in size. There are hundreds of things in it—everything I bought in my life. I'm picking out what I shall take with me. They are all intermixed. There is fabric, Fabergé eggs, cat figurines, all over the place. What should I pick? It's chaos. It's late. I've called a taxi to the apartment. In Paris you have to call for a taxi. I'm going to the airport. The apartment is on a terrace, so the cab is 100 feet away from the door. I have no way to get in touch with him to tell him I'm late, no way to contact him. Friends are there to help pack—helping, but not helping. They are distracted, there to give me a hand, pack, but aren't.

As in most dreams a myriad of elements can be examined and used to help the analytic work. The following are some of the "knowing" aspects of this patient's dream. First, the "Known," representing issues and symbolic signifiers of our mutual understanding of the patient's history and emotional life developed during the treatment. The major "known" aspects were the setting, Paris, and the mentioned objects. For example, the Fabergé eggs were specifically associated with her mother and the mother's need to collect prestigious material objects. Living in Paris and leaving for New York had been discussed in terms of her actual history and in terms of the symbolic self system view of herself as being a different person in New York. These clearly "known" issues were discussed in working on the dream. It was useful to review their relevance to her life and treatment.

One "Kind of Known" aspect was also present. This was the feeling of loneliness and being unaided by friends. While this issue had been discussed, it was never as clearly stated as in the dream. It proved to be important in subsequent work.

The "Unknown," new material of the dream is represented by her feeling of "chaos"—the central emotion of the dream. This was a very different way of speaking about her experience. Exploring this issue proved extremely important for the analysis to move forward.

The "Being Known" aspects of the dream had clear implications for understanding transference and countertransference, helping advance the analysis. The transferential aspect was most clearly represented by her difficulty in communicating with the taxi driver and his distance from her. We discussed this in terms of our relationship and how it could affect our work. Though it was the patient's dream, it helped me see some countertransferential blind spots. We had never discussed at length the cultural differences of being brought up in France and how it might be difficult to understand her. Her aside about having to call the taxi made it clear she needed to explain aspects of her life in France. I learned that she often dreamed in French and translated for me. Did I contribute to this distance and communication difficulty? Yes, in various ways, made clear in working with this dream.

There was also an enactment aspect to our discussing the dream (Levenson, 2009). I did not focus on the intense emotion represented by her speaking of chaos. She had to make it clear to me that she considered this the primary issue in the dream. This led to a very productive period, speaking about what she felt to be her internal and external chaos.

Overall, exploring the "known" and the "unknown" in the dream moved the analysis ahead, helped us understand each other and, with the shared experience of working on the dream, led to a greater working alliance.

Before I examine in detail the known, unknown, and being known aspects of work with dreams, I would like to emphasize that the most beneficial aspect is not the identification and clarification of these features, but the process that working on them stimulates in the analytic dyad.

Stephen Mitchell (1997) stated: "Arriving at a best guess decoding of the dream is neither possible nor desirable; what is important is engaging him (the patient) about the dream in a way that sparks and quickens his own analytic interest in himself" (p. 225). Examining the known, unknown, and being known aspects can lead patients to be more curious about themselves, more engaged in the analytic process. Dreams are excellent vehicles for patients to examine themselves with little value judgment. This work can also be a method for patients to extend curiosity about dream material into establishing ways of thinking and "learning to know" themselves.

Why think of dreams in terms of the known, unknown, and being known? Consider a dream as a painting produced by the dreamer. Can you, the outsider/listener/observer, ever completely know the painting? No, but we can discover aspects of the meaning in the painting/dream. Blechner (2001) astutely pointed out that there are many ways to slice any dream. He terms these different aspects "vectors" representing our different theoretical and technical systems. Discovering the unknown helps develop these vectors. The unknown becoming known can be seen as the most important unifying aspect of work with dreams.

Using dreams to pursue the unknown and make it known has been the focus of analytic work with dreams since Freud (1950) utilized them to uncover unconscious material via associations. Just as our psychoanalytic work has become more varied and complex, so has our use of dreams. The following two examples from the contemporary literature have very different theoretical perspectives, yet both demonstrate how working with the patient and focusing on specific vectors proved extremely productive.

First, Mitchell's (1993) relational work with Robert, who entered analysis because of a sense of inadequacy and anxiety, including limitations around sexual functioning. Two years into treatment, they were working on Robert's tendency to disclaim his resources and potency, keeping alive hope that an ideal father would rescue and confer manhood on him. Robert experienced himself in the consulting room as a frightened little boy, then had the following dream:

> I was looking out across a great expanse of flat land—an enormous plain. Way in the distance was a big mountain, very far away. As I was looking, I noticed a wisp of smoke coming from the top of the mountain, and realized that it was a volcano. As I watched, the smoke thickened and it became apparent that the volcano was about to erupt. It was so far away that I did not feel threatened, although I was fascinated. After a while a crack appeared down the sides of the volcano, and it split in two, with

the two halves falling away to reveal inside a giant ball of molten lava, reddish-orange in color. Losing its containment in the mountain, the ball began to collapse and flow down onto the plain. It was so far away that at first I still did not feel threatened, but little by little the lava began to flow across the plain in my direction. I began to get very anxious and was looking around for a way to save myself. Everything was very flat and therefore unprotected. The red-orange of the lava was a brilliant, terrifying color which began to dominate everything. I started to panic. The dream gets hazy after this, but I think there was a man who appeared and showed me a way to escape through a woods with a stream.

(p. 98)

Mitchell stated: "We lived in that dream landscape for many months" (p. 98). He viewed the dream as a tool to examine various vectors of Robert's analytic experience, especially the multiplicity and integrity of self experience. Working on the dream together, they used the color to lead back to memories of Robert's childhood bedroom and the night his father abandoned the family. This led to discussing conflicted emotions: wanting to protect his mother; being angry at her for pushing his father away; fear of and anger at the father. All of these aspects of Robert's past might have been discovered through other methods, but by working in the dream landscape they were able to "know" them, facilitating the analytic process and greatly helping Robert to see new aspects of his self. Exploring the unknown and making it known was extremely important, but it was also the experience of working together on the dream that impacted Robert's self experience and augmented his sense of efficacy.

Mitchell's emphasis on self experience and the interpersonal is only one vector that can be explored to transform the unknown into the known. Psychoanalysts who subscribe to an object relations orientation have long used dreams to help uncover the unknown (Fairbairn, 1952). Bollas (1987) gave a very interesting example of his use of dreams in working with Jonathan. This patient had great difficulty reporting thoughts, feelings, or associations, but was able to report vivid, complex dreams. He experienced them as dissociated utterances of an unknown speaker that Bollas conceptualized as a manifestation of "the other." Since Jonathan had few associations, Bollas chose the vector of the dream aesthetic, especially the setting, and its continuity over time:

He was in a desert and next to a lake. Sometimes his wife was there with him, sometimes he was alone, once he was there with his mother and his sister. In one dream, the lake was surrounded by a brick wall. He never seemed to take any notice of the lake. He reported its presence, but he never drank from it, for example, and it was the absence of this action which seemed to me more important than what was present in the dream.

(p. 74)

Bollas formulated an interpretation: Jonathan's "not taking any nourishment from the lake reflected the way he split off his needs from potential environmental gratification" (p. 74). Bollas used this and other dreams to explore how "the other" of the patient offered a good setting for nourishment but the subject could not use it. Working within this object relations framework, Bollas helped this restricted patient come to know and address issues that were holding him back in life and analysis. Working with the patient's dreams to transform the unknown into the known can be an essential aspect of analytic work and, in this case, may have been by far the most effective, efficient method.

"Being Known" by the patient is enhanced through working with dreams. There are two major components to the analyst being "known." One is the representation of the analyst in the dream material. The other is how the analyst works with the dreams.

In the dream, the analyst can be represented in various ways. There can be actual presence: "You were sitting in your chair and we were speaking." Or, "I saw you on the street." Or, "I hit you in the chest." One can have a less starring role: "You were in the room, but didn't speak."

Exploring the transference in dream material, beginning to "know" how the patient experiences the analyst, is a crucial element of the work. Bringing this material in dream form can cause less anxiety for the patient. "I thought of hitting you" can be much more difficult to report than a dream with the same content. Dreams let patients speak about the impact the analyst is having on them, and let's the dyad explore the material with less judgment, more curiosity.

There are many examples where the representation of the analyst in dreams is not so direct. These, too, can greatly aid in discovering how the patient "knows" the analyst. For example, the taxi driver in the Paris dream was the key element in opening up this patient's experience of me and how she felt at a distance and had trouble communicating.

While representations of the analyst in dreams can be great indicators of how the analyst is experienced by the patient, how the analyst works with the dream material gives the patient many indications of what the analyst is like as a person, and therefore aids the patient in knowing the analyst. What we ask about the dream, what vectors we choose to explore, are usually clear indications of what we are focused on in the work. As Mitchell (1997) points out, any reaction we have to the dream material can and will be influenced by our relationship with the patient. How we inquire, with what tone, how we formulate an interpretation, can all be great indicators to the patient of who we are in our relationship with them. The most important element is how open we are in collaborating—hearing the patient's thoughts and not being the "expert" in the knowing of the dream.

Using dreams to "know" and better understand patients is only one aspect of the work. Our curiosity can stimulate the patient's. Dreams are also great vehicles for patients to learn how to "know" themselves, try out new self systems, and formulate their thinking about themselves in a psychoanalytic way. Working with dreams can help create a psychoanalytic mind for the patient, one of the most important achievements of a psychoanalysis. Whether we think of this goal in terms of the classical concepts of Bush (2014), the relational "standing in the spaces" of Bromberg (1998), or Fosshage's (1997) "change of mentation," helping patients learn how to think differently is a primary treatment goal.

Dreams are spaces for analysts and patients to meet and, in Winnicott's sense, "play" with material. Dreams can be played with more easily than actual reports of interactions and, therefore, can lead to patients trying new ways of thinking about themselves and their interactions. Processing the dream information can help patients begin to think in a more examined way, with the patient using the analyst as a model and becoming part of the discovery process. Over time, the patient may take over more and more of the exploration, trying out their hypotheses.

John illustrates this taking a more exploratory role and using a more psychoanalytic mind. This 50-year-old man had been in treatment for a number of years, struggling with self image and fears of inadequacy. He had a very close, almost maternal, relationship with his female boss. She changed jobs, pulling away from contact with him, yet he longed for her, looking for her in places he believed she might visit. "Sharon was in the dream. I was in her proximity. So was her husband. This is a struggle for me to recount the dream, overcome the resistance. He approaches me. I hear 'You should let her go,' meaning, don't pursue her."

What was most interesting was how John worked with this fragment. He said: "These are the features of the dream: first, why is John in the dream? Could be he's an observer. Could be he's me because he has the same name. Also could be my brother or father. It's also about contact for me. Back to my decision. It's definitely my voice saying 'let go' of her. It can also be moral behavior. He could also be you. Words come from me. Though it could be someone else. No, it was me. After the dream I think I'm saying it to myself, "It's time to let go." It was like a 'stage of growth.' It's a step forward for me. This is done, a forward step. I'm saying to the self, 'This is my part of the process.' It's also very important, since it's a maternal figure."

John was able to work with the dream from an observing perspective and use his knowledge of himself and how to work with dreams to formulate an understanding, examine relational issues, and experience it as forward movement. There are many more possible vectors to explore in this dream, but it was particularly important for this dependent patient to experience his dream as being his voice and to have a positive interpretation of it.

Patients' dreams are opportunities to work with them on the known, the unknown, being known, and learning to know. They provide occasions to work together on "knowing" the patient and relating to each other through an open, shared experience. This exploration aids the psychoanalytic process and is an excellent tool that both patient and analyst can use to further the change process.

References

Blechner, M. (2001). *The Dream Frontier*. Hillsdale, NJ: Analytic Press.

Bollas, C. (1987). *The Shadow of the Object: Psychoanalysis of the Unthought Known*. New York: Columbia University Press.

Bromberg, P.M. (1998). *Standing in the Spaces: Essays on the Clinical Process, Trauma and Dissociation*. Hillsdale, NJ: Analytic Press.

Bush, F. (2014). *Creating a Psychoanalytic Mind: A Psychoanalytic Method and Theory*. London and New York: Routledge.

Fairbairn, W.R.D. (1952). *An Object-Relations Theory of Personality*. New York: Basic Books.

Fosshage, J. (1997). The organizing functions of dream mentation. *Contemporary Psychoanalysis,* 33(3): 429–458.

Freud, S. (1950). The interpretation of dreams. In J. Strachey (ed. and trans.), *The Standard Edition of the Complete Psychological Works of Sigmund Freud* (Vols. 4&5). London: Hogarth. (Originally published 1900.)

Levenson, E.A. (2009). The enigma of transference. *Contemporary Psychoanalysis,* 45(2): 163–178.

Mitchell, S.A. (1993). *Hope and Dread in Psychoanalysis*. New York: Basic Books.

Mitchell, S.A. (1997). *Influence and Autonomy in Psychoanalysis*. Hillsdale, NJ: Analytic Press.

Petrucelli, J. (ed.) (2010). *Knowing, Not-Knowing and Sort-of-Knowing: Psychoanalysis and the Experience of Uncertainty*. London: Karnac Books.

Chapter 2

The escape from alligator mom

Robert U. Akeret

> We are not only less reasonable and less decent in our dreams. but we are also more intelligent, wiser and capable of better judgement when we are asleep than when we are awake.
>
> Erich Fromm

Not all dreams have equal value. "Life crisis dreams" occur when we need all the help we can get. They can offer a whole new way to understand the crisis and start the process by which it can be resolved.

Life crises differ from everyday problems in severity, complexity, and duration. They may last days, months, even years. There is a tremendous amount at stake. It could be the fate of our marriage, our career, the way we feel about ourselves and our life. However traumatic the life crisis might be, the potential for radical personality change is never greater.

Seth was in the midst of such a crisis when he came to see me. Married only three months, he had abruptly become impotent. His wife was threatening to leave if he did not start "functioning properly." His mood swings ranged from a deep sense of worthlessness to omnipotence. He feared he was losing control and would collapse into madness, spending the rest of his life in an asylum.

A tall, soft-spoken man of 25, Seth had the haunted look of an El Greco figure. The cast of his hooded eyes, hunched shoulders, and heavy movements all suggested deep depression. To my surprise, he was a well-established filmmaker, a line of work that I associated with confident men.

"Hi. I'm Dr. Akeret. I think you know that Paul, your friend, called me to see if I had any free evening hours to work with you. He said you were a rising star in the film industry, recently married, and having sexual problems. Specifically, you are unable to maintain an erection. Is that right?"

"Yes," Seth replied. "I wonder why I ever got married. I'm so afraid of women—ever since I believed my mother was trying to poison me. I think that's why I can't maintain an erection. Might that be right Dr. Akeret?

The escape from alligator mom 23

"I guess your penis has pride," I said, tongue in cheek. "It doesn't go where it's dangerous!"

"Pride—Wow. I never thought of that. My penis has pride. You know it may also be smart," Seth said, grinning. That made me smile. He may be depressed, I thought, but he's also playful. "Paul said you helped him a lot with his sexual problems. Do you think you could help me?"

"Maybe I have already. There's no mystery about why you can't stay erect. Also, think about this. There's no such thing as an 'afraid of women' gene. You learned to be afraid of them and what you learned is not fixed in stone. It can change. So tell me, Seth, how do you cope with your fear of women?" Seth closed his eyes and seemed to be in conflict. Then he opened them.

"Fantasies—that's how I cope. I make up these stories. You see it's not just the thing with my wife that's killing me," he said, almost in a whisper. "It's my fantasies, those awful fantasies. They've come back to haunt me again."

"Tell me about them," I said.

"You don't want to hear them," he replied. "They're too ugly."

"Let me decide that, okay?" I said—mildly I thought. Seth winced, as if I had challenged his basic judgment. Clearly the duress of his impotence had made him acutely sensitive to anything resembling criticism. "You'd be surprised what I hear in here," I said gently. "Nothing human shocks me."

Seth took a deep breath and let it out slowly. "All right, you asked for it. The one that really turns me on is the Bleeding Woman fantasy. That's when I bind a naked woman in a harness and insert a glass tube into her jugular vein. Then I slip a metal pole inside her vagina, which arouses her, but as soon as she becomes aroused, she starts to squirt blood out through the neck tube. The more aroused she becomes, the faster her heart beats, the more blood squirts out of her. She is in utter terror, caught between sexual ecstasy and her imminent death. When I imagine the blood streaming down her breasts, I get really excited. I start masturbating and come with the sound of her screams ringing in my ears. I've had that fantasy since I was fourteen."

"You must have quite a mother," I said.

"What makes you say that?" he responded, looking surprised.

"Just a wild guess," I replied, with just a suspicion of a wink. "Tell me about her," I said softly.

"She almost always had a man living with her—a man she could criticize until he finally found the strength to leave. My father left when I was two. He told me once about coming home night after night, finding me hungry, strapped to a chair in filthy diapers, shit smeared all over me. She had a harness that went around my chest, over my shoulder, like you put on a bulldog, and a leash clipped to the back. She would tie the end to whatever was handy. Then she could do whatever she wanted to do. When I was around five, I was convinced she intended to poison my milk." Seth described how mother was unpredictable, alternating caresses with ungovernable rages. She had read widely in the classics of literature, philosophy, and psychoanalysis. When she found out Seth had married, she flew into an apoplectic rage. She sent his wife a letter, 100 pages long, with the stated purpose of bringing about a meeting to enlighten her about Seth's true self. He said he was "unloved and unlovable."

Four dreams

Dream 1: Abortive journey dream (5th session)

> There are a whole bunch of people and I seem to be the leader. I don't seem to have any clothes. We're in the woods trying to find a path to somewhere like a boat landing. I know the path. They don't. Several places in the path are marshy. Other places have boards as support. The path is also grown over with trees, sort of like a tunnel through the woods. I do something I've done before in dreams. I run along and jump. My feet don't touch the ground. I glide over the bad places in the path. I expect the people I'm with to be a lot more impressed than they are. There are a set of stairs going up to this boat landing. There's a nun who says we can't go up. I argue with her for a long time. I get very angry. I try to slap her, but her habit is like a Russian icon—metal cover. I don't know whether my hand is hitting metal or whether something in me is keeping me from hitting her. I cut my hand holding the metal and get furious. I tear all the stairs up so then we really couldn't go up the steps.

The dream captures the beginning of Seth's psychoanalytic journey toward separation from his mother. He battles with his mysterious, powerful, castrating mother. She is invincible, almost untouchable. His encounter with her reduces him to a raging infant who destroys the very steps that could lead to freedom and autonomy.

Seth's inability to muster strength against his mother is also related to his dissociated, unconscious need to remain with her. This crippling, paralyzing ambivalence makes separation from her impossible. The dream predicts correctly that the major work in his analysis will be resolving his complicated, destructive, yet nourishing relationship with her.

Dream 2 (74th session)

> My mother is luxuriously settling into a tub full of suds. I begin to tell her something. She breaks in, saying she wants me to repair the refrigerator. I get angry that she doesn't listen to me, that she wants me for herself.

The escape from alligator mom   25

I tell her I have a life of my own, and a wife. Now I'm angry and that makes her angry. She crawls out of the tub like an alligator and crawls up my legs, growling. I'm terrified that she is going to eat off my penis. I grab her by the hair and hold her off. I manage to wrestle her to a standing position and tip her out the window. I think I have killed her at last, but I'm not sure. She is lying on the ground in a blue kimono. The police are there, represented by the great Chinese detective, Charlie Chan. He realizes my mother's fall is not an accident. My mother begins to move. She seems to be in first-rate shape.

In this dream Seth attempts separation from his mother in the only way he knows—destroying her. He confronts her by stating he wants a life apart from her. She retaliates by turning into a castrating alligator. He is not alone. He has an ally, Charlie Chan, who sees what Seth is trying to do. Mother is as indestructible as she is destructive. What is clearly dissociated is Seth's need to remain attached to her. He cannot cut the umbilical cord. He wants separation but is not ready for it.

I remember going over the dream with Seth and asking, "Why do you think it is so difficult to separate from your mother?" He replied, "I wish I knew. Doesn't make any sense. She was so lethal, so controlling."

"What did she offer you? What did she think about your talents?" I pushed. Seth closed his eyes and was silent for what seemed like an eternity. " 'You're one in a million,' she told me, over and over. 'But you are nothing without me.' "

Dream 3 (116th session)

Somehow I am convinced to leave my loft and return to live with my mother. I do not give up my loft as I feel a possible temporary nature about this move. I arrive at my mother's with a suitcase full of clothes. She hangs them in a closet. In the next scene I am coming home from school with my blue jacket on. It has been raining so water drips from my jacket. She tells me to take off my jacket and hang it in the kitchen immediately. This makes me angry since I don't think the water was doing any real harm. I remember that I could drip water in my loft and I did it simply because I wanted to. She is being too grouchy.

In the next scene I am going to the fifth grade. I get to the corner and say to myself, "What am I doing? The whole thing is ridiculous." I almost start to cry. I don't want to be going to fifth grade. I want to be in my beautiful loft where I can paint and be happy. I go and tell mother I'm going back to New York. I say, "Do you realize I'm only in fifth grade and when I graduate I will be 31. Who will want a 31-year-old grammar school graduate?"

She brings out something that looks like a secondhand adding machine. She tells me it is a super-special kind of palette for me to use when painting. Aside from realizing that I never use a palette, I catch the note in her voice that is clearly meant to inspire guilt. I tell her I cannot accept it. If I take it and stay I have sold myself. If I take it and go I have sold myself. She acts injured. I expect her anger. She goes into the bathroom, I think to kill herself. I pack my things. She has salted my clothes in various places, making packing difficult. There are several closets full of clothes. I expect to have trouble finding everything since I am sure she has hidden things to keep me from leaving. I find everything. I begin to worry she is angry and about to come after me. I run out of the door and almost fall two floors to the street. I realize I must grasp the ladder and climb down in an orderly way to make it at all.

In this dream Seth returns home in order to discover what there is for him in his mother's world and what there is for him in the world he is creating separately from her. As in a play, in various scenes he explores and discovers he does not want to remain attached to her. He longs for the freedom of his own world, where his jacket can drip water, where he can paint and be happy. He recognizes the trap set by mother with her super-special palette, something that would greatly obligate him to her. He anticipates her anger when he rejects her, but that expectation no longer causes him to collapse. He persists in his plan to leave. Even mother's threat of suicide fails to deter him. He recognizes that too hasty a separation might be dangerous, so he grasps the ladder and climbs down in an orderly manner.

Dream 4: The Prince's sword (147th session)

There are three of us: my father, a king, a great fighter defending his kingdom; a sword master, without armor, tall, self-possessed, a teacher; and myself, the Prince. We are in a dark, cave-like place defending the kingdom against invaders who come through a cleft between some rocks. My father is on the floor of the cave fighting the invaders with a two-handed sword. The invaders are dressed in a more primitive Viking style with chainmail skirts and black leotard garments—all in a quality of disarray. My concern is that since there is to be a definite protocol of fighting, I should know the proper time for me to enter the conflict. My other concern is my sword is long enough, but rather like a tape measure. I think if I swing it hard enough, it might cut, but probably it's harmless. I ask my father if I cannot have a worthwhile sword so I can be of some real value. He gives me a long dagger, but this is far short of being any kind of effective weapon against a two-handed sword. I ask my father if the sword master cannot give me a sword. I have to ask several times, but he finally says yes. The sword master gives me a beautiful, silver-like sword that is long, trim, cleanly designed, and sharp. Its design is in perfect keeping with the image of the sword master. I realize I lack the skill of using it. I think I will ask my father if the sword master can give me lessons so I can learn to use it well.

Rather than despairing over the inevitability of castration by mother, Seth now turns to men for help in becoming potent. The invaders appear in feminine leotards, wearing impenetrable skirts, and are clearly symbolic of mother. The dream focuses on the possibility of male help in combating mother and becoming a whole man. He is limp and harmless, but wants to be a potent warrior. Father, the king, can only offer inadequate help. The sword master (his analyst) gives him the effective weapon he craves. The silver sword is beautiful, trim, cleanly designed—exactly the image of the man Seth wishes to be. He wants to be handsome, potent, incisive, and effective. Within the dream Seth realizes his wishes cannot be achieved magically. He must take lessons.

Conclusion

This chapter portrays the whole course of an analysis being lived and revealed through a series of life crisis dreams. Dreaming aids in the process of knowing and being known. Fresh dream symbols and new insights continually push the analysis along, speeding and deepening it. Seth's life crisis dreams had the structure of a film script, reflecting the fact that he is a film maker.

Years later, I received a Christmas card from Seth that he had designed. On it was a magnificent, silver sword painting, with these words: "From one sword master to another. I have been married for ten years and we have two kids. I continue to make documentary films about issues that concern me deeply. You will be happy to hear I am now making a film about how dreams have influenced world leaders throughout history."

Reference

Fromm, E. (1951). *The Forgotten Language.* New York: Rinehart.

Chapter 3

Failure to launch
Waiting to be known/dreading being known

Stephen Hyman

Failure to launch is a syndrome that brings many young adults into therapy. Self-defeating behaviors are prevalent. These patients flounder attempting to complete college or graduate school, have difficulty getting or keeping jobs, and experience commitment conflicts regarding intimate relationships. Often they live at home with worried, frustrated, confused parents who see them as lazy, manipulative, oppositional or purposely hurtful. The "children" think about getting their own apartment. This chapter discusses why they do not, indeed cannot, leave home.

Coexisting, seemingly contradictory characteristics of many late launchers are reflected in the following quotations: "I have to get my mother to understand me. She's the only one who will know how to fix me." This statement was from a 19-year-old woman struggling with depression and separation anxieties. She is "waiting to be known"—unconsciously hoping to receive the missing empathic attunement from her mother that, she feels, will give her what she needs to move forward in life. Her wish involves a rescue fantasy that disavows a self-determined life—a dynamic that creates challenges in treating delayed launchers.

The second quotation is from a 30-year-old man: "Of course I had to end the relationship. If she ever found out that I have such a low-level job and never graduated from college, she'd know what a fraud I am." These words exemplify the very mixed feelings many of these individuals have about being known. Feelings of inadequacy and insecurity are evident. Fear of failure and avoidance of shame define their relationships and constrict personal strivings in school or work. The unique sense of personal pride that accompanies successful navigation of obstacles is eliminated by defensive disengagement.

Treatment considerations must recognize the important gaps in self-awareness that hinder the development of self-direction in people who are stalled in their progression toward adulthood. As discussed by Sapountzis (2014), effective treatment for non-reflective patients enables them to examine and ultimately tolerate their conflicting, confusing emotions.

Tampering with attachment to parents upon whom young adults are dependent is no simple matter. Peter Blos (1979) writes that in families where externally-based parental validation overrides internally-based self-validation, prolonged adolescence serves the emotional purpose of averting "the crisis of a crushing realization that the world outside the family fails to recognize the imaginary (idealized) role which the child has played for almost two decades in the family. For these people one might say that their great future lies behind them when they reach the threshold of adulthood" (pp. 44–45).

Popularized examples of parent-centered childrearing include helicopter parenting and tiger mothering. These and other practices inhibit children from developing a realistic sense of self based on learning from experience.

The focus of this chapter is on treatment but clinicians and parents should be attuned to societal, economic, and cultural influences that have contributed to considerable changes in the typical pathways that lead to adulthood. Five traditionally accepted markers of maturity include: completion of education or training for a career; moving away from home; being financially independent; having intimate relationships and getting married; and having children. Over the past 40–50 years there have been dramatic changes in the age at which young adults have launched into adulthood. In the 2010 *New York Times* article 'Why Are So Many People in Their 20s Taking So Long to Grow Up?', Robin Marantz Henig (Henig, 2010) cites revealing statistics. Based on 1960 US census figures for the milestones given above, 77 percent of women and 65 percent of men indicated they had reached all five of the above markers by age 30. In 2000, fewer than 50 percent of 30-year-old women and 33 percent of men had done so. Adulthood is occurring later than ever, not only in the United States but also in most western European nations. The trend toward later attainment of the milestones of independent living provides a backdrop for us to keep in mind in our work with people in the 18–30 year old age range.

Most of today's parents didn't consider or even hear of a gap year. There is a growing trend among high school seniors and college students to take a year off from formal education to explore and experience life options before moving ahead with education, careers or marriage.

How long after you reached age eligibility did you get your driver's license? This achievement literally puts people in the driver's seat on their road to independence. Statistics compiled by the University of Michigan's Transportation Institute (2011) reveal that from 1983 to 2010 there was a steady trend of fewer 16–24 year olds getting their licenses.

What do you think the changes have been in the age of getting married? In 1970 the median age for women was 21, for men 23. By 2009 it was 26 for women, 28 for men.

As widespread as these changes are, it's often jarring and disturbing to parents faced with the reality that their 20-something child is following a timetable so different from the one they followed.

Researching these changes led psychologist Jeffrey Arnett (2000) to introduce a revision in the developmental stages leading to adulthood. He proposes a bridge stage between late adolescence and young adulthood, covering ages 18–30, which he terms emerging adulthood. He suggests that men and women in this stage are more self-focused than at any other time, less certain about their future, and more optimistic. Their optimism is often based on idealistic expectations that may not take realistic obstacles into account. It's not uncommon to hear comments like: "You can be anything you want to be. Look at Bill Gates, Mark Zuckerberg, and all the bloggers making tons of money."

For parents, educators, clinicians, and young adults, there are many questions about the long-term impact of these changes. Henig, the *New York Times* writer cited above, asked: "Is emerging adulthood a rich and varied period for self-discovery as Arnett says it is, or is it just another term for self indulgence?" (Henig, 2010). Looking at changes in progression to adulthood from a broader historical perspective, we learn that attaining milestones at a later age than in the past continues a trend that has been developing over the last century. Sociopolitical, economic, employment, technological, and educational forces accounting for this change include universal education and the widespread acceptance of the college degree as required for most higher-paying jobs resulting in financial security. In addition, medical and health advances have led to an increase in lifespan and have extended biological deadlines to a point that people in their late 30s and 40s who are just starting to have children still have enough years ahead to look forward to seeing their children grow and even to having grandchildren.

Besides these influences, psychologically-based concepts of childrearing have contributed to the general acceptance of shielding children and teens from adult responsibilities they were expected to assume in the past. Romeo and Juliet were 13 and 18 when they were depicted as protagonists in Elizabethan adult conspiracies and life responsibilities. We don't have to go back that far to realize that child labor—another force for children to assume adult responsibilities at an early age—was widespread throughout American history. It was not until 1938 that federal regulation of child labor was achieved. The Fair Labor Standards Act set minimum wages and restricted employment of children under the age of sixteen in industry.

Changing parental attitudes and expectations have played important roles in the gradual reforms that have occurred in children's lives. One of the most important voices in shaping contemporary parenting was Benjamin Spock.

A pediatrician by profession, he sought psychoanalytic training that was strongly influenced by Anna Freud's parent-child interaction work to broaden his understanding of the kinds of parenting that would reinforce healthy personality development of well-adjusted, confident children. Spock influenced the parenting of generations of Americans, and the work of current parent educators.

In his 1946 book *Baby and Child Care*, which has sold more than 15 million copies worldwide and is still in print, Spock emphasized supporting parents to trust their instincts regarding childrearing. This message was in stark contrast to the rigidly defined, authoritarian practices that were in vogue. These ideas had a receptive audience with young parents, many of whom had experienced privations and anxieties related to the Second World War.

Stressing the importance of recognizing the individual physical and emotional needs of each child, Spock and later psychodynamically-oriented parent educators encouraged parents to be more flexible in feeding and toilet-training regimens; to show more open displays of affection to children; and to support children to develop a spirit of individuality and independence.

Psychologically-based childrearing practices that stress parental nurturance of children's individuality and creativity have been criticized for encouraging parents to be too focused on making children happy and tension free. This viewpoint has been blamed for encouraging overly permissive, indulgent parenting that cultivates narcissistic, self-centered children who expect immediate gratification and have limited experience with facing the challenges in life that are critical for developing effective frustration tolerance.

A recent *New York Times* magazine article by Jessica Bennett (2017) highlighted this issue. It reported on a number of colleges that offer courses to "de-stigmatize" failure. The article quotes a Smith College leadership development specialist discussing students who are "unable to ask for help when they need it, or so fearful of failing that they will avoid taking risks at all" (p. 2). Risk-taking aversion is a frequent symptom of late launchers.

It's especially relevant for mental health professionals to recognize how popular psychological ideas about childrearing are being translated into actual parenting. Advice to parents should be sensitive to their needs as well as to the needs of their children. If we are to help children contain anxieties, develop frustration tolerance, be willing to experience failures as part of new learning, or embrace their curiosity, it's vital for parent educators to support parents in their own development of these same qualities. Mentalization-based parenting programs such as those described by Arietta Slade (1999) and Norka Malberg, Natalia Stafler, and Ellie Geater (2012) exemplify parent-centered programs that teach mothers to mentalize the needs of their young children. This support enables parents to grow and, in turn, foster their children's maturational potential.

As noted by Jeffrey Arnett, reaching adulthood at a later age is not necessarily an indication of personal maladjustment, nor a harbinger of societal decline. When we work with these late adolescents or young adults, a sensitive evaluation of causes for their behavior is required. We need to understand whether this pattern is symptomatic of psychic conflicts with separation and individuation, or a route toward adulthood that, albeit circuitous by parental standards, is guided by autonomously-based choices that afford valuable life experiences.

For young adults with a limited sense of selfhood, leaving home to go to college or for other reasons places them out of the direct range of parentally set scripts they may have resented but upon which they have become dependent. Without a reasonably stable, internal compass to guide their actions they are vulnerable to being overwhelmed by anxieties and conflicts that come with independent decision-making. Panic attacks are often reported. They leave college, returning home. Some enroll in schools near home. Some are brought into therapy.

Case example

Twenty-three-year-old John and his mother attended his first therapy session together. This was agreed upon when his mother called to make his appointment. She emphasized that although therapy was for John, she had to be involved directly since "He lies to me about everything. I can't believe anything he says. I want to be sure you get the truth about how serious his problems are."

On the phone Mrs. R explained that John flunked out of college, came home, and was currently commuting to a local college. He expected to graduate in two weeks and was accepted into a graduate school that was to begin immediately after graduation. A few days before she called me, John informed his parents that he would not be graduating because he did not complete several courses in the past year. They were furious. They and John were trying to have graduate school admission deferred until he could complete these courses.

In the first session John acknowledged his self-defeating academic patterns. He spoke of his conflicted, tense relationship between him and his parents. More striking and disturbing than the content of what John said was his detached, affectless attitude toward his dilemmas.

John said he felt confused about the events in his life but appeared unaware of potential problems until they reached a crisis point. "I'll get the work done to graduate and then everything will be fine once I begin my graduate studies," were the words he'd mouth when questions about his future were raised. His denial process was widespread. He showed very little curiosity about knowing himself. When asked what he worried about, he responded immediately that he didn't want to worry. Indeed, he was quite pleased that he was able to not worry.

In contrast to his current non-caring manner, Ms. R recalled that John had been a sensitive, caring child. She recounted how, as a two-year-old, he began to cry watching *The Lion King* in response to the lion king father dying. Through his tears he blurted out his apparent realization that, "Daddy will die someday." Upon graduation from fifth grade he sobbed: "I'm growing up too fast. I'm not a kid anymore. Life is going to be over soon." These recollections by John and his mother led me to wonder what had happened to his natural childhood capacity to be aware of the complexities of life, to worry, and to be attuned to his emotions.

During treatment, as his parents' non-empathic position became evident, I felt confused and uneasy. I questioned myself about being up to the task of working with John. I wondered if his dissociation and chronic lying were reflective of a delusional process. At times I was frustrated with his parents and John. Mostly, I wondered why John was so *not* worried.

Nancy McWilliams (2016) discusses the challenges of working with self-defeating patients. She highlights how masochistic, self-defeating patients dissociate from anxious affect with a blasé attitude and place their anxiety onto therapists. I realized I had become the repository for John's frustration and anxiety. How to offer him a fresh perspective on his mental functioning, and to help him feel what he was inducing me to feel, in a way that he could tolerate, was a significant challenge.

As I got to know John, it became evident that he was highly intelligent and articulate. Two themes emerged:

1. John felt that if he followed the path his parents set for him he'd have "a factory worker's rote, assembly line life."
2. A quote from John reflects his risk aversive approach to life: "In life you get one swing at bat. If you miss the ball or don't get a really good hit you're out forever. So when you get to bat your life depends on that one swing." Considering the rules of his "league" I could understand why he'd be very reluctant to even enter the game.

Gradually John became curious about himself and his puzzling actions in college. This curiosity was reflected in his presentation of and willingness to work on dreams. They became his pathway to knowing himself. References to dream themes and the unconscious meaning of this creative, symbolic imagery were central throughout treatment.

Dream I

An early dream was reported after we began to meet twice a week. "I'm running in the street and I got shot. I'm dying. I remember waking myself up."

(Q) "I don't know why I got shot but I was really scared."

(Associations) "When I was young I was afraid of break-ins in my house."

As we talked about the sudden, ambush-like nature of the attack, John commented, "Maybe graduate school will be overwhelming." After a brief silence he added, "That may be good that I'm a little afraid of it ... I remember after getting shot that I was scared to die but I was figuring out a way how not to. It was a strange feeling." I commented: "Although it felt strange to realize your life was literally in your hands, you did something to wake yourself up. So you did save yourself."

Dream 2

"I'm looking outside my window. Something was making the trees go into the air and explode into fireworks."

(Q) "I'm watching it happen and it felt cool, real good. Partially I knew it was a dream."

(Association): "I like fireworks. It reminds me of the 4th of July, my favorite holiday. It's for the Declaration of Independence. That was well written ... Maybe it's about my struggle with independence. I like being with friends and family but I don't want to be bland or just normal."

The violent, explosive nature of this dream seemed similar to the atmosphere of the previous dream in which he was shot. His associations here were to independence but the dream also involved the tree being suddenly and violently torn from its roots.

Dream 3

"I'm in a hotel room with friends. I looked into the mirror and I was Asian. I could see my face was strange. It was me but I was Asian. I'm thinking have I always been this way? I'm touching and looking at my face. Like something in my physical body has changed. Have I always been this way or is this all of a sudden?" John began to laugh and commented that this was confusing.

(Associations): "I guess this is a self-image kind of thing. Asians are supposed to be very good students. But they always follow rules. I'm not like that."

Dream 4

"I was watching a tornado. It was scary. I enjoyed watching it. Things were getting blown away. I was like riding this tornado and I thought it was cool. Seemed like entertainment."

(Q) "I guess I'm not taking the damage seriously ... I'm not aware of any danger or anything until I'm speaking about it now."

Besides the upheaval in his external world, these dreams also reflected the internal turmoil that plagued him. At one point John commented that he wished his parents could be "in my head for just three minutes. Then they'd realize what a strain life is to me and how I can't just do what they want me to do." These dreams allowed him, and me as well, "to be in his head." Their symbolization contributed to our awareness of the limited coping resources he had to contain unconscious anger, fear, and internal turmoil he experienced when faced with conflict. They also revealed his resiliency, capacity for self-examination, and ability to be cautiously open to tolerating emotional upheaval involved with change.

Blos (1979, p. 50) discusses the two tasks of treatment with patients who are struggling with delayed adolescence. The first goal is to increase tension tolerance. The second involves exposing narcissistic defenses through self-observation and introspection. Focusing treatment on John's dreams attended to both goals. In his dreams he could represent symbolically tension-filled experiences that could not be tolerated in real life. The dreams introduced him to his detached defense against experiencing fears and resentful rage. Narcissistic defenses of denial, grandiosity, and projection of blame were depicted in ways he could consider consciously. Gradually he became able to identify defenses as they occurred.

Most importantly, the dreams were his creations. No one was telling him to dream or what to think of each dream's unique revelation about his internal mental/emotional experience. John's ability to use the safety of the therapy relationship to express and listen to his dream mentation was a significant way for him to develop a sense that he had a unique SELF, a self that could be, in fact demanded to be, understood and valued no matter what ideas, feelings, wishes, impulses, fears, and horrors he harbored.

Late in what was supposed to be John's graduating semester, there was a déjà vu event. He learned, or at least acknowledged to his parents and to me, that he had not received credit for two courses he had taken in his junior year. Making up these credits required attending summer school. His graduation was uncertain until the week after he was to enter graduate school. That school allowed him to start classes pending college graduation, which he finally accomplished. This kind of down-to-the-wire living had become John's modus operandi. (An older adult patient with launching difficulties once poetically remarked that he "*needed* disaster to go faster.")

Unpredictability and turmoil were constants for John. I had to contain my own uncertainty. Should I believe what he told me about completing course-work, about reasons for missed sessions, about successes he reported on his job, or about his activities with friends? I never knew. What I did believe were the revelations about his internal emotional world that were reflected in his confused impressions about being grown-up and by his very creative, meta-phorically rich dream life.

By entering graduate school John was at least approaching the launching pad. I saw him for a few sessions during his first semester. The challenging yet stimulating nature of his courses and his respect for several professors contributed to his motivation. He was cautiously optimistic about keeping up with the work.

At the end of the school year I met with John to ask for his authorization to discuss our work in this chapter. He indicated that he had completed the first year academically. Recalling his dreams, he commented that he was "no longer a bystander to tornadoes." About his relationship with his parents, John noted: "You know if a year ago someone would have said to them that I'd have successfully completed a year of graduate studies, did assignments on time, and went to all my classes, really liked it, and had grades that put me in the middle of the class, you would think they would have been ecstatic. Well they don't bug me as much as they did but they still say that if only I worked harder I would be more highly ranked ... But I'm not letting them get to me. I guess I'm feeling that this is where I belong and that makes a big difference." That statement reflects the kind of conviction that is inspired by realistically being known by oneself.

Addendum

During the one and a half years that John was in therapy, he took important steps toward independent functioning: he completed college; made a good adjustment academically in graduate school; reported being able to make decisions more autonomously rather than in opposition to his parents' values; and was feeling more confident and pleased with himself.

While preparing this chapter, the editors suggested and I agreed that it would be important to have an understanding of what in therapy contributed to John's rather significant growth. I decided to contact him two years after therapy ended. He readily agreed to meet to discuss this question.

(John): "Therapy definitely helped ... Saying stuff out loud that I had never said before began to sound inherently dumb ... I had a rationale for believing my fears that you get only one shot at life ... When you keep thoughts to yourself they sound so logical, so truthful ... I realize it was a paranoid spin on a real feeling that I was having ... I still feel that it's insane for a 21-year-old to have to make a huge decision about choosing a career. This forced timeline was making me crazy. Talking about my worries helped me to reframe my way of thinking. It was an erosion process to change the way I looked at making decisions. You would say that worrying the way I did about the future can make the worries happen. Gradually I realized that expecting the one option of having a factory worker-like life was paralyzing me … I was so scared of making any decisions … I really thought of them as ideas. I didn't think they really affected my life. But talking about them in therapy made me realize that I was living these ideas. I anticipated the worst and felt that couldn't be altered."

John's comments about his experience in therapy indicate the gradual growth of self-reflective ability that emerged from listening to his inner self. In the presence of a therapist who took him seriously and non-judgmentally, John became more able to listen to himself from a perspective that allowed him to question his rigidly ingrained self-limiting precepts and consider the possibility of alternative narratives for his life.

Tallman and Bohart (in Hubble, Duncan, & Miller , 1999) discuss therapy as "a resource that facilitates, supports or focuses clients' self-healing efforts" (p. 102). John's words reflect the maturation of his considerable self-healing capacity.

Further comments by John referred to lingering aspects of his pessimistic, one-chance-in-life outlook: "Social commitment is my next hurdle … Boredom and sameness and assembly line living scare me … Thoughts of having a wife and family bring back that feeling." These ideas reflect John's growing awareness that his struggles are not over, but he has a future orientation that includes the possibility of marriage and children. He can verbalize fear that a committed relationship will inevitably result in a rote, meaningless existence where his choices and passions would be sacrificed to "picket-fence living." In the past John had been disconnected from the link between his self-defeating actions and his emotional conflicts with self-determination and autonomy. He still has vulnerabilities but his comments indicate preparedness to face future relationally-based conflicts with greater self-awareness.

(Dr. H): "What in therapy contributed to reframing your way of thinking?"

(John): "First you weren't my parent. Also, I wanted therapy to work. I didn't like what was happening to me."

The presence of strong desire to change is a critical motivator for patients to open themselves to new possibilities. John's observation about me not being his parents speaks to his powerful internal struggle with his parents. He was so enmeshed with them that he was unable to recognize his own contribution to his plight and see alternative paths. Within the safe emotional space afforded by therapy he became able to consider utilizing his agency to make changes.

(Dr. H): "How was this therapy different than previous therapies you had?"

(John): "I had some therapy as a kid and the big thing was how to medicate me for ADD. They were treating the symptoms rather than the problems. I didn't like the medicine. It made me feel like a zombie. I didn't eat and felt robotic."

John's words emphasize the need for therapy to be focused on what's relevant to patients. He recalls therapy as a child as literally revolving around forcing medicine down his throat. That interaction replicated his relationship with his parents and perpetuated his oppositional defensiveness. His involvement in our therapy would be meaningful only if he could experience it as being for him, focused on his welfare, not aimed at getting him to change in any way that was not determined by him.

(Dr. H): "What do you recall about the dreams you had when you were in therapy and what are your dreams about now?"

(John): "The dreams were a way of me realizing how I was crippling myself. Funny I don't have or I don't remember my dreams now. I guess I don't need them to remind me about what I'm doing now."

Psychodynamic focus on dreams tapped into John's creativity, and his ability to symbolically represent and recognize his unconscious struggles as depicted by his imagination. The fact that his dreams were his creations and no one was telling him what to dream contributed to his openness and curiosity to learn about himself through them. Therapy provided him with tools to decipher the meanings of dreams and to recognize that he was the architect of his self-defeating actions. John no longer needs dreams, originating in his unconscious mind, to alert him to what he is not aware of. Self-healing is carrying with it conscious awareness of his emotional life and thus a greater possibility for him to trust himself to be the architect of his future.

References

Arnett, J. (2000). Emerging Adulthood: A theory of development from the late teens through the twenties. *American Psychologist,* 55(5): 469–480.

Blos, P. (1979). *The Adolescent Passage.* New York: International University Press.

Bennett, J (2017). Learning to fail. *The New York Times*, June 25, pp. ST1–ST2.

Henig, R.M. (2010). What is it about 20-somethings? Whey are so many people in their 20s taking so long to grow up? *The New York Times Magazine*, August 18.

Malberg, N., Stafler, N., & Geater, E. (2012). Putting the pieces of the puzzle together: A mentalization-based approach to early intervention in primary schools. *Journal of Infant, Child and Adolescent Psychotherapy*, 11(3): 190–204.

McWilliams, N. (2016). Self-defeating patients: Implications for psychotherapy. Conference presentation at Adelphi University, Garden City, New York, April.

Sapountzis, I. (2014). The space to be: Commentary on "School refusal and the parent–child relationship." *Journal of Infant Child and Adolescent Psychotherapy*, 13(3): 193–197.

Slade, A. (1999). Representation, symbolization, and affect regulation in the concomitant treatment of a mother and child: Attachment theory and child psychotherapy. *Psychoanalytic Inquiry*, 19: 797–830.

Tallman, K., & Bohart, A.C. (1999). The client as a common factor: Clients as self-healers. In M. Hubble, B. Duncan, and S. Miller (eds.). *The Heart and Soul of Change: What Works in Therapy?*, pp. 91–131. Washington DC: American Psychological Association.

University of Michigan Transportation Research Institute (2011). Driving forces: Fewer young, but more elderly, have driver's licenses. *UMTRI Research Review*, 42(4): 1–2.

Chapter 4

On knowing the future

Brent Willock

I dreamt I was on a hill, participating in a clinical discussion with colleagues and students. Someone I regarded as a senior to me, though he seemed no older, shared that he often found it helpful to tell patients that things were going to be alright. This gentleman reminded me of the well-known psychoanalyst, Robert Langs. When I was younger, I had written a book review of his two volumes on the *Technique of Psychoanalytic Psychotherapy*. Subsequently I enjoyed a brief correspondence with him. His comment was quietly accepted by the group. It stirred clinical associations in me, moving me to speak about a patient.

Meghan assumed I always knew precisely what her agitated thoughts and feelings meant. She believed I knew exactly how long it would take her to complete her analysis, and whether and when it would result in her finding true love, vocational success, and overall fulfillment. If I responded with less than a crystal clear answer to her queries in these areas, she would angrily feel I was withholding, or being a new version of her "useless father." We survived these encounters. There continued to be much I did not know. I would have liked to help her get to the other side of her agony much faster.

Meghan had virtually no sense of her mother having been at home. She did, however, have some videotape evidence that mother had been there. Meghan watched that home movie over and over, hoping to gain greater understanding and connection to her formative years by studying it. Beyond that movie, Meghan knew that meals regularly appeared. From this remembered fact, she deduced that her mother must have been in the house. For one preciously memorable lunch, mother really was present. On that occasion, Meghan arrived home from school to find that mother had prepared Meghan's favorite meal. Topping off that delicious surprise, mother had set the television set on the kitchen table to play her daughter's most beloved show. Meghan clung to that recollection, along with one other in which mother attended to Meghan's needs. Much as she cherished these reminiscences, she was painfully aware that a few crumbs do not a loaf make.

When Meghan demanded I provide instant answers, it felt as if she wanted me to serve up her favorite repast, as if this action would create a restorative oasis in the deadly desert of daily existence. She wanted my rapid response to be perfectly attuned to her needs, satisfying in every respect. My A-plus delivery would prove not only that I was there, but also that I had been present all along, working wisely and lovingly on her behalf, rather than being absent or preoccupied with my needs and interests.

Meghan needed me to be in a state of primary maternal preoccupation (Winnicott, 1960) and reverie (Bion, 1962), instantly accessible and optimally responsive (Bacal, 1985) whenever she needed me. Frequently she felt I was not there for her. She angrily likened me to her father whom she experienced as having abandoned her in her adolescence, after her parents' marriage dissolved. Her vicious rage at my vacancy was so profound that we suspected it was rooted in her earlier experience, or non-experience with her mother.

In Meghan's quest for certainty about her future romantic and vocational prospects, occasionally she turned to highly recommended psychics, astrologers, and other paranormal practitioners. These specialists seemed to have uncannily accurate knowledge of crucial details of her childhood. They provided the precise predictions she craved. They would tell her that in X months she would begin an important romance, in Y months she would have a career breakthrough; and so forth. Meghan derived immense relief from these reassurances about her future wellbeing in these two areas that, in keeping with Freud's dictum, mattered most to her: love and work. Their insights and predictions enabled her to relax momentarily from her usual state of agitation, secure in her belief that life would, in the not too distant future, be alright.

At times I felt not only impressed but also envious and competitive with regard to the psychic powers of these confident clairvoyants that Meghan respected so highly and appeared to benefit from so much. Generally, however, I was grateful for the relief she harvested from their uncanny knowledge of her historical and contemporary circumstances and future.

In my dream about the outdoor clinical discussion, at the risk of talking to that group for far too long, I proceeded to share some related material about another patient, Marina. She, too, was long suffering but, unlike Meghan, was more prone to sobbing and wailing than raging. She felt her mother never loved her and remembered her as having been painfully dismissive. Her father did love Marina, but she believed his love was more about what she could do for him, rather than his having genuine interest in her.

As Marina went deeper into her analysis, she felt she made good progress. Unfortunately, those advances led to more profound pains emerging. At times Marina felt her sorrow was bottomless. She desperately stated that she could not survive another issue emerging.

Marina knew Meghan and shared with me that they frequently talked about how they did not know what they would have done without me. They felt I was the good parent they never had. I would hardly have guessed Meghan felt that way, for she often told me if I had informed her at the outset that treatment would be this long, frustrating, and painful, she would have quit after the first session. Here, too, she conveyed her belief that I knew in advance precisely what her analysis would entail.

Marina's fears also focused on Freud's comprehensive categories: love and work. When she feared she might not survive her agony, she needed me to tell her she would be okay, that she would make a lot of money, and/or find the man of her dreams. If I responded with anything less than exactly what she wanted to hear, she would have none of it. She did not want empathy regarding how frightened she was. She did not want to hear about why, considering her developmental history, she might crave such reassurance. She insisted she needed me to directly say she would eventually feel good, find a wonderful husband, etc. If I refused to provide precisely what she wanted, I would be compounding her debilitating anguish, possibly pushing her over the edge.

I felt Marina wanted me to participate in a psychodrama. As we often do in child analysis, I decided to play my assigned role. Remembering Sandor Ferenczi, Michael Balint, and other remarkable psychoanalysts saying that the more adult analysis resembles child analysis, the better it is, I felt supported in shifting my analytic stance to play the requested role, engaging much as I might when child patients ask me to be the witch, the teacher, or the mother. When I spoke my lines, Marina immediately felt immense relief. She thanked me sincerely for being "good dad." Occasionally she asked if I really meant it, but always she was able to pull herself together and get on with her day—far more so than if I had not performed properly as her good father.

In one session, Marina cried at just about everything, including good things. She did not know why she was sobbing. Lately she finds herself grossed out when she sees couples kissing on television. "I don't even know if I want a man. Does this mean I'll live forever alone? I don't want that." I told Marina she had been struggling for a long time to feel better. Finally feeling she has gotten her life together, she is now like someone who has been swimming for a long time after her boat capsized. Finally pulling herself up on a raft, she is so happy to be safe. It will take time to catch her breath and recover from her ordeal. Consequently, she wants nothing other than to calm down and restore herself. She does not want an activity, a romance, a holiday. Marina agreed that was what she was feeling. "Do you think it'll change?" Yes, I replied, without hesitation. "Ok," she responded, sobbing. "I never had reassurance from my parents about anything. That's why I've been so scared. They never said it'll be ok, just catch your breath, it may take a year or whatever. I've had a very hard life. You know that better than anyone. Finally the struggles are over. I need to rest, take time for myself, and it's ok. Thank you for the reassurance. It will change, won't it?" (Yes.) "Ok, now I can leave."

After awakening from my dream in which I had shared my thoughts about my two patients who craved reassurances that the future will be alright, I recalled a dear supervisor, Naomi Lohr, telling me, "You have to lend your patient your omnipotence." Working on a psychoanalytically-oriented inpatient ward, Dr. Lohr lent hers to many fractured souls, and many students. Meghan and Marina certainly wanted me to lend them my omnipotence. Astrologers and psychics provided this service for Meghan. With Marina, I lent omnipotence quite concretely in accordance with her plea in our 'play therapy'. With Meghan, it was more a matter of surviving her relentless rage, being sufficiently omnipotent not to be destroyed by her intense, often sadistic assaults.

On one occasion, as Meghan was preparing to leave our session and the city for a few days, she looked deeply broken, frustrated, and despairing. I knew she was in for days of agony until our next appointment. I shared with her that I had once visited an old folks' home where an Irish musician was performing. Some residents were demented. All had significant challenges. The music enlivened them. They resonated with familiar songs, tapping their hands and feet, moved pleasurably and meaningfully by the music. In his upbeat banter, the singer said, "We Irish say things are desperate but not hopeless." That "interpretation" struck a very meaningful chord with Meghan. The next week, she said those words had been resonating with her helpfully. A "meal" had appeared when she needed one, when she was almost beyond hope of any nutriment arriving. Rather than disastrous, things were going to be alright.

Marina was nervous about an upcoming business meeting. Believing her mother in heaven had evolved into the perfect being she was meant to be, Marina shared that she "asked mom to attend the meeting. I felt her on my shoulder, watching out for me, meaning that everything will be fine." Marina appeared to be internalizing this needed psychic (selfobject) function.

With respect to the grassy hill where I spoke intensely to the group in my dream, I afterwards associated to the Hill of Calvary where Jesus was crucified, and also to the grassy knoll near the Texas book depository where John Fitzgerald Kennedy was assassinated. Two good father figures, both executed. At least one of them was omnipotent.

I spoke so long in the dream that, over time, the discussion group had largely dispersed. I continued to chat with one colleague about Marina as we walked away across the field. That grassy plane was like the one I cross on my way to work. In my dream, we have similarly to be careful to not step in a large puddle. Another member of the group was quietly listening (observing ego?) as the three of us walked along. My colleague asked, "Do you want a community consultation?" He was inquiring as to whether in discussing my patients I was seeking feedback. He also seemed to be wondering if I were suggesting it would be valuable for our community to create more mutually beneficial consulting opportunities.

My nocturnal reverie was what Masud Khan (1962) called a good dream. Upon awakening, I thought it might be serving up my topic for an upcoming symposium on the topic of Knowing and Being Known. Wondering if I had any ideas worth sharing at that gathering had been on my mind the previous day (Freud's day residue). The dream, and some sleeplessness that followed it, was probably not just about that approaching conference. Something had occurred that made me worry about my wife's health. I could be the one wanting to hear from a wise, caring authority that everything was going to be alright. I thought of Meghan and Marina as being concrete in their demands that I tell them that they were going to be okay. Now it appeared to be me desiring similar reassurance that everything would be alright, that my wife would be okay, that I would be okay. We crave containers for that which we cannot hold. How wonderful it would be to have some equivalent of Robert Langs/good dad reassure me that everything was going to be just fine.

Post PS

What do we do when we are not quite so concrete and literal as Meghan and Marina were? What do we do when we no longer believe mom's kiss or dad's reassuring words will guarantee the fairytale endings in which we will live happily ever after? What do we do when we are no longer so much in the Paranoid-Schizoid (PS) Position where omnipotence rules one way or the other, either in our secure relationship with the good breast or in our terror of its replacement, the malevolent mammary? What happens when, for better and worse, we think increasingly from the more complicated Depressive Position?

Struggling to answer that question, I recall what another patient, Pablo, shared with me recently. He had reason to be concerned he might suffer serious physical deterioration in the years ahead. When he was a young boy, he had developed a chronic gastrointestinal condition that made life challenging. He felt he was hated by his mother for being a burden rather than being the ideal child who would never cause any difficulties and would always agree with and support his parents. Pablo was not sure whether his psychological problems had begun long before he was confronted by the challenges of his illness. At the very least, he was certain his suffering had been grossly exacerbated by the onset of his malady.

In Michael Balint's (1979) framework, Pablo's feelings about his mother's reaction to his affliction reflect the basic fault we experience when we become aware that our parents can, or have, dropped us. He felt broken and doomed. Suicide seemed attractive. Homicidal impulses provided some enlivenment. Despising his parents, he believed the sentiment was mutual. For years he raged intensely about them, a bit like Meghan, though not so ferociously or constantly.

Balint (1955) discussed attempts to cope with the basic fault by ocnophilic (clinging) and philobatic (adventurous, counter-dependent) means. Pablo experimented with both those orientations. Eventually he reached a more transcendent solution. He began believing he would be okay if physical deterioration set in because, he realized, what was more important was to still feel loved. He had never felt that was a possibility. The physical dimension was becoming less significant. He now had a sense of a loving, internal object that he experienced in relation to his live-in partner, children, friends, analyst, and self. More securely in the Depressive Position, he was beginning to perceive the situation as dire but not hopeless. No longer alone in a persecutory world, a sufficient supply of mutually flowing love bridged the basic fault that, prior to analysis, had to be filled in with psychotropic medications, alcohol, and electroconvulsive therapy. Pablo now knew things would be alright.

Kohut (Strozier, 2001) said his own fear of death was mostly related to fearing abandonment by selfobjects. Meghan, Marina, Pablo, and most patients would understand that terror. They would say they dread, or are reeling from abandonment by loving others, initially and foundationally their parents. Meghan, for example, believed her rage protected her against terror of death related to her sense of having been emotionally deserted by her mother at birth, if not before.

Useful terms like selfobject sometimes seem abstract. My three patients might more easily understand Balint's empathic observation that something went terribly wrong very early in these patients' relationships with their parents that must, at all cost, be righted. They would also probably resonate deeply with the message the Beatles transmitted via their song, *All You Need is Love*. From our lengthy work, these analysands would know that prescriptive title applied not only to now, but also to their distant, lonely pasts—pasts that were not really past but painfully present.

Marina came to realize her aching longing for a wonderful husband, or for me to play the role of good Dad, was more about her wish to avoid experiencing how unloved she felt by her parents. "The man" she yearned for would bandage that old wound, preventing her from having to know how traumatized she felt by parental shortcomings. She felt she could finally face those awful feelings because she now had me and others who were there for her.

46 Brent Willock

In another superb song, Paul McCartney shared his good fortune that in his times of trouble Mother Mary comes to him, whispering words of wisdom. For many decades Mother Mary did not come to Meghan, Marina, and Pablo. They were, instead, alone with the uncaring, bad breast. Marina visualized this persecutory object as Cruella de Vil, a woman infamous for her evil, icy stare in Walt Disney's movie *101 Dalmatians*. At other times, perhaps indicative of her foothold in the Depressive Position, she emphasized her mother's dead fish eyes. These mirrors of the soul, having lost their sparkle, were reminiscent of André Green's (1986) evocative description of the emotionally *Dead Mother*. Marina's mother's deceased fish eyes triggered horror and despair in her daughter rather than irrepressible demands for the good breast or the good father to appear and perform.

What, then, is alright if it is not simply happily ever after? What is alright when it is not, and cannot be assured by an omniscient other? Pablo suggests it is being in touch with healthy successors of the benevolent breast, that is, the good internal object and its external manifestations in loving others. This relational matrix helps us accept the fact that pre-Depressive wishes for all illness and unhappiness to be banished, now and forever, will not be fulfilled. It permits us to resonate with the wisdom of the Rolling Stones and tolerate the reality that you can't always get what you want, but if you try sometimes you just might find you get what you need.

You can't always even know what you want but if you try, as we surely do in psychoanalysis, you might come to know what you need. Slowly but surely my patients (and I) were learning this crucial lesson. The path to this knowledge and wisdom can be a long winding road, a difficult slog, as we work through the terrors of the basic fault, come to know the nature of the rent in the fabric of our being and how, at last, to mend it, in increasingly healthy ways.

Reflections

From the emotional wave I experienced when I presented my paper at the symposium several weeks after my dream, I came to know that I had wanted a community consultation. In my sleep, I thought I was mostly sharing some clinical vignettes, hoping to contribute something to a mutually beneficial dialogue amongst colleagues concerning professional matters. What I received from the community of analysts in real life was something more personal and profound. The good object arrived, like Meghan's memorable meal, at a moment when I scarcely knew I was craving it. For me, this was a good dream, and a very good community.

To dream, perchance to know. Dreaming about patients, we come to know more not only about them and their needs, but also about ourselves and our

On knowing the future   47

longings. Sometimes dreams' benefits are only fully realized when we share them with a significant other. From anthropologists we learned of tribes that routinely make time and space in their daily lives in which to share dreams with their collective. When we tell our dreams, it is usually to a romantic partner, friend, or psychoanalyst. Less commonly, we may share these nocturnal reveries in a group. That, too, can be very beneficial.

Peremptory needs to know the future may drive our patients to demand or plea for us to be omniscient, to be what Jacques Lacan (1998) called "the subject supposed to know" (p. 268). Frustrated by our shortcomings in this regard, they may turn to psychics, astrologers, and other fortune tellers for the certainty they crave. In psychoanalysis, this yearning may gradually diminish as these patients come to know something more profound and trustworthy. Becoming aware of and working through the traumatic shortcomings of past relational experience, they acquire a new internal relational matrix forged from good aspects of prior relationships, now less occluded by rage and despair, combined with currently benevolent relationships, very much including the psychoanalytic one. Now they have something inside that is 'good enough' (Winnicott, 1971). While this internal presence may not be omniscient, it goes a long way toward encompassing and transcending the traumatic past, the imperfect present, and the unknown future. In fact, the future is, in a sense, now known as a time when things will be 'alright' even if they may be very difficult at some times, in some ways.

References

Bacal, H.A. (1985). Optimal responsiveness and the therapeutic process. *Progress in Self Psychology*, 1: 202–227.
Balint, M. (1955). Friendly expanses—horrid empty spaces. *International Journal of Psychoanalysis*, 36: 225–241.
Balint, M. (1979). *The Basic Fault: Therapeutic Aspects of Regression*. London: Tavistock Publications.
Bion, W.R. (1962). *Learning from Experience*. London: Heinemann.
Green, A. (1986). The dead mother. In A. Green, *On Private Madness*, pp. 142–173. London: Hogarth Press,.
Khan, M.R. (1962). Dream psychology and the evolution of the psycho-analytic situation. *International Journal of Psychoanalysis*, 43: 21–31.
Lacan, J. (1998). *The Seminar of Jacques Lacan: The Four Fundamental Concepts of Psychoanalysis* (Vol. 11). Jacques-Alain Miller (ed.), Alan Sheridan (trans.). New York: W.W. Norton.
Strozier, C.B. (2001). *Heinz Kohut: The Making of a Psychoanalyst*. New York: Farrar, Straus, and Giroux.
Winnicott, D.W. (1960). The theory of the parent-infant relationship. *International Journal of Psychoanalysis*, 41: 585–595.
Winnicott, D.W. (1971). *Playing and Reality*. London: Tavistock Publications.

Knowing through appearances

Chapter 5

Secrets of eating and eating of secrets

Daring to be known

Jean Petrucelli

One could infinitely jest—how can a body be known when a body does not always know itself? There are internal conflicts between body-states. There's the body being known, or often only sort-of-known, to the person who inhabits it. Then there is the body and its "behaviors" being known or perceived in the world, subjectively and objectively. Your mind may take you in one direction in terms of "knowing" but the body—having a mind of its own—may take you down another path, doing things you might prefer it "not to."

Daring to fully know and be known involves a level of attunement to the body and its responses. This entails embracing the vulnerability of a body self. For some, seeing the body as an extension of the self changes the perception and meaning of things and the way a person views their body. This is made more difficult by the cultural imperative to "look" a certain way. Youth and thinness are celebrated. For many, it would be a "radical" idea to simply love your body without losing weight. It would be an even more "radical" idea to appreciate untapped imperfection. For a body to know itself it must feel lived in. To live "in" our bodies, we must be able to tolerate knowing ourselves.

Our culture follows a tacitly accepted set of rules for women in the limelight. They must be thin and not eat a normal diet. These imperatives are seen as "normal," not dangerous. Americans are obsessed with obesity. Most overweight people in the media or pop culture hate their bodies. Shows like *The Biggest Loser* parade contestants around like circus animals—celebrities— who flog themselves in nationally televised weight-loss commercials. We have come to expect the spectacle of the miserable overweight person and emaciated bodies culturally sanctioned. Both result in negative body image, low self-esteem, and increased body dissatisfaction. On either end of this spectrum of body size, shame is held in secret eating and eating secrets.

The secrets that eating disordered patients bring to therapy reveal a basic ambivalence between urges to retain and expel. Their relationship to secrets could be thought of like their relationship to food—the tensions of wanting and not wanting to know themselves and be known through revealing their secrets to another; doing and undoing, depriving, and over-sharing. The core of their identity, their most "secret self," is felt to be spoiled or dirty in knowing and revealing itself to an Other.

Bodily esteem and size have become one and the same. Eating disorders fall in line with what society "expects" of people in the spotlight—a love of "thinness" while simultaneously conveying they are immune to, or even repulsed by, the *means* of achieving it. Throughout visual culture, objectification—which we might think of as relational impingement, if not relational trauma—reminds women that they are being scrutinized and sexualized. It supports women being both cut off from their bodies, regarding them as mere aesthetic wrappers of the self and, at the same time, deeply pre-occupied with them, perceiving their bodies as central signifiers of identity (Baker-Pitts, 2015; Petrucelli, 2015). Focusing on one's body as object inhibits self-awareness and leads to stultifying self-consciousness.

Eating disorders are a silent form of destruction—of vitality and hope for meaningful existence. They create the illusion of time stopping. Past, present, and future collapse. Insidious negative self-talk is too loud, the aftermath of trauma too pervasive, and affects too overwhelming. The body itself becomes the theater of war (McDougall, 1989) wherein feelings, memories, longings, and stories that have led to symptoms feel so dangerous that they are dissociated from behaviors.

The largeness of life on stage can be paradoxically myopic, with celebrities feeling stuck, trapped in the narrow, isolated world of loneliness and despair. Consider the tragic death of British music performer, Amy Winehouse. She died in 2011 from complications relating to bulimia—a secret not publicized, though recognized by many. On the night of her death, Amy drank two bottles of vodka while watching YouTube videos of herself. As well documented as her struggles with alcohol and drug addiction were, the "little" fact of her severe, untreated, decade-long, bulimarexia was rarely mentioned. Though the official cause of death was listed as alcohol poisoning, Amy's body was weakened and medically compromised from her eating disorder. We can learn much from her painful life. Among these things are the ways in which her dependence on alcohol, drugs, and disordered eating—her compulsive reliance on substances—were attempts at regulating a profoundly compromised experience of self. Anxious, isolated, alone—yet sparkling, kind, and immensely talented—her vitality was quashed as her fame increased. One can speculate that "fame" provided her with pseudo-company—illusions of companionship and love—that highlighted her aloneness and lack of real sustaining support or connection. It was a substance-induced high rather than sturdy vitality; a binge on whip-cream rather than a satisfying meal;

illusory contact rather than authentic relatedness (Schoen, 2016, personal communication).

People struggling with eating disorders keep their rituals and disordered behaviors secret—a double life of sorts. Symptoms like starving, bingeing, and purging represent unlinked states of mind. Through the effort to self-protect from historical or current trauma, individuals with these disorders are protected from the felt impossibility of holding two incompatible modes of relating. Dissociation is not knowing there is a secret you are keeping. Bodily symptoms are used not only to manage overwhelming feeling states or numb access to parts of oneself, but also to compensate for lack of capacity to know and deal with conflict. Unable to reflectively experience a part of oneself or another, patients with an eating disorder (ED) have difficulty experiencing a mind of their own.

Symptoms are used to maintain a state of mind, full of fantasies of possibilities of a moment or a life, without what "*feels*" unbearable (Petrucelli, 2004, 2010, 2015). The person in the ED "body-state" believes there is no other way. This is knowledge borne of the absence of experience. Anorexic patients refuse food to keep their desire "alive." Rather than saying she does not eat anything, she keeps some space for her desire to live (Fink, 2004). If she says she eats "nothing," then nothing is the object that holds her desire, and keeps her "feeling" something.

We could ask people struggling with EDs to truly *imagine* what it is like to have a healthy stable body that can be trusted. Can they know what it feels like to be alive, feeling longing and desire? The ED becomes a hyperaware "solution" to not facing the consequences of living life in the body if she *does not* and *cannot* know what that experience is. The resulting hyper-deadness (anesthetization) that follows from starving, bingeing, or purging, forces her to focus on nothing but her symptoms even if she would *prefer* not to. It allows her to believe she is "getting away with something" (Phillips, 2010). In reality, she has protracted the torture, deferring the moment of punitive truth of accepting imperfection. In the illusion of pseudo desire, appetites and their bodies can *seem* bearable.

"*I can have all the food I want and never face the idea of the thing not chosen. I can be thin and control my body and no one can hurt me.*" Regardless of symptom, patients with eating disorders feel at the mercy of feelings, enslaved by an inability to contain desire as regulatable affect. It is, rather, experienced as an overwhelming state in which one wishes and hopes to have everything all the time—commonly known as "greed." Particularly regarding human contact, greed overwhelms the patient who therefore attempts to control "appetite." Trying to eliminate the potential for traumatic rupture in human relatedness, she replaces relationships with food, a self-contained solution not subject to others' betrayal (Bromberg, 1998). The desire to have it all runs into pressure and the need to choose. This necessity creates either a refusal (no more appetite and frustration) or, if the ED patient chooses, she must contend with the loss of the thing not chosen. External indifference and non-recognition that this is a loss leads to dissociative "indifference" and making sure that loss becomes impossible by foreclosing desire (Bromberg, personal communication, 2016).

To make meaningful choices, one must feel meaningfully related to others. That requires giving up omnipotent fantasies of having it all (or, alternatively, depriving oneself of all), and dealing with the losses that reality—real dependency needs and the pleasures and pains of real relationships—entails.

People with eating disorders can be of "many minds" that are not supposed to interfere with one another. When they try to protect themselves this way, self-development and a sense of coherence are derailed. In contrast, when a person's self and body-states are linked—and when these links do not threaten core, internalized attachment relationships—they have access to all parts of the self and can smoothly transition between them without succumbing to the narrow tunnel of a particular self or body-state filled with shame or self loathing. This capacity allows for real contact with others—to take in what they have to offer and survive how they may fail or disappoint.

In treatment, the body speaks through the patient's narrative, but it is the felt experience within one's own body and between bodies that is ultimately the vehicle for discourse. The patient's hyperawareness of the outside as a potential threat or impingement, and the deadness and lack of vitality inside, are excruciating. These states are passed back and forth between the patient's varied internal states and between patient and therapist.

Amy Winehouse reminds me of my patient, Bella. Both their desires were never met and transformed in the mutually regulating context of good enough caretaking. When Bella's mom was pregnant with her, she was told she was having twins. During gestation, one died. The family story was that "due to the way the babies were positioned, Bella *ate* all the food" or, as her father chided: "You ate your twin with your ravenous appetite!" Believing the lost sibling was a boy, Bella feels a mixture of guilt and glee.

As a child, Bella preferred pirouettes to math. The middle child between two other sisters, she carved her identity out of negative attention-seeking, from forest fire setting at age 10 to car crashing under the influence at 17. In her early 20s, she had two hospitalizations. She oscillated between alcohol and opiate addiction, bingeing, purging, restriction, and exercise addiction. Her appetite for trouble was as voracious as her food craving. Strikingly beautiful, feisty, antsy, and jumpy, she pulls for images like a "white rabbit" with long blonde hair and petite body. Recounting her drug history, she quotes Jefferson Airplane lyrics: "One pill makes you larger, and one pill makes you small ... The ones that mother gives you, don't do anything at all"—forewarning me I was in for a wild ride and nothing I could "give her" would work.

Bella's thinking is black and white, her actions impulse driven. She lacks empathy and self-reflexivity. She does whatever she can to anesthetize her unfettered energy and anxiety. With her sisters, she is extremely competitive and condescending. Her first treatment dream involved one sister vomiting in the bathroom in their beach house and not cleaning up her vomit. Bella's association? "What an amateur she is!"

Intergenerational transmission of body dissatisfaction and Bella's inability to live in her body are traumatic and profound. Her mother had seven cosmetic surgeries. With mother's suggestion, Bella had four surgeries by age 24, including breast reduction, then implants. Having lost sensation in her breasts, they have become objects of someone *else's* pleasure—one of many ways Bella sees and treats herself as an object. In her performing career— and perform she does for all around her—she caters to the whims of narcissistic others who surround and rule her. When not on stage she isolates, avoids social interactions and commitments, and does not make sustainable friendships. She would rather preserve the integrity of an initial encounter by denying herself further ones.

Before our work, Bella had two failed residential treatments, several therapists, and was bingeing and purging 4–6 times per day with a "driving under the influence" charge. I saw her twice weekly. We made a contract to use her birthday, six months away, as a timeline to decide that if her symptoms hadn't changed, she would consider a third rehab. We focused on stopping the alcohol first, utilizing AA and group therapy. Abstinence meant less calories, a secondary gain in her mind. She has remained sober for five years. Alcohol was not her primary addiction—food was. She stopped all ED symptoms for three months, gaining a few pounds, as is to be expected. Unable to tolerate this "new" body, Bella began bingeing and purging once a day. We made another contract. She could binge and purge 1–2 times a week—no more. We explored why she stopped ED symptoms for three months. She revealed that her desire to be the "good girl" in therapy motivated her, but not sustainable as her sense of agency and integrity had not yet developed.

Bella's extremely needy, intrusively unaware mother's own mother died when Bella's mother was 12. Nurturing and self-care conflicts abound, so contracts with Bella often do not work. I try to help her establish a sense of agency and integrity which could slowly extend into other areas of her life—having a voice, doing healthy performances, with manageable schedules, setting boundaries, identifying her anger, regulating self care, and saying no when necessary. Try as I might, this often failed. We considered residential treatment. Instead, Bella got pregnant and had an abortion. Was she letting me know her body was still enacting self-harm while trying desperately in a maladaptive way to change her self situation? If she got pregnant, she could quit performing and this new guy would take care of her. She did not really want to be with him, but did not know how to get out of her rut. For Bella, actions have always spoken louder than words.

Fast forward another year: Bella went from purging 3–6 times a day to sometimes once a week, desperately holding onto her "old solution": the possibility of purging when overwhelmed. Her body-state believed she could purge if *needed*—even though she now knew it didn't work. She wanted more in life, but this "*just in case I need it*" idea still floated in her head and body.

Terrified of failing, she typically fails in advance. Consequently, we stopped officially contracting. That does not mean we stopped talking about it. One day I repeated something to her I had said months before. She asked, "Am I ever going to stop purging?" I answered playfully: "Well ... you can't be my only patient that NEVER stops purging!" She said, "OMG! I have been your BEST WORST patient." This realization and enactment hit us both. Secretly she had found a way to be "the best" at something with me—without failing in advance. As long as she stayed symptomatic, she maintained her BEST WORST status. I had unconsciously validated it by giving her a platform to feel "special" with me. I felt terrible, but strangely elated—as did she. It was HER realization ... with agency. Being headstrong served *her* now. So she stopped purging and just celebrated a four-year anniversary of being free of bingeing, too.

Real recovery from eating disorder takes a long time. Patients (and therapists) struggle to tolerate ambiguity, uncertainty, and their limits and vulnerability. Clinicians are taught to remain "rock" steady (Hoppenwasser, 2008), but steadiness means remaining keyed into our experiences of being in and out of sync, becoming aware of our moments of dissociation, shifts in our self and body-states, and the collision of our dissociative lapses with patients. There is no leaving the self out, and no seeing yourself either. The beauty is in seeing this messy complexity from the vantage point of human imperfection. Owning our pieces and having the courage to stay real helps prevent more shame in patients. This may be their first experience of feeling real—vital.

In moments of intense vulnerability, new relational experiences can be taken in. Superficial relating can shift to sustaining connection. Sometimes this occurs in playfully poignant ways. Being Italian and Jewish affords me two "luxuries," *tsuris and agita*—the ability to worry and have guilt. During a heated exchange with a patient whom I was extremely worried about, she turned and said daringly in an irate huff, "Do you know what my name means in Hungarian?!! ... STORM!!! I could destroy you and blow you away!" To which I replied, "Okay ... But do you know what MY name means in Italian? ... LITTLE ROCK!!!!! ... and I'm not moving ... so there!!" (Petrucelli, 2016). Not the response she was expecting. We laughed. Over time, over cultures, between "our names," between us, a bedrock of mutative impact was being built. This experience of our names became a new way to be known together, an exchange felt within our bodies, the kind of experience that Amy Winehouse never had a chance to develop in an impoverished, abusive relational world.

This chapter touches on the complex dialectical relationship between eating disordered patients' bodily experiences, with loss of vitality, and new ways of relating that can facilitate uncovering secrets and secret lives so they can move, as Bromberg (2011, p. 42) saliently wrote, from "*being*" the secret to "*knowing*" the secret. Knowing oneself involves valuing imperfections and coming to terms with limitations, giving up illusions of omnipotence and specialness—however unsettling.

References

Baker-Pitts, C. (2015). "Look at me—What am I supposed to be?" In J. Petrucelli (ed.), *Body-States: Interpersonal/Relational Perspectives on the Treatment of Eating Disorders*. London: Routledge.

Bromberg, P. (1998). *Standing in the Spaces: Essays on Clinical Process, Trauma, and Dissociation*. Hillsdale, NJ: Analytic Press.

Bromberg, P. (2011). *The Shadow of the Tsunami and the Growth of the Relational Mind*. New York and London: Routledge.

Fink, B. (2004). *Lacan to the Letter*. Minneapolis, MN: University of Minnesota Press.

Hoppenwasser, K. (2008). Being in rhythm: Dissociative attunement in therapeutic process, *Journal of Trauma and Dissociation*, 9(3): 349–367.

McDougall, J. (1989). *Theaters of the Body*. New York and London: W.W. Norton.

Petrucelli, J. (2004). Treating eating disorders. In R. H. Coombs (ed.), *Handbook of Addictive Disorders: A Practical Guide to Diagnosis and Treatment*, pp. 312–352. Hoboken, NJ: John Wiley & Sons.

Petrucelli, J. (2010). Things that go bump in the night: Secrets after dark. In J. Petrucelli (ed.), *Knowing, Not-Knowing and Sort-of-Knowing: Psychoanalysis and the Experience of Uncertainty*, pp. 135–150. London: Karnac Books.

Petrucelli, J. (2015). Mermaids, mistresses & Medusa: 'Getting inside out and outside in' the relational montage of eating disorders. In J. Petrucelli (ed.), *Body-States: Interpersonal/Relational Perspectives on the Treatment of Eating Disorders*. London: Routledge.

Petrucelli, J. (2016). Body-states, body-image, and dissociation: When not-me is 'not-body.' *Clinical Social Work Journal*, 44(1): 18–26.

Phillips, A. (2010). On getting away with it: On the experiences we don't have. In J. Petrucelli (ed.), *Knowing, Not-Knowing and Sort-of-Knowing: Psychoanalysis and the Experience of Uncertainty*, pp. 165–174. London: Karnac Books.

Chapter 6

The analytic dialogue
Looking at and listening to each other

Anita Weinreb Katz

I would like to introduce another theme to Knowing and Being Known: Seeing and Being Seen. Working with one patient's presentation and fashion statements, in addition to listening to words and feelings, I will show how analysts can help patients open their eyes to seeing and being seen in new ways.

Clothes "make clear reference to who we are and wish to be taken as while alternatively or simultaneously evoking an aura that 'merely suggests' more than it can (or intends to) state precisely" (Davis, 1992, p. 35). Esther's fashion, posture, facial expressions, and makeup conveyed powerful messages, providing clues to her inner state. As she became more trusting of me, she could take in and accept my interpretations of their meanings.

As Anzieu (2016) states, the first boundary between self and other is skin. The second includes facial expression, posture, and sartorial choices. These boundaries are also ways of connecting to oneself and others. Esther was gradually able to transform both her presentation and her connections with the world.

The therapeutic journey

Esther began what became a long-term analysis at age 25. She struggled with conflicted desires for autonomy and loving connections, harboring fear that to be autonomous, powerful, and beautiful was to risk abandonment or punishment. She had learned to anticipate that both dependency and assertiveness would result in disaster. Plagued by repetitive struggles with weight gains and losses, she was as uncomfortable in body as in psyche. She felt safest when withdrawn, sometimes entranced by recordings of Broadway musicals, enjoying singing along. Her rich fantasy life was filled with exciting sex and vindictive power. Long periods of sleep, enlivened by dreams, were her best source of soothing. Chronically depressed, she was as wary of help as she was desperate for it. She hoped psychoanalysis would help her feel more comfortable with herself and relationships.

At the beginning of our work, and for many years, Esther looked like a waif. Her hair was unkempt. Her clothes fit badly. She slouched. This self-presentation expressed feelings of being unlovable to herself and others. So forlorn and forbidding was her expression that some of my other patients, encountering her in the waiting room, expressed compassion and hope that I could help her.

We connected an accident when Esther was two-and-a-half to her belief that it was dangerous to be spunky. Catastrophic injury to her face occurred when her mother briefly left her alone in the kitchen. Esther climbed onto a counter to reach a can of crayons that she was forbidden to use without supervision. Running off with her prize, trying to catch up with her mother, she fell, tearing her mouth on the can's jagged metal rim. During a 3-week hospitalization, Esther underwent the first of two surgeries to repair cosmetic and functional damage. She has no memory of mother visiting her in hospital. The final repair of her hanging lip had to be postponed until her growth slowed down at age 13. Even after correction, Esther was very sensitive about the remaining scar.

Esther's mother had never dealt with important aspects of her own history. Her mother was frequently hospitalized. When Esther's mother was eleven, her mother was confined to a mental institution until her death. Unable to tolerate her own psychological realities, Esther's mother was limited in her capacity to tolerate her daughter's. She tended to treat Esther's body as if it were her own, touching her scarred lip, lamenting the damage as though it were an intolerable injury to herself. Esther felt her mother acknowledged only one body between the two of them. To want something for herself, like a body of her own, or clothing that she picked for herself, was usually not acceptable to mother.

Esther's father was even less able than her mother to let her be autonomous. Even after she was an adult, he discouraged separation and never complimented her appearance. Searles (1995) stressed the importance of fathers finding comfortable, appropriate ways to experience and express attraction and desire for daughters, seeing this as crucial to the daughters' successful resolution of oedipal issues, as well as an enriching, enlivening experience for fathers. He suggests this works best in the context of good marital relationships. Searles adds that there is a corresponding truth to the importance of analysts finding appropriate ways to experience and recognize the attractiveness and desirability of female analysands. In a paper on fathers facing daughters' emerging sexuality, I explored the importance of analysts affirming, when appropriate, the attractiveness of both male and female analysands (Katz, 2002, p. 287).

Esther got much negative attention from her mother and aunts for her attire. Her mother did not respect Esther's ability to choose clothes. She was humiliated by mother asking a stranger on the subway for advice on what style dress would be good for her daughter. She viewed her own opinion, as well as her daughter's, as worthless.

Only after several years was Esther able to consider that it was her own belief, not mine, that she was a shitty person and that the world was filled with other shitty people. Until then, she simultaneously acted out these beliefs and held them at bay with verbal diarrhea, dreams of shit, and her messy, unkempt appearance. Countertransferentially I feared my couch or myself being dirtied. I felt ashamed of these fears and judgments. We came to realize that her presentation aimed to protect her against anyone invading her body and psyche like her mother did.

Esther's use of evacuation to deal with affect took on new poignancy when she brought in a story her mother told her. When Esther was a baby she smeared herself with feces. Mother, not wanting to touch this shit, got a neighbor to bathe Esther. Esther needed to test whether I, too, was afraid to touch her shit. We explored the possibility that it might be a creative product as well as a disgusting one.

As Esther became stronger and more separate, she allowed herself to spend money more freely—to "enjoy her shit." She felt pleased that she was no longer an anxiety-ridden martyr. She bought an apartment and pretty clothes. She enjoyed showing me these garments and was interested in my admiration and critiques. She felt guilty for having something nice that her mother had not allowed herself.

Among the important beliefs that Esther began to question was her "badness" (associated with "shittiness") that she felt kept her subject to abandonment and punishment. When caretaking is unreliable and autonomy not encouraged—or is even punished—fashion may come to be seen as a punishment for needing care, rather than a technique for ensuring care.

As Esther slowly allowed herself to pursue her dreams, she began to anticipate a long-desired achievement: a PhD in Italian. Although she still wore her pain on her sleeve, or rather on her entire waif-like presentation, she dreamt of being an elegant, Italian-speaking woman. Venturing into an accomplished, elegant persona brought up old fears in new ways.

Throughout analysis, Esther had moments in my office of moving into a state of consciousness that was not expressed in words, but physically enacted in screams, contorted bodily positions, and lopsided grimace of her mouth that recreated the disfigurement resulting from her accident. Now that she was pursuing the doctorate that she had always desired, these moments increased. The possibility of achieving her life-long ambition of being an elegant, scholarly, strong, accomplished woman stirred up the trauma that her spunk, when she was two-and-a-half-years-old, had brought upon her. When her physical contortions subsided, I tried to put into words what I thought she was experiencing, or re-experiencing. We linked this with her choosing rag-tag clothing and messy hair to show me the pain and suffering that were so much part of her life.

Slowly Esther developed a sense of safety with me. She began to believe I liked her, even though she still thought of herself—and on a deeper level, of me—as a pain in the ass, sometimes even dangerous.

Esther was grappling with the right to a separate identity—to be autonomous without being abandoned, demeaned, and criticized. She thought this would be like being reborn. When she finally felt able to communicate this wish, her body expressed pain and rage. She banged her head and legs and rocked on the couch, drooling, gagging, spitting, screaming, and wailing inconsolably. I appreciated the power and pain in these physical enactments and explained them to Esther as communication as well as evacuation.

On one occasion when she sat up and began to hit herself, I told Esther to stop. She did, saying in a childish voice, "That's not good for me, is it?" She found my distinction between communicating with her body and hurting herself useful. Although these physical enactments and altered states of consciousness continued for a while, self-injury stopped. We became able to talk about these dramatic experiences, understanding them as reenacting her experiences in the hospital and, afterwards, at home.

Initially Esther lacked capacity to reflect upon feelings and put them into words. When I tried to do that for her, she felt criticized, using my interpretations to beat herself and hate me. I commented once that she held onto her money instead of buying pretty clothes and enjoying being attractive because of a fear of being depleted of the inheritance that made her feel secure and loved by her parents. She took this to mean that she was a greedy, bad person, harboring that "criticism" for years. Her endless self-critique also served, in true sadomasochistic style, to express her anger at me for my narcissistically wounding interpretation (Katz, 1990).

Eventually Esther allowed herself awareness that her face took on a scowl or glower when she feared she would not be liked or accepted, and that these angry facial expressions sometimes made her fears come true. As she became able to reflect upon how she presented herself, she saw her neglectful grooming and wretched demeanor as a way of "becoming my own monster to scare people so they leave me alone." She was simultaneously saying, "I'm so miserable, please have mercy and take care of me. Be nice. Don't hurt me." Beginning to recognize the down side of her appearance, she gradually became empowered to enjoy presenting herself attractively. This transformation did not entirely rid her of anxiety associated with coming out as a strong, fashionable woman.

After several years, as I reliably survived the rage she was certain would leave her abandoned or destroyed by me, Esther began to think about emerging from her "cocoon." She experimented with new ways of seeking attention. She metamorphosed into a well-dressed, beautifully groomed woman, proud of her toned body. Instead of mainly looking inward, she began to allow herself to look outward. She commented on objects and flowers in my office, and on my clothes. Fashion became a medium for connecting with and separating from me. Although she admired what I wore, there was an underlying current of criticism of my extravagance, naming me her "fashionista analysta." She prided herself on being frugal regarding money spent on clothes—in contrast to the shame she felt when she lost control in public places, becoming enraged when feeling her space was invaded by strangers.

We sensed that Esther's unkempt, shabby clothes represented her adult self crying for mommy: "Look at me. Take care of me." She longed for connection to her mother, to be seen and empowered by mother/me. Through fashion, she enacted her lack of identification with a caring other, and her angry refusal to accept limits. At times she regressed, lying on my rug, crying, "Ma-ma, ma-ma." These actions clued us in to how unresponsive her mother had been when she was an infant. As her enjoyment of autonomy and power in the analytic relationship developed, and psychic space opened up, she could contain and think reflectively about experiences that had previously been handled through evacuation or non-verbal communications, such as fashion.

For several years I had a dog in my consulting room. Esther greeted us daily with, "Hello, Dr. Katz. Hello, Dr. Dog!" This was not entirely a joke. She developed the custom of spending the first ten minutes playing with Dr. Dog. I don't believe I have ever seen more loving, engaged play between person and animal. In this way Esther began to show her loving, joyous side that she had sealed off out of fear that revealing it would forfeit her right to be cared for. My enjoyment contained her joyful experience and helped her to reflect upon herself as a loving subject and beloved object, and to integrate these experiences into her beliefs about herself in relation to others.

Esther was exquisitely aware of my clothes, hairstyle and color, and intrigued by objects in my office, sometimes lovingly stroking them. They functioned like transitional objects (Winnicott, 1971), helping her to connect and separate from me, as well as partaking in a paranoid/schizoid position in which she was taking me over and becoming the powerful one (Klein, 1975).

What we witness in patients (gaze, posture, attire) as well as what they see in us—and how we reflect and interpret this—are significant aspects of the analytic journey. Jarl Jørstad (1988) and others hypothesized that Freud's emphasis on neutrality (and use of the couch) was partially a defense against being stared at. Regarding neutrality, Freud's artifacts belied his admonition that it was essential. Hilda Doolittle (HD) sought analysis from Freud because she was suffering from writers' block. Arlene Richards (2000) refers to Freud giving HD a statue of Athena, the goddess of reason, intelligent activity, arts, and literature at the end of her analysis. This gift conveyed his respect and appreciation of HD's creativity, and his role in freeing her to resume writing.

Once when Esther and I encountered each other on the street, she did not recognize me because of her avoidant gaze. In our next session I brought this up. She explained that she focuses on her path, not the person walking toward her. Informed by Salomonsson's (2014) exploration of defensive gaze avoidance, I suggested that by warding off eye contact, she warded off destructive impulses. We understood that gaze avoidance was automatic when the other is a stranger—someone she feared would look at her critically. This expectation defensively stirred up her destructive impulses. Looking at fashion (hair, clothing) might be easier for most people, less scary, than perceiving their faces, let alone looking into their eyes (the mirror of the soul). This anxiety may be related to fear of love being absent, or present, of engulfment and/or criticism.

Esther's fear that to be strong and beautiful meant to be uncared for gradually gave way to realizing she could be empathic and helpful without giving up the right to either lovingly care for herself or be lovingly taken care of by others. Our work on her loving qualities provided an empowering balance to the painful work of uncovering her needy wishes to never have to grow up, and the terror of her murderous rage. Once she could enjoy being the strong, nurturing one, relationships improved. When she needed care, she learned to elicit it actively instead of by passive coercion via waif-like appearance. In spite of anxiety, she was becoming the sophisticated renaissance woman she always wanted to be.

Not long before her dissertation was completed, Esther told me her mother had knit some clothes, beautiful in design and workmanship. This was not the mother she had described in sessions. We thought perhaps that she knit these clothes before she (Esther's mother) got married. Now that Esther had lost weight, these dresses fit perfectly. One dress had a few holes. Upon my encouragement, Esther had it fixed, then wore it to a session. She was indeed the elegant woman she had been afraid to be!

As Esther's sense of herself became stronger, she had more capacity to contemplate the pleasures and dangers of separateness, mourn parental failures, and forgive them and herself (Klein, 1975). As her body and mind became more harmoniously married, she could perceive, in the present and future, safe avenues for autonomy, beauty, and connectedness. Physical contortions and reenactments of painful early experiences of feeling at risk of accident or abandonment had been replaced by profound sadness as she mourned the trauma that she had endured throughout early life. She is in touch with deep feelings of loss of past opportunities—especially in friendships and romance—and strong enough to endure this sadness.

Conclusion

Patients' facial expression, style, fit of clothing, jewelry, hair, and posture are powerful means of communication, and significant indicators of self-esteem and trust. They enhance the analyst's understanding of the patient and, when worked with, deepen treatment. Through these modalities, Esther opened her psyche to me, an empathic witness, as well as opening her eyes to the world. Coming out of her shell, she enjoyed my looking at her, even when I was sometimes critical.

When I first started seeing Esther, her external appearance communicated a damaged, unkempt, disrespected self. My job was to bear witness to present pain and past trauma. I was a self-object looking at her in a caring, empathic way, including addressing her concrete presentation of conflicts about being a strong, spunky, sophisticated woman. Although there have been significant changes in her life and fashion statements, she sometimes still presents mixed messages. Recently she wore a lovely dress for the afternoon ballet, but covered it with a "shlumpy" sweater many sizes too big. This fashion statement seemed to express both her love and hate in the transference (and perhaps countertransference). I told her it was a reminder that she harbored residual pain and despair. "Write that down," she replied. "It's a beautiful, poignant line." I was deeply moved by her ability, in the midst of pain, to think of my writing project, and connect to me in a generative way.

"There is something reparative in putting myself together in the morning—putting on make-up, trying to figure things out, what scarf to wear—like I care about it. I used to throw myself together," Esther said. When I asked what this meant, she replied. "I wanted my family to see it—a rebellion against my mother. If I tried to look good, it was never good enough, so I rebelled by not trying."

Esther's looking good and being seen as engaged and interested in others was poignantly reflected by one of my patient's reaction. In his session following hers, he entered beaming: "She looks so good—like a totally different person." I beamed back with pleasure at hearing this.

References

Anzieu, D. (2016). *The Skin-Ego* (N. Segal, trans.). London: Karnac Books.

Davis, Fred. (1992). *Fashion, Culture, and Identity*. Chicago, IL: University of Chicago Press.

Jørstad, J. (1988). Aspects of transference and countertransference in relation to gaze and mutual gaze during psychoanalysis. *Scandinavian Psychoanalytic Review*, 11(2): 117–140.

Katz, A. (1990). Paradoxes of masochism. *Psychoanalytic Psychology*, 7: 225–241.

Katz, A. (2002). Fathers facing their daughters' emerging sexuality: The return of the oedipal. *Psychoanalytic Study of the Child*, 57: 270–291.

Klein, M. (1975). *Mourning and Its Relation to Manic-Depressive States in Love, Guilt and Reparation and Other Works (1921–1945)*, pp. 344–369. London: Delacorte Press/Seymour Lawrence.

Richards, A.K. (2000). Hilda Doolittle (H.D.) and Bisexuality. *Gender and Psychoanalysis*, 5(1): 37–66.

Salomonsson, B. (2014). Infantile defences in parent-infant psychotherapy: The example of gaze avoidance. *International Journal of Psychoanalysis*, 97: 65–88.

Searles, H.F. (1995). *Collected Papers on Schizophrenia and Related Subjects*. New York: International Universities Press.

Winnicott, D. (1971) *Playing and Reality*. New York: Routledge.

Dreading and longing to be known

Chapter 7

The little girl and Detective Monk

Ionas Sapountzis

Picture a rather overweight, nine-year-old girl with articulation difficulties, a girl who has experienced learning and social problems and has difficulty expressing herself. Picture a girl who is embarrassed of herself, an adopted girl of different race who lives in a relatively affluent suburban neighborhood where every child, to paraphrase Garrison Keillor, is good looking and above average. Picture a girl who is described as undecipherable by teachers and tutors, a girl who is used to adults being annoyed and puzzled with her, a girl who has received much remedial care and attention but consistently feels she fails to meet expectations. Picture a girl who feels neither liked nor wanted, and has never felt secure in the world, and you can imagine how likely it is for such a girl to feel inferior, unsure of herself, and aware of her "shortcomings." You can also imagine how disengaged and alone she is likely to feel.

She is a girl who seems very playful but does not play; eager to come for sessions but indifferent to everything once in the room; a girl who does not ask questions and does not seek answers; a girl who makes statements but does not seem to expect her statements will be understood. She is a nine-year-old who looks and dresses like twelve-thirteen but acts like six or seven, a girl whose every act seems to be a product of evacuation that serves to deflect and confuse. Her inscrutable expression, part mischievous pleasure and part apprehension, part deliberate indifference and part confusing unawareness, makes one feel that she expects very little, if anything, from others. She is a girl who seems untroubled by the confusion she creates, a girl who thwarts meaning and makes people wish she were elsewhere.

Left on her own she roams from activity to activity, material to material, item to item with disturbing casualness, as if nothing matters, as if nothing can be made out of anything. Left on her own she creates a vacuum, a vacuum she seems to seek and yet feels uncomfortable in, a vacuum that is part defense and part offense. She responds to the confusion and irritation her acts trigger by becoming more chaotic and meaningless, more distant and provocative. She is a girl who seems lost, a girl who cannot organize her world and defies others' attempts to do so. She is an alien in a world she does not understand and does not seek to understand.

Who is this girl? Is she lost in time and space, full of action and impulse, like the children Ekstein (1983) described? She acts as if nothing matters, as if it serves no purpose at all to make sense out of who we are and what we do. Reflecting on how she might feel, observing that she seems as if she does not know what to do in the room and what to make of me, elicits no responses from her, as if these comments were not addressed to her. Over time, I begin to feel my observations make her feel watched and evaluated. I begin to understand how defensive my observations and remarks are, how uncertain and stuck I feel. It does not take long to realize that she is convinced I won't like her, that I am just another adult who is put off and will find her lacking once he gets to know her. It takes me some time to realize she is an angry girl who cannot articulate nor tolerate her anger; that she is a frightened girl who cannot tolerate nor articulate her fears; that she is a girl who cannot contemplate her experiences (O'Shaughnessy, 1981) and needs to distance herself from them.

Her play is a parody, a mockery of play. Shooting hoops quickly evolves into tossing her shoes to the hoop. Glue and clay are mashed together into an amorphous pulp. She puts morsels of clay in her mouth, proceeding to chew them with feigned relish, watching to see how I will react. Pretend money and coins are tossed high in the air and stuffed animals are dropped to make the carpet feel "squishy" as she steps on them. Art materials are swept from table to floor with dramatic, exaggerated gestures, as if they are in the way. The little kilim on the floor is tossed up again and again. She seems intoxicated by the mess she creates. Papers are ripped. Kleenex boxes are emptied with one decisive yank. She is a tornado, undoing everything in her wake, having no intention of returning anything back to its original state. It takes fifteen minutes to restore the room after she leaves.

What is she communicating? What does she seek through deliberately aimless acts that often leave everyone, including her, confused and eventually angry? The little girl ridicules me, my expressions and accent. She seems to enjoy being provocative and turning our sessions into "nothing." She stares at me and burps, burps again, then farts. In a basket filled with markers, she quickly locates the permanent ones and gleefully, with sudden decisive swipes, attempts to mark me. What is she seeking? Is she aggressive and dismissive? Or is she trying, through provocative, unsettling acts, to engage and play with me? For Willock (1990), in this type of acting out behavior, which is indicative of "arrested and distorted development," one can also "detect a potentially healthy element of play" (p. 332). It is an element of play that is easy to miss however, and instead, feel vexed with her and relieved when the session is over.

The little girl is not merely a girl who projects chaos and confusion. More importantly, she is a girl who does not want and does not seek, to introject. She is a girl not dismantled or "unmantled," to use Alvarez's (1992, p. 95) expression, but a girl who is terrified of becoming "mantled," a girl who is uncomfortable with herself and afraid to find out who she is. She is a girl who feels unloved and unlovable (Willock, 1987), a girl who is afraid of being "found" (Winnicott, 1963, p. 185). Her acts, which leave everyone confused and unsure as to what to do with her, confirm her expectations and outlook— namely, that little is communicated with words and, more importantly, that she finds little in interactions with others that make her feel sustained and held. The little girl seems to find temporary safety in the havoc she creates but her escape into the nonsensical comes at a personal cost, that of feeling disengaged in life and not liked by others.

The little girl runs ahead of me to the therapy room, slams the door behind her and locks herself in. The possible meanings of her act, its possible playfulness is easily missed underneath the feeling of being locked out, of having the door slammed in my face with gleeful excitement. The little girl makes herself unwanted and unliked, a frightening reality she cannot *take in* but, instead, has to deny by making everything inconsequential. It is a cycle she repeats again and again as she finds herself unable to cope with demands and expectations. Without being aware of it, she makes communication impossible and is at risk of remaining unfound, "a disaster" in Winnicott's (1963, p. 183) view that will confirm her isolation in the world.

Protective properties of the little girl's acts can easily be lost in the vacuum she creates. If everything is meaningless, if what people say and do is seen as meaningless, then their criticisms of her and their frustrations with her are meaningless, too. They become transformed into irrelevant acts she can make fun of. She is at risk of remaining forever lost in a state of Neverland, a place where nothing grows and nothing is taken seriously, a tragedy since it is her fear of being found of no-consequence (Truckle, 2004) that has brought her to this emotional state. It is easy to misunderstand her unless one is willing to reverse course and see in her provocative acts of confusion, not the aggression but the fear and the desire to engage while remaining hidden, the yearning to be found without feeling exposed.

"Mom, are you ok? Are you ok? Can we race? Can we race mom?" The repeated questions of my then five-year-old daughter as my wife entered home after spending 3–4 days at a hospital, come to me and help me make sense of the little girl's puzzling insistence on playing a physical game with me, like shooting hoops or tossing a nerf ball or pillows back and forth. These are not activities she had shown much interest for in the past. Her insistence on physical play feels rather vexing as my sore back makes me unable to make sudden moves. But my daughter's questions and the excitement and fear she conveyed when she uttered them, make me realize that underneath the little girl's peculiar insistence on physical activity there is fear and concern about my state, and also a wish that this is not the case. After all, only a few weeks prior to our session she had seen her father taken by ambulance to an emergency center.

"Are you ok?" "Can you play?" "Is everything ok with you?" "Are you upset with me?" "Are you giving up on me?" Is this what the little girl is asking? Are her persistent demands fueled by emotions she cannot name nor tolerate? It certainly seems so. I do not say anything about her father having been in an emergency unit and her feeling frightened by his fragility. Instead, I tell her she must have noticed that I was not feeling well that day and she did not like that. I tell her this was very sweet of her and that it took me some time to realize it. The little girl, as she often does when something has been stirred inside her, does not respond to my remark but instead smiles, sits by the table and begins to draw lines in different colors. "Can you tolerate my mess? Can you tolerate me? Can you find me likable despite my acts and in spite of myself?" Is this what the little girl asks when she becomes provocative and seems intent on making a mess? Is this what she is searching for?

These intentions imply a desire, a wish to relate and connect. Wondering about the possible intentions enables me to reverse perspectives (Bion, 1962a) and experience her not as offensive and disturbed, but as a desperate girl, troubled by who she is and fearful of the world. It is only when her acts of "active non-communication" (Winnicott, 1963, p. 188) are treated as acts of indirect communication that they cease to be seen as acts of a deliberate offender. It is only then that her acts begin to be understood as acts of a girl who cannot generate meaningful and validating moments for herself, and finds herself feeling lost in the world and alone. As long as she is frightened of herself and engages in acts that leave her feeling inconsequential, she is at risk of remaining forever hidden, deep in the provocative and burlesque, forever misunderstood, forever finding safety in the nothingness she creates. She runs the risk of remaining in that state until one comes to realize how important her hiding is, how she needs her "psychic retreat" (Steiner, 1993) to preserve herself. For her to not feel threatened by the other she first needs to feel that the other is not put off (Winnicott, 1971a) by her, however provocative she strives to be. This is not simply a matter of tolerating her destructive acts. It is a matter of recognizing the desire underneath them and tapping into the playful element that is embedded in them.

I do not interpret the girl's acts when she pops clay in her mouth, lets saliva drool on the floor, picks her nose, rolls the excrement with her fingers, then with a theatrical gesture flicks it across the room. Instead, I pay attention to the satisfaction she derives in challenging me and I seek to acknowledge it and, in the process, make her feel nontoxic. She burps and I pretend to be horrified. She throws objects on the floor and I exclaim "Ha! Take that, silly world." She puts her finger in her nose and pretends to roll the excrement and I say to her "Really?" I look at her as I open the door to the waiting room and say, as I notice her getting ready to dart for the door, "Get set, run!" A second later, as she reaches to close the door in a hurry, I add, "Aaand lock!" She empties the box that is filled with markers with one swipe. She reaches for the drawing paper and pulls a sheet out of the stack in a manner that ensures everything will land on the floor. I say "Yesss" and clap. She looks at me and shakes her head with disapproval. I try not to flinch when she squirts all the glue and glitter from the containers onto the paper, but I notice that over time she seems less messy, that she listens when I ask her to keep the glue on the paper, to make her deliberate messiness well, more deliberate and less messy. I notice that she listens when I indicate which items she should not throw on the floor and which shelves should be left off limits. I notice she does not reach for the objects that can break but only for those that can create a rather "safe" mess.

Our engagement has begun to feel more playful and anticipatory. Several times, as I notice her getting testy, I lean forward and tell her softly, as if I were sharing a secret, that I have found that she "just loves doing the opposite of what everyone expects," that she is Ms. Opposite. I wink at her and tell her that by that logic, farting and burping can be expressions of greeting me, locking the door is surely a gesture of inviting me in, and tossing papers on the floor and making a mess are her way of telling me that she enjoys being in the room with me. The little girl stares at me with an expression of bewildered amusement, shakes her head, and tells me I need a doctor. "If you tell me I need a doctor it means I am the most wholesome person in the entire world," I say, bowing theatrically to convey my gratitude. The little girl is quick to correct herself: "No, you don't need a doctor. You are very healthy!" And so we continue for a while, with each provocation, each seemingly destructive act being treated as a tease, a challenge to find the playful underneath it and, with that, what she cannot articulate with words. It is a game of hide-and-seek that has become our pattern of engagement in which what I offer her is not my insight nor my capacity to engage in the metaphor (Krimendahl, 1998) with her but my desire to find her and engage with her in the meaningless and seemingly random.

Is it just my impression? Slowly, her determined messiness seems less determined and messy and, more importantly, less needed to create an exchange. The tone of the sessions has become different as she feels I do not recoil from her and I do not feel put off by her. Gone are my attempts to structure her play, to find the *who, what, where* (Slade, 1994) in her acts, to establish causality, find the link, create a narrative. I am the one who seems to expect nothing now, no narratives, the "weird one," as she has called me several times and I remind her that every time she says "weird," I hear "special."

She looks for my responses now. She seems to wonder what I will do, and I tell her that. I tell her that like her, I also wonder what might happen next and what I will do. I realize that I have begun to look forward to her coming, knowing that anything could happen. She has begun to leave behind her casually, accidentally, her little creations, as if she just forgot them—an origami box or star, a small heart cut from construction paper. She leaves the imprints of her hands on papers. She leaves papers on which she has tried again and again to write her name as calligraphically as possible, using as many different colors as possible. She preoccupies herself with no more than two activities per session. When she leaves, it does not feel anymore as if a tornado has just passed through but that, instead, an active child has been there, a child younger than her age but a child nevertheless, who has left behind remnants of her play. She seems less determined to provoke me. She does not seem to need to hide as much underneath chaos.

Is it enough? Is our playful back and forth banter sufficient? Like the young clients in Willock's (1990) paper, the little girl's defiant and provocative acts have been "transformed by means of the analytic relationship" (p. 330) into unmistakably playful exchanges that make us enjoy the presence of each other. For Winnicott (1971b) this is a significant development. The little girl is still a mystery, even to herself, but as she gets older, she needs more than my playfully unpredictable reactions. After all, she is not a 9 or 10-year-old child anymore. She is now a thirteen-year-old who dresses like 14–15. She has gained weight. She still has difficulties in school and few friends. Her face is covered with pimples, a "pockface" as she calls a face she hurriedly draws one day, angrily filling it with marks. She is still playful but her provocations do not serve the purpose of testing me to see if I can tolerate her. Rather, they seem to serve the purpose of escaping what she cannot face and of creating something, anything, to fill the absences she creates. She is still a girl with significant language difficulties which become more pronounced when she has to articulate thoughts and desires. She is still a girl who is frightened by her perception of what she is not and what she fears will never be.

The little girl, who is not so little anymore, is at risk of remaining hidden, forever "unfound" (Winnicott, 1963, p. 187), a tragedy in Winnicott's view, forever unrepresented in her own thoughts. Her parents tell me how difficult she is at home, and how much she lies and does not seem to care. I do not see her as a liar. I see a girl who is troubled to even look at herself in the mirror. I see a girl who avoids turning her face towards me as she enters the room, and when she cannot avoid me anymore, brings her face very close to mine, staring intently to see, I am sure, whether my eyes will waver and look at the pimples that cover her face. It is a pattern that is repeated several times and I feel disturbed, and at a loss for words, just as she is at a loss herself. I am at a loss until I pay attention again, not to what feels disturbing to me but to what feels frightening and the words eventually come: "You stare at me," I say to her, "as if you are wondering whether I like you. Can't you tell, after all these years?" The little girl smiles and slowly moves away from me. Although she says nothing, I have the feeling that my words have "touched" a chord in her. She retreats to an art project, for which she asks my help and she becomes busy making a bracelet and matching necklace while talking about colors, patterns, and school art projects. She is still a girl who cannot express her emotions with words, but she can be reached and does respond to "words that touch" (Quinodoz, 2003). To emerge as an adolescent, the little girl needs to find the language to articulate herself, a language that builds on what she has already started. It is the language that passes, as Quinodoz put it, "through the analyst's memory" (p. 45), a language that often requires the therapist's desire and capacity to dream (Ferro, 2005) the dreams she dares not dream.

The challenge now is not simply to tolerate the slapstick, but the emptiness that now feels palpable. It is important to tolerate her silence without becoming silent myself and without becoming dismissive of her. And so, I simply stay silent next to her, waiting for her to initiate something and help her along by sharing a thought or an observation, if it feels relevant. She often responds with a story of her own about an incident at school or home, something trivial that she narrates with a halting voice that conveys how anxious and uncertain she feels when speaking. She still likes to tease but it now feels less like a manic escape and more like an act of greeting. She shares with me that I remind her of Monk, the TV show detective. She cannot articulate why I remind her of him beyond the regressed statement that we are both bald. Perhaps she does not need to. Like detective Monk, I look for clues and value the trivial and seemingly insignificant. More importantly, I feel her casual statement conveys faith in me. After all, despite his initial uncertainties and predictable fumbles, detective Monk always finds what is going on at the end.

Sharing stories from school, describing movies and actors she likes, telling me about cooking recipes she tried and about Friday evenings with one or two lonely classmates she socializes with, slowly come to characterize the content of our sessions. She tells these stories while painting now, and her painting unfolds the way treatment has—random, childish strokes that she painstakingly transforms into evocative abstracts that surprise both of us. It is an engagement on Row C, as Ferro (1999) pointed out, an engagement in the transitional space between real and not real, the private and the shared.

Although some of her stories from school and her descriptions of events still favor slapstick and can feel manicky, they are a form of play that she creates. She seems to enjoy the experience of being the author of her brief, often incomplete, stories.

The adolescent girl has come a long way since the beginning of treatment. She has moved to the spheres of peer groups and boyfriends, of inclusion and exclusion, of being part of and expressing the desire to be part of, to a place where feeling known is less scary and thus seeking to be known and part of social groups feels possible. She dares volunteer for acting roles and submits essays for the school's paper, daring to risk being seen and evaluated. She is still uncertain of herself and one can see how brittle she is underneath her adolescent mannerisms and fashion conscious style. Confusing moments and misunderstandings with peers, teachers, parents and myself happen every now and then. One can sense in these moments that she is still a girl who cannot contain and reflect on her experiences when she feels overexcited or disappointed, when she feels she is not enough and not like her peers.

Sometimes, as if propelled by an impulse she cannot control, she begins telling me what happened and why it is so difficult to figure out what is happening. She tells me, in an angry voice, about a classmate who invited several others to her house but not her, and about another classmate who posted something very upsetting on Facebook. She tells me about other students who do not come to her support and in her episodic account I hear how wounded and ostracized she feels. But I also hear an adolescent who wants to be included despite her uncertainties, a young woman who perseveres and does not recoil when she does not get the reactions she seeks. Our last year together unfolds in this manner, with many promising beginnings at school and with peers that give her a sense of purpose and being included, and several mishaps that leave her disappointed, angry, and experiencing the weight of emotions and thoughts she cannot make much sense of. But she perseveres and keeps coming, never missing a session, always on time, looking not as much for answers to internal states and interpersonal entanglements as for a place where she feels welcomed and engaged even when she manages to say and do little.

Postscript

I remember one [a patient] who was quite articulate, in fact articulate enough to make me think I was analyzing him quite well. Indeed the analysis did go extremely well, but I was beginning to think that nothing was happening. However, the patient checked all that. After a session he went home, sealed up all the crevices throughout the room, turned on the gas, and perished. So, there was my little successful analysis—a very disconcerting result indeed, and no way of finding out or learning for myself what exactly had gone wrong, excepting the fact that undoubtedly it had gone wrong.

(Bion, 1976, p. 319)

Bion's words come to mind when the adolescent girl, who moved to another part of the country a year before she finished high school, calls me several years later to see if we can resume treatment. Her news is troubling. Despite considerable achievements that included scholarship offers from several colleges, she never felt comfortable on any campus and never really felt accepted by peers. The adolescent girl who is now a young woman has found it very difficult to function in the world and has continued to struggle with herself.

It is impossible as I hear of the difficulties she has experienced not to question the value of the treatment she had with me and wonder whether the playful tone of our earlier sessions served to distract both of us from the "nameless dread" (Bion, 1962b, p. 114) she experienced beneath her seeming indifference to everything—the feeling that others could not make sense of her and did not like her. It is impossible not to feel that I should have inquired more and persisted in my attempts to draw her out of her state of retreat. It is impossible not to feel that I should have been more demanding of her presence and of the treatment I was offering. Yet I know that pressuring her would only have intensified her tendency to disengage. The demand for someone to be more present presupposes that they can assert themselves in life. But for the little girl with her profound self-doubts and long history of finding safety in avoiding challenges and keeping herself hidden, any demands to become more present in the room would have been experienced as persecutory bad objects (Bion, 1962b) that had to be dismissed at all costs.

As the now young woman seeks to start sessions again, I feel touched by her desire to do so and the sense that after so many years something out of our time together has remained and has value for her. What was it? Although I never ask her and she never makes a comment about it, I have the feeling, indeed, the conviction, that what she found valuable during our time together was my willingness to look past her symptoms and focus not on what was missing in her and what was wrong with her, but on what was missing in her life and what she wished to find in her exchanges with others. Is that enough? With clients who seek to understand themselves and expand their perspectives on life, it certainly is. These are the clients who can use the treatment (Winnicott, 1971a) to generate meaning for themselves and implement their insights. Creating that space with them enables them to begin sharing experiences and, over time, make sense of their acts and others' reactions. With clients as avoidant, reactive, and brittle as my patient was, creating such a space may not be enough to enable them to find their way in life. For the little girl who now has become a young woman, that space has always disappeared whenever she felt hopeless and found others not being tolerant of her acts nor interested in her.

What then? Has the treatment been a meaningless experience for her, a waste of time and energy and nothing else? It is a thought that has haunted me, a thought that is likely to haunt any therapist whose patients do not seem to find their way in life despite all the efforts and time. There is, however, a risk that in posing this question about the usefulness of the treatment, one may end up negating the experience such clients had and what they found in their relationship with their therapists. The little girl, after all, valued her sessions and seemed to enjoy the support she experienced over the years.

It has been understood all along that this girl needed much more than one or two hours a week of individual therapy to find her footing in life. She needed the presence and support of others, a therapeutic milieu that would offer her guidance and structure. The little girl who has now become a young woman has always been prone to disengage from others and attack the meaning (Bion, 1957) they create for her whenever she felt threatened and at the mercy of impulses and reactions she cannot regulate or own. She has always been prone to escape what felt overwhelming through acts that however effective in diverting her attention from what she found unpleasant and upsetting, have contributed to keeping her rooted in a reality she could not tolerate and found it difficult to cope with. That, in my view, has been the focus of treatment with her—namely, to seek her out despite her insistence on remaining hidden, to look for what she wishes for underneath her silly mannerisms and dismissive reactions. I have always felt that it is exactly in those moments when she finds herself swept by emotions she cannot control nor tolerate that she needs to find a space for herself that allows her to be (Winnicott, 1971b) without making her feel too exposed and criticized. I have always felt that creating such a space was not a trivial matter for her. I am pretty certain this is why she stayed in treatment for so long and sought to reconnect with me after so many years.

References

Alvarez, A. (1992). *Live Company: Psychoanalytic Psychotherapy with Autistic, Borderline, Deprived and Abused Children*. London: Routledge.

Bion, W.R. (1957). Attacks on linking. In W.R. Bion, *Second Thoughts: Selected Papers on Psychoanalysis* (1967), pp. 93–109. Northvale, NJ: Jason Aronson Inc.

Bion, W.R. (1962a). *Learning from Experience*. New York: Basic Books.

Bion, W.R. (1962b). A theory of thinking. In W.R. Bion, *Second Thoughts: Selected Papers on Psychoanalysis* (1967), pp. 110–119. Northvale, NJ: Jason Aronson.

Bion, W.R. (1976). Evidence. In W.R. Bion, *Clinical Seminars and Other Works.* London: Karnac (1994), pp. 312–320.

Ekstein, R. (1983). *Children of Time and Space, Action and Impulse.* New York: Jason Aronson.

Ferro, A. (1999). *Psychoanalysis as Therapy and Storytelling.* New York: Routledge.

Ferro, A. (2005). *Seeds of Illness, Seeds of Recovery: The Genesis of Suffering and the Role of Psychoanalysis.* New York: Routledge.

Krimendahl, E.K. (1998). Metaphor in child psychoanalysis. *Contemporary Psychoanalysis*, 34(1): 49–66.

O'Shaughnessy, E. (1981). W.R. Bion's theory of thinking and new techniques in child analysis. *Journal of Child Psychotherapy*, 7(2): 181–189.

Quinodoz, D. (2003). *Words That Touch: A Psychoanalyst Learns to Speak.* London: Routledge.

Slade, A. (1994). Making meaning and making believe: Their role in the clinical process. In A. Slade & D. Palmer Wolf (eds.), *Children at Play: Clinical Developmental Approaches to Meaning and Representation*, pp. 81–107. New York: Oxford University Press.

Steiner, J. (1993). *Psychic Retreats. Pathological Organizations in Psychotic, Neurotic and Borderline Patients.* London: Routledge.

Truckle, B. (2004). On becoming of consequence. In M. Rhode & T. Klauber (eds.), *The Many Faces of Asperger's Syndrome.* London: Karnac.

Willock, B. (1987). The devalued (unloved, repugnant) self: A second facet of narcissistic vulnerability in the aggressive, conduct-disordered child. *Psychoanalytic Psychology*, 4(3): 219–240.

Willock, B. (1990). From acting out to interactive play. *International Journal of Psychoanalysis*, 71: 321–334.

Winnicott, D.W. (1963). Communicating and not communicating leading to a study of certain opposites. In D.W. Winnicott, *The Maturational Process and the Facilitating Environment* (1965), pp. 179–192. Madison, CT: International Universities Press.

Winnicott, D.W. (1971a). The use of an object and relating through identifications. In D.W. Winnicott, *Playing and Reality*, pp. 86–94. New York: Basic Books.

Winnicott, D.W. (1971b). Creativity and its origins. In D.W. Winnicott, *Playing and Reality*, pp. 65–85. London: Routledge.

Chapter 8

I won't know you if you won't know me

Irrelationship and the benefits of bad relationships

Mark B. Borg, Jr., Grant H. Brenner, and Daniel Berry

"You've never really appreciated how much I do for you," Joe complained to Chad. Something had shifted in their relationship, but neither knew what or why. Joe has always taken care of Chad in every way he knew how: emotional, financial, and daily needs. Suddenly, however, Chad's pointed gratitude for Joe had become dampened, leaving Joe feeling hurt, angry, and frightened. Why *frightened?*

Joe and Chad's interactive pattern, known as *irrelationship*, comes into play when a couple is overwhelmed by the anxiety they feel as they encounter risks associated with intimacy, particularly the vulnerability essential to empathy and emotional investment in another. In irrelationship, compulsive caretaking jointly enacted in dissociated-self-states provides a means for the couple to defend against this anxiety.

Harry Stack Sullivan (1953) referred to dissociation as "Not-Me" states—states whereby we protect ourselves from intolerable anxiety by becoming "not ourselves." Irrelationship is a relational version of dissociated self-state—a *Not-We* state, a Not-Relationship, so to say.

The impulse to enact irrelationship dates from early childhood when emotionally distant caregivers stimulate fear of abandonment in children. If unrelieved, this anxiety is brought into adulthood. If these trust issues remain unresolved, irrelationship will be repeated with virtually anyone signaling a desire to get close. Irrelationship is therefore thoroughly *relational*. It is not a syndrome, illness, or pathology, but a dynamic individuals enact together.

Irrelationship aligns with the psychoanalyst's interest in anxiety-reducing coping mechanisms that impede growth. To be caught in irrelationship is to be locked into an endless transference enactment. Reenacting fear that the world (as represented initially by unreliable caregivers) is falling apart results in jointly creating a defense system that prevents its members—caregiver and child—from testing the world (i.e. significant or potentially significant people in one's life) as children and as adults to find out if one's "security apparatus" can be lowered safely.

Origins of irrelationship

Harold Searles (1979) believed that a child's first task is to provide therapy for primary caregivers. We come to believe early in life that survival depends on our success as "therapists." We rapidly learn our parents' relational rules and strive to adhere to them. These rules are so fundamental to our environment that we generally remain unaware of them unless they're explicitly brought to our attention. Some rules, such as never asking for anything for oneself, or being scrupulous about showing appreciation for anything our caregiver does, leave us feeling isolated and empty, but we follow them to ensure our need for safety is met. As we mature, the same rules continue to shape our interactions. For example, if I made myself responsible for cheering up my depressed mother, as an adult, I'll be the romantic partner who's always "up" and holding things together in time of crisis. Or I'll be the person who takes it upon himself to make co-workers feel better when they're feeling "down," or things in the workplace aren't "going right." If this pattern goes unchallenged, I'll remain locked into it to the point that I'm unable to distinguish my caretaking routine from true connection and intimacy, and will have no insight into what drove my becoming a caretaker in the first place.

The parent/caregiver will come to depend on the child's caretaking to distract from negative emotions, thus signaling to the child how important this caretaking is. Irrelationship provides a means for both child and caregiver to distance themselves from anxiety. It interferes with development of thought patterns and behaviors in the child that are necessary for discovering how to build intimacy and genuinely meet his or her own emotional needs. Whether the role is that of the "performer" invested in fixing or rescuing mother, or that of the "audience" whose role is to be (or pretend to be) receptive to the parent's ineffective caregiving, the irrelationship configuration is an emotionally stifling straitjacket built for two. It provides for interactions that are safe from the vulnerability connected with intimacy.

Joe and Chad's irrelationship storyline

Joe and Chad were Broadway star wannabes who came from Middle America. Both hoped the move to New York would put behind them bad feelings left over from failed past relationships. Meeting in a therapy group wasn't love at first sight, but the attraction was resonant enough to augur satisfying companionship along the difficult road to stardom.

They *were* a good fit, but not for reasons they imagined. Joe's father had been a not particularly successful salesman who spent most of his time on the road, leaving his wife in charge. As the oldest child, Joe frequently found himself in a "supporting role" opposite his mother who felt abandoned, resented her husband's absences, and showed signs of clinical depression. Because he was the oldest, Joe felt obligated to relieve her distress by trying to cheer her up and taking on some of the caregiving needed by his siblings. To an extent, he was successful, although this resulted in years of resentment and estrangement between himself and his father over Joe having taken on roles proper to his father.

Chad's parents divorced when he was three, leaving him alone with an anxious, detached father whose insecurity about his parenting of Chad was relieved only by young Chad constantly reassuring him he was a "great dad." This did little to change his father's emotional state, but it did nudge his father into seeing that Chad's material needs were met, although only barely at times. (Though his father's parents financially supported him, they were largely absent from his life.)

Almost from their first conversation, Chad and Joe supported each other's pursuit of an acting career. Joe landed a supporting role in a highly publicized Broadway revival, while Chad continued working temp and catering jobs, interspersed with small, infrequent acting gigs, usually Off-Off-Broadway. Over the years, Chad increasingly saw himself as a failure, a spectator of his partner's success.

Their initial agreement to support one another devolved into irrelationship. Emotionally isolated from his partner, Joe turned increasingly to alcohol, compulsive sex, and spending. Chad's ever-increasing feelings of inadequacy made him regret meeting Joe or even coming to New York. Finally they called Dr. Borg, asking for couples' therapy.

From their first session, Joe came on with a flashy big star performance complete with an entrance suitable for a Broadway musical. His well-torqued song-and-dance routine, long deployed to counter Chad's negative feelings, was refocused to mesmerize his therapist. It was the wrong routine for therapy: Chad's boredom with it was well established, while I (Mark Borg) found it disrespectful and contrived. Thinking that Chad and I "didn't get it," Joe ratcheted up his performance, sometimes to the level of frenzy, sometimes interrupting himself to criticize Chad for not appreciating "all I've done for you," sometimes prefacing that with, "You're just like every guy I've ever been with." Through it all, Chad usually sat, scornful or unresponsive. He validated "all that Joe does for me," but without any warmth or gratitude.

After several months, they reached a crisis. Chad raised how fed up he was with Joe's caretaking and with his own grateful audience role. "It stopped feeling like we were sharing anything long time." Joe was shocked to learn he had been playing to an empty house. Their disconnect, they started to realize, had been in place long before either was ready to recognize anything was amiss.

Joe was not ready to surrender his "all I do for Chad" position. Instead, he added that I, their therapist, should consider myself fortunate to have such a famous client.

Chad took a different transference position. He passively resisted Joe's behavior by creating a new repetition scenario. As a child, Joe had felt that if he did not take care of his mother, he would die. Chad's passive stance created a sea change in their irrelationship dynamic that made space for me, their therapist, to participate in a way that exposed their pain—a risky maneuver that fortunately proved productive.

Interpersonal psychoanalyst Edgar Levenson (1972) believed that change in a system can be created through a practitioner's "ability to be trapped, immersed, and participating in the system and then work his [or her] way out" (p. 174). Consistent with this analysis, I allowed myself to become enmeshed in a repetition of Joe's terror by enacting a fear of failure as their therapist if I proved unable to convince Joe to accept the treatment.

Joe needed to believe that *his* intervention was vital to saving Chad from being destroyed by his career disappointment. Chad feared that Joe would be devastated if he realized he didn't succeed at "saving" Chad, much as Joe's routines as a child didn't save his mother when her husband abandoned her.

Over two years, I increasingly felt my treatment strategy was not succeeding. The position I had taken within their enactment gave me the sudden insight that they were enacting their transference-countertransference *jointly.* Their battle wasn't *against one another*. It was a repetition of battles against loss fought in early childhood.

After months of Joe's performance playing to Chad's silence, I broke through my increasingly uncomfortable countertransference position by telling Joe, "I think the time has come for you to do something about your selfishness." Both looked at me, dumbstruck. I continued, "Yeah, Joe, you do a lot of giving—till it hurts you, Chad, probably hurts everybody you're around. You're so full of your own 'generosity' that nobody else can give anything to *you*. By hogging the stage this way, you tell Chad, and probably everybody else, that that they have no value to you except as the audience for the Joe Show. I think it's because you're terrified that Chad will fall apart if you let up—just like you're still blaming yourself for not fixing your mother after your father left. Your biggest success as a performer isn't on the stage. It's how you've succeeded in isolating yourself in your one-man show without giving Chad even a bit-part."

Obliterating my posture of neutrality busted open Joe and Chad's irrelationship song-and-dance routine. Taking that risk paid off quickly. For the first time, Joe began to realize how exhausting it was for him to be "on" all the time. Making this admission cleared the air enough for him to see that performing for Chad gave him job security in their relationship without looking closely at what was driving it or the damage it caused. Chad was no innocent bystander. His role as victim-who-didn't-get-better-passive-aggressively denied Joe the satisfaction of "fixing" him. Their joint buy-in into irrelationship allowed them to ignore the divergence of their lifepaths and the anxiety and pain this caused them. When they entered therapy, they were pretty sure their trust in one another was not salvageable. As they uncovered their irrelationship routine, they began to recover what they had once shared and still longed to—empathy, intimacy, willingness to take emotional risk—all of which rekindled their excitement about one another.

Hidden in plain sight

Joe and Chad are a textbook example of what *Not-Relationship—Not-We—* looks like: keeping the world from falling apart becomes the reason for being together. By enacting a three-way irrelationship routine, Joe, Chad, and I each lived out caregiving roles.

Phillip Bromberg (1998) describes this process as it relates to the analyst–patient relationship: "As a patient's self-experience becomes sufficiently processed between them, the patient reclaims it, little by little, increasing not only his tolerance for self-reflection and intrapsychic conflict but also a sense of dynamic unity—the capacity to feel like one self while being many" (p. 310). Reclaiming Chad's self-experience means acknowledging and accepting the value of the other as well as reclaiming his own needs, dissociated since childhood. Allowing the authentic presence of another person broke through years of the self-sufficiency delusion, allowing a return to self-states that were open and responsive to the care each offered, including the therapist.

If we look at the Joe-Chad routine as "the patient," we can see that increasing acceptance of self- and self-other experience allows for diverse self-experiences ("self-states") which their anxiety had driven Joe and Chad to dissociate. "But first, the analyst and the patient have to live together through the mess" (p. 311). Over time, Joe and Chad each took responsibility for his part in their dysfunctional relationship. No matter how it appeared (Joe as success, Chad as failure), each had taken on a caretaking role that got in the way of building the relationship they wanted. The recovery process dismantled their delusion so they could re-appropriate how important they were to one another. "Meanings can be negotiated, shared and safely contested" (Jessica Benjamin, 2013, p. 365). Through this process, we created a space where we could be safely together/apart—neither symbiotically engaged in joint psychological defense, nor purposely distanced. We were free to care for each other even through the rough spots that are part of every relationship. Joe and Chad had found relationship sanity.

References

Benjamin, J. (2013). Thinking together, differently: Thoughts on Bromberg and inter-subjectivity. *Contemporary Psychoanalysis*, 49: 356–379.

Bromberg, P.M. (1998). *Standing in the Spaces: Essays on Clinical Process, Trauma and Dissociation*. Hillsdale, NJ: Analytic Press.

Levenson, E.A. (1972). *The Fallacy of Understanding*. New York: Basic Books.

Searles, H. (1979). *Countertransference and Related Subjects*. New York: International Universities Press.

Sullivan, H.S. (1953). *The Interpersonal Theory of Psychiatry*. New York: W.W. Norton.

The analyst's ways of knowing and communicating

Chapter 9

Knowing and being known
The effect of the analyst's affection[1]

Dan Perlitz

"At least two kinds of knowledge, two kinds of representations, and two kinds of memory are constructed and reorganized in dynamic psychotherapies. One is explicit (declarative) and the other is implicit (procedural)" (Boston Change Process Study Group, 1998, p. 904). Implicit (procedural) knowing is largely informed by affect and its communication—a far larger domain of mental process than the explicit (Boston Change Process Study Group, 2007). This chapter focuses on one dimension of implicit process: how the psychoanalytic therapist's affection, if available, influences therapeutic process.

I sense from the phenomenology of my personal experience that there is a constant, largely non-conscious process whereby I monitor emotions of others, particularly the presence or absence of affection. In every interaction, the questions "Do you like me?" and "Do I like you?" are being processed, alongside whatever else is taking place in my mental activity. This is a central aspect of relatedness that is ever-present, and rightly so, for the presence or absence of affection is a key signal of intersubjective safety. All mammals rely on ingrained, species-specific cues of approach and avoidance. Dogs know each other through the intimate smell of each other's bodies, but this only takes place once they have detected, through facial cues and body language, the other's willingness to be known (smelled) in safety. Similarly humans know each other more easily and deeply once we sense there is safety denoted by cues that speak of the other's affection. This process takes place in analysts as well, creating an important part of the therapeutic intersubjective field.

Neuroscience confirms the central importance of emotion in giving purpose and coherence to cognition (Damasio, 2011), from which we can deduce that the analyst's specific emotions, including affection, if available, can influence the analyst's knowing and the patient's knowability. Mirror neurons, facial recognition, recognition of prosody and tone, and other innate human capacities assess cues for implicitly knowing each other in the analytic dyad, particularly each other's affective states. Given the importance we now attribute to implicit process, it is incumbent on psychoanalytic therapists to explore the entire emotional spectrum of our experience, including affection in its many forms and nuances. Registering whether patients have affectionate feeling for us, and their nuances if present, is a key part of implicit knowledge and a significant factor in how deeply patients can allow themselves to be known.

I use "affection" rather than "love" to encompass the wide range of this part of the emotional spectrum. By affection I mean affiliative, accepting, caring emotional states ranging from mild fondness to intense love. Affection contains the felt desire to come closer. Its intensity and nuances let us know how possible, intimate, and vital our connection can be, and how deeply we can know each other. I would therefore modify Hanna Arendt's statement, "It is good to be recognized, it is better to be welcomed," to, "It is good to be welcomed so we can risk allowing ourselves to be recognized." This is why Donna Orange and I arrived at the term "affectionate understanding" (Perlitz, 2016) to denote therapists' affection and cognition acting synergistically, so vital to the psychoanalytic endeavour to know and heal patients. Empathy is necessary for knowing the other. "Affectionate understanding" blends empathic knowing and emotional responsiveness, informing the therapeutic field in a recursive, mutually influencing matrix typical of complex, non-linear systems (Marks-Tarlow, 2011).

Understanding without affection is "hollow" (Bacal & Carlton, 2010, p. 141). Phrases like "empathic understanding" and "attuned to" are often used to imply not only the analyst's understanding but also affection, without acknowledging the affection part of the experience. "Affectionate understanding" describes explicit and implicit relational responses and ways of knowing conducive to successful psychotherapy.

The analyst's affection generally acts non-consciously, a supportive foundation for foreground interaction. Although it can form a vitalizing enactment (Fosshage, 2007), its more important function is to provide a vitalizing background. I do not claim affection suffices for therapy. It is possibly not always necessary. I do not view it as pure but rather as part of the analyst's responsiveness that may include hate (Winnicott, 1949). Nuanced and fluid, affection waxes, wanes, and evolves over time in complex ways. Often a hard-won achievement, it does not always develop.

Being held with affection provides confidence that we are in a relationship that can tolerate revealing shame-laden and/or disavowed aspects of ourselves. "The courage comes because the patient, still injured and terrified but no longer completely alone, comes to have a sense that perhaps she or he will not be left to perish, to die alone" (Orange, 2011, p. 99). Enabling this deep connection, the analyst's affection draws the analyst closer to the patient.

Contemporary psychoanalytic theories, to one extent or another, recognize empathy as key to understanding patients. Although it is often wrongly conflated with kindness, empathy is neutral as to intentionality. It can be accompanied by and put in the service of intentions of many kinds (Bernie Madoff had superb empathic skills) as well as emotions of many kinds, including fear, anger, and hate, as Kohut emphasized. Patient's perceptions of whether they are deeply understood by their analysts are vital to the therapeutic process. Alongside that is the patient's need to locate the analyst's emotional reaction towards him. Valorizing and exploring empathy or other kinds of understanding without also exploring the analyst's specific emotions truncates the intersubjective field. It can be difficult to decide whether affection is cause and/or effect of our empathic process and analytic work, for in complex, non-linear systems cause and effect can be recursive and interchangeable.

The importance of the analyst's affection has often been noted, but infrequently expounded upon. Its recognition waxed and waned repeatedly in the psychoanalytic cannon. Freud and Ferenczi, once Freud's closest disciple, parted over numerous issues. Ferenczi's view of the essential need for the analyst's love colored all these divergences. His banishment from psychoanalytic orthodoxy submerged this aspect of the analyst's affection, although it would arise again and again. Michael Balint (1936), W.D. Fairbairn (1952), Hans Loewald (1960), and Sacha Nacht (1962) illuminated aspects of the analyst's affection and its importance. More recently Cohen (2006); Novick and Novick (2000); Fosshage (2007); Gabbard (1994); and Daniel Shaw (2003, 2007) have written on this subject, but its importance continues to be marginalized (a contemporary version of abstinence and neutrality).

It is interesting to speculate how Bion would have recast his rich theoretical ideas in the context of current perceptions of implicit, affective communication. One of his key concepts was "the function of linking one object with another" (Bion, 1959, p. 308) and "the patient's desperation to attack the link between two objects" (p. 308) which he viewed as a casual mechanism in the production of psychosis. He interpreted one patient's symptoms as the feeling that he (Bion) was bad "and would not take in what he wanted to put into me" (p. 309), basing his understanding on the importance of the analyst's (or mother's) capacity to take in and metabolize the patient's (or infant's) destructive projective identifications and sadistic attacks, the prototype of which, for Bion, was Klein's concept of "sadistic attacks upon the breast."

Were he writing now, with our current knowledge of infant development, affective science, and neuroscience, I believe Bion would have located the good-enough analyst (or mother) in the context of good-enough affective capacity and communication, and affection/love as the band of the emotional spectrum forming the foundation that would largely determine "if the mother can introject the infant's feelings and remain balanced" (p. 313). Bion may have added to "and remain balanced," an affectively neutral statement, the idea of maintaining her love for her infant. He may have recognized that transforming beta elements of "raw sensory data into units of meaningful experience he termed alpha elements" (Ogden, 2004, pp. 288–289) requires an intersubjective field in which the analyst's/mother's affection/love provides a reliable, vitalizing foundation.

I believe Bion would have evolved his concept of "O" to incorporate the nonverbal, bodily based, preconceptual qualities of affective states. He emphasized knowing and accepting "O," "the reality that comes before conceptualization, the reality of what is, a reality that we do not create, a reality that precedes and follows us, and is independent of any human act of knowing, perceiving or apprehending" (Ogden, 2004, p. 290). Many patients have been traumatically expelled from their own emotional experience and lead impoverished lives in which their "O" is not accessible—lives in which they may be able (not always) to think about their experience, but cannot be in it. The endeavor to experience emotional truth, Bion's "O," is greatly facilitated if the therapist's affection undergirds the process—affection that is unwilled, itself part of the therapist's "O."

The availability of the analyst's affection is independent of theoretical outlook. Slavin (2007) described a young woman who consulted him about studying psychology: "I was impressed by the personal awareness she showed in the way she spoke and commented that she must have had a good analysis. She said she had. With my own thinking at the time quite caught up with the relational perspective that was exploding all around, I said offhandedly that her analyst must not have been very classical. "No," she said, "she was very classical. She almost never answered questions and I never really knew very much about her. But I found it very helpful." I asked what she thought was helpful. Linda replied immediately, "She loved me, I knew she loved me" (p. 198).

For facilitating the analyst's affection, I propose three key elements: the analyst must strive for empathic understanding; the analyst's attitude must be imbued with hermeneutics of trust; and there must be good-enough satisfaction of the analyst's self-object needs. Striving for empathy in an overarching spirit of the hermeneutics of trust constitutes not only the optimal approach to understanding patients, but also transforms the analyst's emotional organization so as to enhance the possibility of the analyst's affection emerging. A forward edge perspective (Tolpin, 2002; Geist, 2011) is squarely located in the hermeneutics of trust, understanding even the most destructive behaviours and mental processes as positive attempts to survive and thrive. This attitude facilitates the analyst's affection, helping shield us from abhorrence or hate for destructive elements in the patient's adaptations, moving us in the direction of appreciation and acknowledgement of positive attributes. Striving for empathy moves us into the patient's shoes, facilitating the analyst's affection, particularly as we integrate empathic understanding of our selves and the human condition in which we and our patients are embedded. Since authentic affection cannot be manufactured or willed, good-enough satisfaction of our self-object needs is necessary to engender affection for patients. Striving for empathy and adopting a hermeneutic of trust expands the range of what is good-enough to achieve satisfaction of the analyst's self-object needs.

These principles are in the direction of attunement and empathic understanding of patients. This necessary foundation for the relationship comes before the possibility of mutual recognition and grappling with doer/done-to complementarity (Benjamin, 1990). Empathy informs analysts as to when it is optimal to engage more fully with the struggle of mutual recognition, the timing of which is part of the art of psychoanalytic therapy. The analyst's ongoing affection for the patient is a vital support for the dyad's cohesion in the face of the intersubjective negotiation of conflictual phenomena, realizations, and integrations. I hope to demonstrate these ideas in the following vignettes.

Helen

In her mid thirties, Helen began seeing me three times weekly during a crisis. She was in a fragmented state, often unaware of where she was, unable to sleep or eat comfortably, experiencing waves of crippling anxiety. Intelligent and attractive, she had been in a variety of therapies since age 20. A few months after we started, her anxiety and dissociative symptoms abated. She was functioning "like I used to." For two years our interaction remained lukewarm as I listened to her as empathically as I could as she told me how difficult and unchangeable her life continued to be. I felt caught in a holding pattern, assiduously working to maintain empathic understanding of how she wanted to use me to maintain her equilibrium. She was thankful she was functioning, *"not falling apart."* I was hesitant to disturb her fragile equilibrium.

One day in year two, the intensity of our emotional field suddenly changed. Helen came in, sat across from me, looking away, and said, "OK so it's happened," in a grudging tone. The room felt charged. After some hesitant, anxious enquiry, it turned out she had started to have erotic fantasies about me and felt in their grip. Thus began many months of exploration over what this meant for us.

Being the object of this young woman's erotic fantasies was pleasing. What facilitated the emergence of my much deeper affection was her trusting me sufficiently that she could be so vulnerable as to disclose these feelings—a much more powerful self-object experience for me—allowing for a more vitalized, intimate process that continued to grow despite her erotic fantasies about me disappearing after several months. This is an example of the necessity to satisfy, in a good-enough way, the analyst's self-object needs to facilitate affection for the patient. Thankfully there are many such opportunities. Patients coming for the first time seeking help may be enough, by virtue of the implicit message of the analyst's goodness and importance. Beyond this, a great gift bestowed on us is our patients' trust that we have the capacity to tolerate their painful states, to stand as reliable witnesses and companions to their suffering. This too can be a self-object function for the analyst.

Helen exemplifies the value of the continual struggle to know someone deeply, from inside them, and to understand their subjectivity in the context of a hermeneutics of trust. "When the hermeneutics of trust includes a forward edge perspective, we are inclined to discern the patient's thoughts, feelings and actions fondly rather than experiencing a sense of suspicion or negativity inherent in most pathological perspectives" (Geist, 2016).

Helen writes eloquently. The following is a poignant expression of the effect of my affection for her that she perceives from cues that generally remain implicit. This is one of less than a handful of times that my caring was made explicit by her.

> I just want to feel like I am less worthless. (I don't feel totally worthless but I do feel like my life is so small.) I want to be able to believe, along with you, that I can trust in myself and also in others, and that if things are hard, or if they don't work out, it's ok and I will find my way without having to suffer so much loneliness. When you give me certain looks it's like you're including me in a world that I want to belong in. You have this way of making me feel special sometimes, almost like you feel that you are lucky to have me around, that you may be thinking, "Damn, I'm lucky this patient walked into my life because not only is she so attractive, she's just so wonderful and it's so good to be able to try and help her, she really deserves to get better." I guess you're transmitting to me what I wish my dad transmitted.

Sam

A 48-year-old gay man, Sam, was referred to me by a trauma therapist. Her effulgent praise of my work with previous patients she had referred was a powerful self-object experience for me. I liked Sam before I set eyes on him!

In our first session, with a small, ever-present smile, Sam told me details of his life, including that although *they* called it a *suicide attempt* the year

Knowing and being known 95

before that landed him in hospital for a week, he simply had taken too many pills. "I had a perfectly normal childhood. My mother was taken to hospital a few times. She tried to commit suicide a couple of times, but it really wasn't anything big. We really were a very normal family." Also, "I've always been gay but it was no big deal. My family was OK with it. I've never really had a partner—but then look at me. Who would want me? I'm pretty ugly," said with a big laugh. Any exploration of his sense of being ugly was met with laughter that I didn't understand the gay world and how *looks are everything.* He typically worked long hours, came home and drank two bottles of wine while watching music videos and pornography, falling asleep after 2am.

Whenever I alluded to loneliness, Sam dismissed it. "I've learned to accept it. It's no big deal." He never cried in our sessions. Once in the two years we met a bleak statement leaked from behind his carapace of smiles: "I'm hopeless, aren't I?" His look of despair lasted only seconds, but could pierce stone.

I became increasingly dismayed with our inability to delve into Sam's loneliness, self-deprecation, and denial of what it meant to have his mother repeatedly attempt suicide, or his own attempt. That he could never use me to explore the misery of his life left me feeling futile, despairing, fearful, and resentful that he did not allow me in, that I was helpless to influence his downward spiral. As his sessions approached, I felt tired and burdened.

Suicidality, a difficult issue for any therapist, is poignant for me given my life experience. I didn't realize how important this might be in working with Sam. One and a half years into the therapy, I started to get sleepy during sessions, at first occasionally, then constantly, once nodding off briefly. I have successful relationships with other suicidal patients. It was Sam's impenetrability that left me feeling hopeless and narcissistically deflated. Our "feeling about feeling" (Doctors, 2007, p. 34) can be overwhelming, causing us to protectively distance ourselves. This is the opposite pole to good-enough satisfaction of our self-object needs enabling us to feel affection.

After a session no different than many others, I received the following email: "I wish to discontinue therapy immediately. Thank you for all you have done to try to help me. I feel we have reached an impasse, going in circles, accomplishing nothing."

In retrospect, I was unable to focus on Sam's desperate need to maintain his isolation and self-devaluation. It was there in his "Who would want me? I'm pretty ugly;" in his denial of his mother's suicide attempts and his serious pathology that manifested in suicide attempts, and much more. This contained forward-edge elements, no matter how paradoxical this might seem. It was there that therapy needed to begin, where Sam needed to be known. I should have better understood the tremendous impact his suicidality and barriers to intimacy had on me. Instead I felt compelled to distance myself, became drowsy, full of fearful resentment, the opposite of an affectionate urge to come closer. Empathy requires us to span the space between. It can only happen if we feel affection. I should have referred Sam to somebody who might have endured with him better until affection could emerge. Instead I continued a futile struggle which ended in one more experience for him of failed hope. I think I let him down badly.

It would be easy to describe Sam as a patient who can't be helped. However, he had kept coming—his attempt to break through isolation. I believe these outcomes should be understood not only as empathic failures, but also as a failure of the analyst's affection developing, often antecedent to empathic failure, so that affectionate understanding escapes us.

To mitigate the therapeutic failure that Sam experienced with me, and because it is such an important part of the analyst's emotional response, I believe it is essential to detect whether or not we are feeling affection for patients, and the nuances of this emotion, given that it functions generally at an implicit level. I try to find ways to ascertain my available or lacking affection. One way I do this is by engaging in a thought experiment in which I introspect what it would feel like to touch my patient's skin. I rarely touch patients, aside from a handshake with some. I have discovered vast differences in my fantasized tactile experience with different patients, and with the same patient at different times, from revulsion to warm comfort to pleasure. There is a visceral quality to touch that gives an immediacy to what has been non-conscious. Often I am surprised by what is quite disparate from my anticipated reaction.

Conclusion

Contemporary psychoanalysis emphasizes the emotional connection of analyst and patient. A great deal has been written about implicit process, implicit relational knowing, and right brain to right brain emotional interaction, *but* this discourse has been largely non-specific as to what *kind* of emotional interacting is useful, as if the connection itself is what is important without qualifying its specific nature. The analyst's affection is often alluded to but not clearly articulated, continuing the legacy of difficulty acknowledging it. Our emphasis on the importance of love for normal child development contrasts sharply with its de-emphasis when considering psychoanalytic process. It is easier for analysts to reference erotic feelings for patients (Gabbard, 1994). The canon concerning countertransference focuses on the problematic, the obstructive, and how this contributes to impasses, disruptions, and destructive acting out, failing to adequately articulate the analyst's affection, its availability, nuances, and importance.

Kohut's patient, Howard Bacal (Bacal & Carlton, 2010), experienced Kohut's affection at the end of a session:

> One of the most therapeutically salutary responses Bacal experienced Kohut offering him was an encouraging arm around the shoulder, at an especially dispiriting time, when they were facing yet another 2-week break … He conveys that had Kohut interpreted his need for such a gesture rather than offering it, he would have experienced it as a somewhat hollow response. In his analysis with Kohut, he discovered that neither Kohut's offering of empathic attunement nor interpretation constituted the only ways that *he* experienced Kohut being optimally responsive to his therapeutic needs.
>
> (p. 141)

"Hollow response"—a charged phase letting us know the power of Kohut's gesture. It let him know and feel Kohut's affection, concern, and caring. Bacal's purpose in describing this vignette was to address optimal responsiveness. I believe it would have greatly enriched our understanding of the essence of what was optimally responsive in Kohut's gesture had Bacal addressed Kohut's affection. Bacal and Carlton never use "affection," "warmth," or any similar word to convey that moment's emotional import. Instead they become emotionally hollow linguistically. "Therapeutically salutary" and "optimally responsive" are formal descriptors of Bacal's experience in contrast to the language of affection—caring, tenderness, love, warmth, any of which would have captured that moment's essence. We are deprived of the rich experience we might have had were our psychoanalytic culture more conducive to Bacal saying something like, "His arm on my shoulder let me feel his affection for me. The memory of this gesture has stayed with me my whole life."

In Bacal's (2017) moving "Credo, My Psychoanalytic Adventure—A Quest to Conceptualize Therapeutic Efficacy," published seven years after the article referenced above, he again discusses Kohut's arm around his shoulder:

> For me, the optimal response from Kohut was not in his words—it was, as Elliott Markson (1978, personal communication) so aptly puts it, in the "music." Markson was referring to the quality of the therapeutic effect that the analyst's verbal communications may embody, which may transcend the meaning of the words themselves. Kohut would usually listen quietly and receptively and respectfully, sometimes for a long time, before he spoke. What he actually said—and he offered many carefully considered observations and explanations—was usually of secondary importance to me. I can barely recall any of it. But the melody that went

along with what he spoke about harmonized with what I needed at the time: acceptance and optimism, delivered with warmth and kindness.

(p. 14)

The "music," the "warmth and kindness," conveyed Kohut's affection. This was the central element that led to his gesture, and the dominant memory that Bacal retained of his therapy.

Geist (2016) referenced Henry and Judy Gruenbaum's paper, "A Good Therapist is Hard to Find." They interviewed analysts ten years post-analysis, asking them to recall the most meaningful aspects of their treatments. No analyst remembered interpretations. All pointed to the occasional, heightened, intimate interaction as most meaningful. For Geist, these were moments where analysands felt affectionate connectedness.

Kohut (1984) had an inkling of this dimension that he was unable to articulate before he died. He referred to a South American analyst who finally said to her patient, "obviously in a warmly understanding tone of voice" (p. 92), that she felt her announcement about being away had decisively shifted the patient's basic perception of her. Kohut's phrase recognizes the importance of the analyst's affectionate understanding. However, his word "obviously" makes this passage easy to overlook, as if it were trite. Later in that chapter Kohut states:

I am convinced, furthermore that the analyst could have spoken the same words without the patient's wholesome response to the interpretation if she had failed to transmit her correct empathic perception of the patient's devastated state via her choice of words, the tone of her voice, and probably many other still poorly understood means of communication including bodily movements, subtle body odors, and the like.

(p. 94)

His prescient grasp of later more fully understood modalities of emotional communication is remarkable, privileging implicit over explicit, claiming emotional *tone* and human warmth, i.e. affection, is key.

Kohut postulated that empathy is the psychoanalytic information-gathering methodology. In considering effective psychotherapy, he did not explicitly marry the analyst's affective response to empathic ability. However, as the above-noted excerpts from his writings imply, he had a keen sense of the importance of the analyst's communicated warmth and affection. I believe he was heading toward articulating that linkage and would have found "affectionate understanding" an apt term. Both the analyst's affection for and understanding of patients are vital for effective therapy.

Note

1 This chapter builds on and elaborates ideas in *Beyond Kohut: From Empathy to Affection* (Perlitz, 2016).

References

Bacal, H. (2017). Credo: My psychoanalytic adventure—A quest to conceptualize therapeutic efficacy. *Psychoanalytic Dialogues*, 27(1): 1–19.

Bacal, H., & Carlton, L. (2010). Kohut's last words on analytic cure and how we hear them now: A view from specificity theory. *International Journal of Psychoanalytic Self Psychology*, 5: 132–143.

Balint, M. (1936). The final goal of psycho-analytic treatment. *International Journal of Psychoanalysis*, 17: 206–216.

Benjamin, J. (1990). An outline of intersubjectivity: The development of recognition. *Psychonalytic Psychology*, 7S (Supplement): 33–46.

Bion, W.R. (1959). Attacks on linking. *International Journal of Psychoanalysis*, 40: 308–315.

Boston Change Process Study Group (BCPSG). (1998). Non-interpretive mechanisms in psychoanalytic therapy: The 'something more' than interpretation. *International Journal of Psychoanalysis*, 79: 903–921.

Boston Change Process Study Group (BCPSG). (2007). The foundational level of psychodynamic meaning: Implicit process in relation to conflict, defense and the dynamic unconscious. *International Journal of Psychoanalysis*, 88(4): 843–860.

Cohen, Y. (2006). Loving the patient as the basis for treatment. *American Journal of Psychoanalysis*, 66: 139–155.

Damasio, A. (2011). A reply to Jaak Panksepp. *Neuro-psychoanalysis.* 13: 217–219.

Doctors, S. (2007). On utilizing attachment theory and research in self-psychological/intersubjective clinical work. In P. Buirski & A. Kottler (eds.), *New Developments in Self Psychology Practice*, pp. 23–48. Lanham, MD: Jason Aronson.

Fairbairn, W.D. (1952). *Psychoanalytic Studies of the Personality*. London: Tavistock Publications.

Fosshage, J. (2007). Searching for love and expecting rejection. Implicit and explicit dimensions in co-creating analytic change. *Psychoanalytic Inquiry*, 7: 326–347.

Gabbard, G.O. (1994). Sexual excitement and countertransference love in the analyst. *Journal of the American Psychoanalytic Association*, 42: 1083–1106.

Geist, R.A. (2011). The forward edge, connectedness, and the therapeutic process. *International Journal of Psychoanalytic Self Psychology*, 6: 235–251.

Geist, R.A. (2016). Unpublished Discussion of D. Perlitz's "Beyond Kohut: From Empathy to Affection." October, *International Association for Psychoanalytic Self Psychology Conference.*

Kohut, H. (1984). *How Does Analysis Cure?* A. Goldberg & P. Stepansky (eds.). Chicago, IL: University of Chicago Press.

Loewald, H.W. (1960). On the therapeutic action of psycho-analysis. *International Journal of Psychoanalysis*, 41: 16–33.

Marks-Tarlow, T. (2011). Merging and emerging: A nonlinear portrait of intersubjectivity during psychotherapy. *Psychoanalytic Dialogues*, 21: 110–127.

Nacht, S. (1962). The curative factors in psycho-analysis. *International Journal of Psychoanalysis*, 43: 206–211.

Novick, J., & Novick, K.K. (2000). Love in the therapeutic alliance. *Journal of the American Psychanalytic Association*, 48: 189–218.

Ogden, T.H. (2004). An introduction to the reading of Bion. *International Journal of Psychoanalysis*, 85: 285–300.

Orange, D. (2011). *The Suffering Stranger*. New York: Taylor & Francis.

Perlitz, D. (2016). Beyond Kohut: From empathy to affection. *International Journal of Psychoanalytic Self Psychology*, 11(3): 248–262.

Shaw, D. (2003). On the therapeutic action of analytic love. *Contemporary Psychoanalysis*, 36(2): 251–278.

Shaw, D. (2007). Prologue. *Psychoanalytic Inquiry*, 27(3): 187–196.

Slavin, J.H. (2007). The imprisonment and liberation of love: The dangers and possibilities of love in the psychoanalytic relationship. *Psychoanalytic Inquiry*, 27: 197–218.

Tolpin, M. (2002). Doing psychoanalysis of normal development: Forward edge transferences. *Progress in Self Psychology*, 18: 167–190.

Winnicott, D.W. (1949). Hate in the counter-transference. *International Journal of Psychoanalysis*, 30: 69–74.

Chapter 10

Winnicott's true self/false self concept

Using countertransference to uncover the true self

MaryBeth Cresci

Beginning in the late 1930s, Winnicott proposed a new way of looking at early child development that dramatically changed psychoanalytic theory. Although he attempted to frame his ideas in a manner that would not deviate far from the psychoanalytic establishment, he actually made revolutionary proposals that suggested fundamental changes to both Freudian and Kleinian theories. We are familiar with his many evocative statements such as: "There is no such thing as a baby," only a "nursing couple" (Winnicott, 1952, p. 99). His emphasis on the baby's use of the mother to create the illusion of safety and autonomy brought a new dimension to our understanding of early development. As these ideas were applied to treatment, new emphasis was placed on the analyst–analysand relationship. Winnicott's focus on having the analyst provide a holding environment deviated considerably from the emphasis on the analyst's neutrality, use of interpretation, and lack of gratification of the analysand's instinctual desires that characterized Freudian and Kleinian theories.

A concept particularly indicative of Winnicott's novel approach is his distinction between true and false self. True self is the "experience of aliveness" and potential for expression and development that children possess innately. Within the right environmental circumstances ("good-enough mothering") this potential can come to fruition, facilitating the child's developing personhood. If children are not provided with secure, loving environments, they adapt to their caretakers' needs and constrict their own development. In conforming to parental demands, they develop false selves that guard their true, inner selves from assault. They may become cut off from their own desires and wishes (Winnicott, 1960a, p. 148).

Even though Winnicott tried to ignore theoretical distinctions and conflicts, this developmental sequence was almost diametrically opposed to the Freudian structural model (Freud, 1920, 1923). In that framework, the child's id is a seething cauldron of unconscious desires needing to be tamed and brought into some kind of relation to the surrounding world. Ego and superego enable this process. The ego helps the child test reality and find ways to sublimate or neutralize drives. The superego provides a critique of the child based on the parents' values and inhibitions. In this model the child's innate desires must be directed to socially acceptable purposes rather than be allowed to manifest indiscriminately.

Another model, interpersonal psychoanalytic theory, has some similarity to Winnicott's framework in postulating that all individuals have multiple self-states, referred to as "me" and "not me" states (Hirsch, 1994; Bromberg, 2010). To a greater or lesser degree, these self states are dissociated from each other. Hirsch discusses how they may be entirely out of awareness, yet be relived in interpersonal relations. He refers to the person's character or false self as a "compromise between the striving of the patient for separation, self-development and optimal enrichment and the requirements of the environment of the significant others" (p. 784). Bromberg suggests that not-me states are a self-cure that may be worse than the disease. These self states, dissociated by both patient and analyst, are enacted between them without cognitive representation. Interpersonal theory sees dissociation, rather than Freudian repression, as the primary means of defense. As with Winnicott's true/false self, interpersonalists advocate that both states need to be acknowledged and integrated. "It is through the open, joint processing of each partner's not-me experience that the potential for expanded symbolization of self-meaning occurs" (Bromberg, 2010, p. 21).

This chapter examines how clinical theories and developmental models affect our ability to know patients, their histories, and stories. What difference does it make if we believe they are unable to express their true selves and can only show false selves to the world, compared to believing they are motivated by libidinal and aggressive drives that have created internal conflicts and anxiety? How do we use our sensitivities and countertransference reactions to arrive at understandings? Do our emotional reactions to patients coordinate with our theories of personality development or have more validity than our theories? Clinical examples will highlight these questions, helping us better understand how we come to know our patients.

Edgar and Eleanor

When I first met Edgar, I found his appearance notable. His pointed nose, round belly, and protruding front teeth were accompanied by a squeaky, whiny voice when he got excited and emotional. In contrast, Eleanor had a hearty laugh and pleasant demeanor. They had come for couple therapy, citing difficulties in communication. These professionals met through work, married late, and were now retired. Edgar resigned prematurely due to conflicts with fellow employees who, in his portrayal, picked on him. He felt loyal to his few friends and obsessed about friends who had dropped him.

Edgar's sense of being abused by others was a dominant theme. He maintained the self-righteous indignation of a wronged person and struck back with vitriol when he felt attacked. He preferred to spend most of his time alone, expressing himself in writing. He had a vulnerable side, a sense of humor, and an ability to speak in poetic language that highlighted his intelligence and depth. He described himself as living in a dark forest, looking to Eleanor to help him clear some space to let in light and air. Edgar's parents, Holocaust survivors, had shared their stories of abuse, terror, escape, and survival with Edgar when he was young. This traumatic history made him suspicious of authoritarian political movements and anxious about his safety.

Eleanor was feeling very frustrated in the marriage. She had been obese most of her life and felt unattractive and unlovable. She learned to use charm to ingratiate herself and be liked. Recently she had engaged in a rigorous exercise and eating regimen, losing her excess weight. Her wish to please people resulted in feeling caught between Edgar's preferences and those of her friends and extended family. Typically, she believed she and Edgar had reached an agreement about an activity they would participate in with friends only to find that he didn't believe he had agreed. She then felt caught between his newly expressed conditions for participation and the commitments she had already made to others. Eleanor also felt burdened by Edgar's depression and reclusive lifestyle. She was his primary source of companionship. His frequent requests that she listen as he read his writings, and his reluctance to join friends in social activities, limited her ability to be out-going and active.

In our sessions, patterns emerged. Eleanor had difficulty with silence; Edgar was comfortable with it. Eleanor usually started sessions with a current instance in which she felt caught in a conflict between commitments she had made with friends and Edgar's newer reactions to the plans. He would then attack her for making undue assumptions about his viewpoint, putting her family and friends ahead of him, not recognizing how he had been attacked by a friend at their last meeting, etc. There was something tyrannical and desperate in his efforts to control her behavior. It was clear he needed her full attention and love and was having trouble sharing her. We recognized he achieved power through silence, counter-balancing her more active decision-making style.

This treatment is still in the early stages. These issues are far from resolved. Our sessions are opening areas of light and air in the marriage. Eleanor can express frustration when Edgar suddenly wants to change their social plans.

At the same time, she is more aware of how he feels unsupported by her when he feels attacked in social situations. He ruefully admits he depends on her more than he should and blames her for not protecting him with other people. They are becoming more aware of how they can enhance or limit each other's ability to enjoy life and make the most of their relationship.

Discussion

That brief summary of the early stages of treatment provides a prelude to considering how I am developing an understanding of these two people and their relationship. Does Winnicott's true/false self dichotomy help? As I see his concept, it advocates that therapists should look for the better inner qualities of the person that are being obscured by an outer layer of defensiveness and personality structure. From this perspective, his concept is very useful. It enables me to see Edgar as having once been a frightened child who learned from his parents that the world is dangerous. While his intelligence and capacity to express himself in creative ways are part of his inner core, his fear and paranoia have made it difficult to open up to people and form friendships. With these thoughts in mind, some of his abrasiveness and tendency to strike out when feeling attacked are not as off-putting as they would otherwise be.

It is easy to see Eleanor as overlooking conflict, trying to make everyone happy. This is the only time she can be at ease. Otherwise she sees herself as unattractive and unappealing. Her true self is most likely more assertive and decisive than she is with Edgar or with friends and family. She has curbed those capabilities in the interest of being loved and appreciated. In the countertransference, she is easy to like and feel empathy toward because her efforts to please make her a cooperative patient. Nevertheless, I wish she would speak up and express her own needs rather than kowtow so much to others.

Andrew

Convinced he was most unlucky, Andrew came to see me. Retired from middle management, he has a comfortable life. He is proud of those accomplishments. Five years before we began, Andrew was diagnosed with prostate cancer. He underwent radical prostatectomy and lives with fear of recurring cancer. He feels totally emasculated because the procedure affected his ability to sustain an erection and have intercourse. He tried various options and found he can only maintain an erection with an injection. Embarrassed to explain this problem to potential partners, he has not tried to consummate the sexual act with anyone.

Andrew never married. He has always had problems with erectile dysfunction, especially in the early stages of dating. He consulted therapists in his 20s but continued to have the problem occasionally and to feel very ashamed. He did not have an ongoing relationship with anyone until his 40s. At that point he met Sandy and lived with her except for a few separations he initiated. Initially attracted to Sandy, they occasionally had sex. She was non-orgasmic and not particularly interested in sex. Over the years her mental health deteriorated. Fired from several jobs, she withdrew into a paranoid state, and became delusional. Andrew is her only social contact. He is embarrassed that he is living with a woman with limited functioning who refuses to leave home and join him for family events. Occasionally he has angry fits in which he insists she move out so he can find a more suitable partner. However, depending on her to soothe and praise him, he fears letting go of her because his loneliness would be overwhelming.

Andrew is also distressed that his extended family feuds. His successful professional brothers are married and have grandchildren. These two families have had serious disagreements. Andrew has tried to be a peacemaker with little success. Even though both brothers talk to him and invite him to family events, the entire family rarely gets together. Andrew feels caught in the middle even though no one seems particularly concerned about having him take sides. Since he has no children and finds his relationship with Sandy very limiting, he feels angry that his brothers are not providing him with the warm, welcoming extended family he desires.

Andrew provides minimal detail about his early life. He describes his father as an artist who befriended and worked for celebrities. He was often away in the retinue of these people. He was very critical of his sons and abusive to his wife. Andrew says his mother was a kind, loving person, disrespected by his father. He identified with her and felt that he too never added up to much in his father's eyes. He believes many of his negative feelings about himself are derived from his father's attitude toward him.

On the other side, Andrew has some feelings of superiority that at times he displays toward me. For instance, he possesses considerable information about his illness and other medical topics. It is important to him to impress me with this knowledge and take satisfaction in teaching me something I don't know. This also gives him some sense of mastery over his illness and general health.

Andrew takes some pride in being a good friend and caretaker to individuals who are unable to function well. He explains his continuing to live with and support Sandy as a desire to help others. He has helped several female friends financially when they were in dire straits. He feels more competent and masterful when he is able to take care of others. He also believes these relationships can become quicksand from which he cannot extract himself.

Discussion

Andrew is dealing with a serious problem in recovering from prostate cancer and the surgical side effects. His seeing only dire aspects of his prognosis and his inability to consider means of dealing with his erectile dysfunction have made it difficult to be as empathic as he wishes me to be. He fits the self-defeating, masochistic pattern that Nancy McWilliams (2016) clearly describes. Seeing himself as a victim in every area, he emphasizes his suffering in the unconscious hope that this will result in someone providing him with a solution.

McWilliams distinguishes depression and masochism: "The unconscious pathogenic beliefs of the depressive individual might be described as 'My caregiver is gone and I'm alone, and it's my fault because there is something bad or inadequate about me, and, given that failing, I'm destined to lose my relationships and be ultimately rejected and alone.' The unconscious cognitive schema of the masochistic person would be something like 'My caregiver is gone and I'm alone, and it's my fault because there is something bad or inadequate about me, *but maybe if I demonstrate that I'm suffering enough she will come back and take care of me*'" (p. 5).

McWilliams addresses countertransference dilemmas with self-defeating, masochistic individuals: "Even at the very beginning of a therapy relationship with a self-defeating patient, we may face a tension between, on the one hand, entering fully into the patient's felt experience at the price of a nontherapeutic collusion, and, on the other, remaining unmoved and seeming to 'blame the victim'" (pp. 9–10). My experience with Andrew is similar. I feel his strong pull to have me see him as a helpless victim. He implies he has no control over events in his life, depending on me to solve them or give up along with him. If I suggest he can make changes, I am seen as unappreciative of his overwhelming struggles.

In some ways, my negative countertransference is helpful, enabling me to avoid joining Andrew in his hopeless despair. I can have a more realistic perspective on his medical prognosis and see ways in which he can help himself once he recognizes that he is frightened of change and possible failure. In other ways, my countertransference can be problematic. Andrew can believe I don't take his difficulties seriously enough and don't see him sufficiently as a tragic victim fighting insurmountable odds. Being able to see how defeated Andrew feels while still believing there are at least partial solutions enables me to offer him new visions rather than leave him—and myself—in despair.

How does the true/false self paradigm apply to Andrew? By focusing on his struggles with a critical father, a submissive, abused mother, and two domineering older brothers, we can imagine a child who felt insecure and unprotected, particularly from the men in his family. While his true self might have included capacities to be assertive and fully engaged intellectually and socially, he was frightened to join this competitive milieu. Instead, he clung to his mother, who offered only limited solace. Andrew's false self includes strong elements of dependency, hopelessness, and underlying resentment that he received so little love and attention. By recognizing the inner qualities of the true self, it is possible to feel more positively about Andrew, more optimistic that he can harness his capacities to improve his life.

General discussion

What is the advantage of using the true/false self paradigm to understand and work with these individuals? This framework sees people as having potential to be fulfilled, productive, and creative if their true selves are allowed to develop in a good-enough environment. Difficulties arise when children need to hide or subvert their potential to accommodate demands of parents and other significant figures. Edgar, Eleanor, and Andrew all realized some part, but not all, of their potential. Their unhappiness arises from ways they have had to redirect their desire for growth and fulfillment to maintain connection with parents. These accommodations were carried into adulthood, affecting their ability to lead fulfilled lives.

We can conceive of Edgar's true self as artistic, creative, and strongly sensitive to others' feeling states. To protect himself from traumas experienced with his parents, he found it safest to withdraw from others as much as possible, responding vehemently with his sharp intellect when feeling under attack. Eleanor grew up in a large family of out-sized siblings and found that her true self, one of competence and enthusiasm, was not supported or acknowledged. She needed to become a helper in order to have a significant role in her family. Andrew's true self includes intellectual capabilities and desire for meaningful relationships. His false self focuses on his failings and need to bolster self-esteem by taking care of dysfunctional others. Realizing that these individuals have not been able to fully express their true selves enables me to recognize that much of my negative countertransference is to those aspects of their personalities protecting their frightened or overwhelmed true selves. This understanding prevents my countertransference from becoming the whole experience or something I try to ignore or deny.

Winnicott (1960b, 1964) described healthy mother–baby relationships as situations in which the baby's needs and aggression do not destroy the mother. There is a component of this in treatment as well. Each patient described above has the potential to want me to take care of them and solve all their problems. Providing good enough rather than perfect mothering is a means of negotiating their unrealistic desire for easy, painless solutions.

In contrast, the classical Freudian model suggests therapists need to maintain a neutral balance between id, ego, and superego. In the most traditional models, countertransference is seen as an unresolved conflict that will interfere with treatment if it is not addressed in the therapist's own analysis or supervision (Freud, 1912). As countertransference has been recognized as an inherent part of treatment, it has been acknowledged as a legitimate reaction to patients' personalities. Most recent perspectives see the therapy relationship as co-constructed with both therapist and patient having reactions to the other based on realistic and transferential elements (Hoffman, 2006).

The value of pairing the true/false self paradigm with our awareness of countertransference feelings is that it provides a clearer explanation for the origins of negative countertransference as a reaction to patients' false selves. It allows therapists to seek connection with patients' true selves while recognizing their false selves make it difficult to avoid negative countertransference.

In a moving paper on countertransferential hate, Winnicott (1947) describes acknowledging his own hatred toward an adolescent patient. Putting this young man out of his house, he explained to his patient that he was full of hate for him at that moment. He says we may need to avoid expressing our extreme countertransference in the immediate moment when the patient is unable to tolerate it, but that eventually it needs to be discussed and acknowledged. I imagine this progression is similar to a parent eventually describing to a child how difficult it was at times to respond in a totally selfless way to the child's discomfort when he was sick or crying for hours at night.

As we acknowledge negative countertransference we develop a more sensitive way of knowing our patients. Pairing awareness of our negative feelings with Winnicott's concept of true/false self allows us to know patients more profoundly. Negative countertransference is a reaction to their defensive false selves. Positive countertransference is likely to be a reaction to the patient's true self that is partially hidden but can be encouraged to express itself. Experiences of irritation and annoyance allow us to recognize that patients use false selves to defend against challenging, frightening worlds. Patients and analysts discover how these false selves have limited patients' options to develop their true personhood in treatment and the world.

References

Bromberg, P.M. (2010). Minding the dissociative gap. *Contemporary Psychoanalysis*, 46: 19–31.

Freud, S. (1912). Recommendations to physicians practicing psychoanalysis. In J. Strachey (ed.), *Standard Edition of the Complete Psychological Works of Sigmund Freud* (1955), 12: 108–120.

Freud, S. (1920). Beyond the pleasure principle. In J. Strachey (ed.), *Standard Edition of the Complete Psychological Works of Sigmund Freud* (1955), 18: 1–64.

Freud, S. (1923). The ego and the id. In J. Strachey (ed.), *Standard Edition* (1955), 19: 147–154.

Hirsch, I. (1994). Dissociation and the interpersonal self. *Contemporary Psychoanalysis*, 30: 777–799.

Hoffman, I.Z. (2006). Forging difference out of similarity: The multiplicity of corrective experience, *Psychoanalytic Quarterly*, 75: 715–751.

McWilliams, N. (2016). *Masochism revisited: Some thoughts on addressing self-defeating patterns.* Unpublished.

Winnicott, D.W. (1947). Hate in the countertransference. In D.W. Winnicott, *Through Paediatrics to Psychoanalysis* (1958), pp. 194–203. New York: Basic Books.

Winnicott, D.W. (1952). Anxiety associated with insecurity. In D.W. Winnicott, *Collected Papers* (1975), pp. 97–100. New York: Basic Books.

Winnicott, D.W. (1960a), Ego distortion in terms of true and false self. In D.W. Winnicott, *The Maturational Processes and the Facilitating Environment* (1965), pp. 140–157. New York: International Universities Press.

Winnicott, D.W. (1960b). The theory of the parent-infant relationship. *International Journal of Psychoanalysis*, 41: 585–595.

Winnicott, D.W. (1964). *The Child, the Family, and the Outside World.* New York: Penguin.

Chapter 11

Knowing him, knowing me

Harriette Kaley

The narrative shows how analyst and patient got to know themselves and each other as they grappled with Oliver's dramatic history, his dreams, and the transferences and countertransferences that pervaded the treatment.

Introduction

At a recent conference in Iceland, this chapter appeared with two others on a panel labelled "Transformations." The chapter is not actually about transformations. It's about a series of quiet, painstaking illuminations about me and my patient Oliver.

They are ephemeral, those illuminations. In the course of a treatment now past its third year, at three times a week, there were many illuminations, but also many foggy patches. It is impossible to describe fully the questions, the insights, the certainties, the uncertainties that came up, the sense of knowing him and knowing myself that gave way in the next session to a sense that I did not know in any useful way who this man in front of me was. When knowing actually did seem stable and dependable, I wondered if I was deluding myself, or perhaps engaged in self-congratulatory, possibly countertransferential foolishness.

It cannot all be captured, but there is value in considering a clinical report that examines what I thought I was coming to know about him, and about myself, and what that had to do with knowing him. The truth, at least at present, is that knowing him is an ongoing battle, an intermingling of his struggle to be an integrated person with my efforts to grasp who he is. Before even beginning this report, I acknowledge the danger in thinking I know Oliver or even myself in relation to him. There always needs to be an undercurrent of humility about that.

Oliver is male, single, gay, now 42 years old, European-born, well-dressed, vaguely Protestant. I am female, widowed, heterosexual, now 82 years old, a New York Jew. We are very different. Yet for him to know himself more honestly and fully through the analytic encounter is the fundamental purpose of our work. Moreover, that encounter had to be with me, differences and all. Through that encounter, we have come to know that the worldly, well-travelled cosmopolitan man he appears to be is constricted, hidden, isolated, and yet deeply yearning. I've come to know that I had harbored biases that I didn't know existed in the world, let alone in myself, and can care for—perhaps the better word is love—someone as hard to know as he is.

I kept a kind of journal and took copious, almost verbatim notes, and drew on them for this chapter. In addition, I was sustained during this work by my longstanding consultative relationship with a gay analyst well known in our psychoanalytic community. He helped with certain specific aspects of gay life and community—for example, matters related to HIV/AIDS. Mostly he deepened my work with Oliver.

For example, when I felt, as I often did for the first few years, that my patient would be better off with a gay male analyst, the supervision helped me see it as countertransference. Ultimately I was able to really grasp that it was, in fact, a distancing device. I now think of it this way: if I were disqualified by not being a gay male analyst, my difficulties in the entanglement with him were natural and immutable, were they not? Instead, grasping it as countertransference, the difficulties became a clinical problem to be resolved, a clinical problem that required hard work but that demanded to be worked through. Happily, as I was writing this, I realized I simply no longer have that distancing thought. It seems it simply was worked through in the course of the therapeutic process.

Another time, I repeated in supervision a conversation neighbors of mine had engaged me in, during which I'd suddenly realized they were trying to commiserate with me for my son being gay. My consultant helped me metabolize that disturbing experience and use it to deepen my grasp of what it means to be a gay person in a mostly heterosexual and often homophobic world. It made Oliver's wariness as he moves through a mostly straight world into something I understood far more empathically.

Clinical process and progress

An only child, Oliver is tall, with receding dark brown hair, neatly trimmed beard, and straight white teeth. Despite his ever-present personal discomfort, he often has a lively, bouncy way about him, and is gifted with a particularly pleasant speaking voice: deep, resonant, flexible, coupled with a very slight unplaceable accent. Though most people would agree that he is today an attractive man, thanks to genetics supplemented by his assiduous work in gyms, he is haunted by recollections of himself as a skinny teenager. He's always neatly and appropriately dressed, even when casual, even when it turns out—as it often did — that he's wearing the kind of outfit he calls drag. He considers the large tattoo on his right leg to be daring. When he pointed out that trousers conceal it at work, he unwittingly underscored the ways in which he was still semi-closeted.

I learned a lot about him early on, since he's often quite voluble, with excellent English. He's had, for example, romantic/sexual entanglements on several continents. But after six months, he startled me by announcing that he had been just "telling stories."

As time went on, I understood that he was right. There was such eventfulness to his daily life, so much affect, such grieving for a recently deceased partner, such anguish about his compulsive online sexual practices, such uncertainty about a new relationship, that it concealed a certain shallowness. He was in those early days of the treatment excited by glamour and celebrity, however superficial. He was, for example, happily excited when he encountered a celebrity in the elevator to my office. Moreover, despite his intense puzzlement about himself and his avid recounting of confusing thoughts, feelings, and activities, he often somehow deflected delving into the material. He "shut off" without querying it, focused on the "good" in despicable partners, and spent inordinate amounts of time and energy on the insignia of social status and on appearances, his own and that of others. I heard little about his work for an organization he thought of as elite but where his skills seemed under-utilized. That was acceptable to him at the time. Though interested in promotion and status, the focus of his attention was elsewhere.

Nevertheless, shallowness notwithstanding, he came to sessions dependably, dreamed, mulled over his thoughts, worried about his feelings, and reported fantasies. He seemed a fine analytic patient: committed, earnest, complicated, tremendously neurotic, and determined to get better.

Our work required that I enter a world I'd known only minimally and indirectly: a male world, a very gay world, a world with heartbreak alongside a very considerable emphasis on surface, class, and sex. He assured me it was a world very heavily populated.

Oliver lavished concern on details of appearances, his own and that of other people. He could, for example, be withering about someone wearing out-of-season footwear. I often in those days marveled at the blurriness of the line between pure snobbery and discriminating taste as he settled for image and appearance at the expense of attributes that he otherwise valued, like loyalty and fidelity. He seemed to long to be a comfortable participant in the ethos of Fire Island, the fabled gay seaside enclave he visited in summer, with its emphasis on pleasure, good looks, and affluence. Though by itself that ethos is not necessarily a bad idea, for him it was too often anxiety provoking, too much in conflict with his other values. Sometimes he understood that dressing up and being "cute" were narcissistically gratifying games without much depth. Sometimes he could get quite ruefully dismissive of his own snobbishness, perceiving it at such moments as petty. But most of the time it all felt to him truly sophisticated.

Oliver's world had an impressively single-minded focus on sex. He spent hours "bingeing" on Internet porn and using Internet sites to arrange hook-ups which often he pursued almost to the point of consummation, then abruptly dropped. He talked a lot in sessions about his sexual history and peccadilloes; his painstaking assessments of his own and his partners' attract-iveness; reported details of his masturbatory activities; of his preferences in male bodies, what turned him on and what didn't, whether he came or didn't. Initially amazed by his candor, I reminded myself that he was simply doing what he was supposed to be doing: telling what was going on in his life and how he thought and felt about it. He was not trying to shock, seduce or titil-late. Sometimes he educated: I hadn't known what butt plugs were. Sometimes he filled in details: hook-up sites, porn, masturbatory practices.

His sexual and romantic worlds didn't much overlap, though both were filled with contradictions. He loved dressing up, wearing dramatic well-tailored vested suits to work and formal dress to the opera, loved being with a boyfriend well known enough in the gay community to be recognized on the street. But at the same time, he was a homebody who loves to cook, bake, and cuddle, is often quiet in company even to the point of seeming shy, and was in essential ways still closeted. The most important contradiction was his increasingly close relationship with a man with whom he was unable to have satisfying sexual relations. Oliver wants intercourse, and wants it with someone he considers "hot." His boyfriend, Oliver thinks, is not hot. The boyfriend himself acknowledges he is "not a very good top." Oliver's discom-fort about his secretive "hooking up" outside that relationship was matched only by his partner's anguish when he discovered it.

Given all this—his apparent openness, the narrative richness of most sessions, and his story-telling as a way of seeming accessible while remaining unknown—it took time to grasp just how hidden and guarded he was.

It was more than three years into the treatment when there came a great rush of revelation. Earlier, Oliver had described his sexual behavior as something robotic that just got triggered by his being horny and was satisfied simply by finding an outlet. In what I took as a significant gesture towards being known, he described how he had "learned to be gay" in the bathhouses of London and Paris. In those venues, sex was separate from affection, from relationship, from ongoing life. There was impersonal desire with impersonal partners, a focus on ejaculation, on enticing transient partners. The reinforcement that sexual satiety provides, regardless of how it is provided, virtually imprinted this early learning (Kaplan, 1965)[1]. Oliver often dreamt of "tracks" of some sort. They embody his sense that he got "tracked" into a very specific, narrow way of being a sexual person. Early in the treatment, his bathhouse activities had simply been part of his stories. Later, he feared they had trapped him into a tight, constrained set of "habits" that he could briefly suppress by acts of will but could not change. Much of our work has been around trying to understand that pattern and trying to introduce flexibility into it.

Another revelation came in response to a dream Oliver had. A girl was puking. Oliver held a bag for her. It was more about the bag than about the puking. The bag was about keeping things tidy and contained. It was also about something sexual because, after all, puking is a bodily function. After some temporizing, he said there was something he hadn't yet said. Hesitatingly, he stated there was one sexual practice he liked that he couldn't get many guys to engage in with him. It involved peeing on him. With one man he'd known and been able to negotiate with comfortably, Oliver had climbed into a bathtub and gotten his face peed on, with a blowjob somewhere in there. At one point, someone, probably me, used the name of this sexual practice: Golden Shower. He smiled. I asked why. He asked if I knew what puking was called. It seems it's called a Roman Shower. So the dream was trying in different ways to help him talk about something he was half trying to hide. I think the part that was trying less to hide, the "Roman" part, served defensively to sanitize, even glorify, the practice. Roman, in that context, evokes not just puking and toilet functions, but patrician banquets.

Listening to the dream, I was fascinated by its clever allusions to the sexual practices. But afterwards, from some dim corner, an outdated, strait-laced, proper petit bourgeois remnant awoke in me, a remnant of me in my early days. He likes having someone pee in his mouth? Yuck!! Is that OK? I now think that is what eventuated in me wondering at that particular time if he'd be better off with a gay analyst. In other words, a distancing operation had set in. I grappled with that riveting but distancing Yuck! factor. This elegant man liked that? I was startled at my own capacity to be startled by it—as well as tremendously interested in such an unexpected wrinkle in Oliver's erotic life. And then, knowing that I had not expected such a tightness in myself, I was humbled at the recognition of the limitations of my much-valued open-mindedness. It was one of the moments that taught me a much-needed lesson about myself.

The simple fact of recognizing this discordance helped me resolve it. When I acknowledged it, there was no choice but for me to deal with it in myself so that I was then able, non-judgmentally, to grapple in sessions with

Oliver about what the practice and this particular incident of it meant to him dynamically. How, clinically, did we do that? We returned to the incident associatively, referred to it repeatedly, with curiosity and interest, but with suspended judgment. We talked about the man who was his partner in the incident, about his sense of safety with that man, about their similarities and differences. In the end, without whitewashing the peeing part out of existence, we came to understand that the important things for Oliver were not just the act but the way he had reached equilibrium with his partner, in an evenhanded, anxiety-free negotiation that preserved his valued sense of agency.

Conclusion: where are we?

I could cite other interactions, but space and time are short. The question remains: how much knowing has developed? For Oliver, most of it has gone unarticulated, but his life has changed. He bought a home, fulfilling one of his criteria for adulthood. He is in a long-term relationship, with lots of the sexual knots still to be untied, but for the first time he is with someone who is, as we keep saying, "a nice guy," a decent man who treasures him. He's more casually dressed, significantly less preoccupied with affluence and social class. He's more open, less closeted. He's more questioning, more thoughtful about himself, not merely trying to play out his fantasies, but trying to understand why he is having them. He recently took his boyfriend to meet his parents. Afterwards, the two of them vacationed and "had fun." It is new to him, this egalitarianism that having fun requires (Panksepp, 1998). Even without negotiation, he was neither dominated nor submissive.

It turns out that the illuminations that occasionally flashed across the therapy as we grappled with what was going on—What is this all about? What is going on here?—in the long run demonstrated that getting to know Oliver and getting to know myself are two sides of the same coin. For both of us, getting to know him is an ongoing project that requires my willingness to know and use myself, so that nothing—not my defenses, not my anxieties, not my own past—gets in the way of engaging deeply with him (Levenson 1993/2018). I know that his tacit understanding that I, too, am learning about myself through our interactions, and am gratified by the process, helps him brave the explorations of himself that he has in the past avoided whenever he could. I know, too, that we are engaged in a process that is reparative to me in much the way the therapy is to him. Engagement with him has been illuminating for both of us.

Perhaps in the end it might yet turn out to be transformative.

Note

1 See especially Kaplan (1965, pp. 39–41), for a discussion of how sexual satisfaction fortifies the sexual activities, including fantasies, that have led to it.

References

Kaplan, D. (1965). Homosexuality and the theatre. *Tulane Drama Review*, 9(3): 25–55.

Levenson, E. A. (1993/2018). Shoot the messenger: Interpersonal aspects of the analyst's interpretations. In D.B. Stern & I. Hirsch (eds.), *Further Developments in Interpersonal Psychoanalysis, 1980s–2010s: Evolving Interest in the Analyst's Subjectivity*, pp. 84–97. London and New York: Routledge.

Panksepp, J. (1998). *Affective Neuroscience*. New York: Oxford University Press.

Chapter 12

Spiritual knowing, not knowing, and being known

Nina E. Cerfolio

For seven years I lived in a liminal space between life and death, feeling closer to the latter than the former, my foothold in this world tenuous (Cerfolio, 2016). When I was healthy, I had the luxury of forgetting that my immune system functioned as a precise, intra-related cascade. Suddenly at the age of 45, I quickly transformed from a vibrant, high-achieving psychiatrist and ultra-marathoner—running 10 miles during breaks between caring for patients—to a sickly, immunocompromised, bedridden patient. My illness began in 2005, when I was engaged in humanitarian work with war victims in Chechnya, where Russian authorities saw aid workers as challenging their Chechen policy, and I was poisoned with what I suspect was anthrax.

As a result of becoming ill, I experienced a spiritual awakening that was essential to my recovery. The awakening consisted of an active awareness of connecting to transcendent aspects within myself, be it God or the Cosmos. Anthrax was the nuclear bomb that shattered my defensive sense as being a warrior-king. Part of my being a warrior-king was my counterphobia, running into my fears with a macho attitude, not being fully aware of the imminent danger. My assumed invincibility was stripped away by becoming ill. Slowly I began to embrace the beauty of my vulnerabilities. This recognition catalyzed my shift into a higher spiritual state of enhanced love, with a previously unknown state of limitlessness.

Seven years of spiritual growth during my illness culminated in a mystical encounter with a wild, gray whale (Cerfolio, 2017). In 2012, while I was paddleboard surfing for the first time on the Pacific Ocean, a pregnant whale suddenly spyhopped me. Spyhopping occurs when a whale vertically pokes its head out of the water to get a better look at the activity on the surface. The whale I have come to call Molly—a magnificent, 50 feet long, baleen whale—moved with the grace of a hummingbird. She spyhopped not once but twice, first 15, then 30 feet away from me, without creating a single ripple beneath my board.

With her vertical half-rise out of the water, Molly's upper body filled my entire field of vision, and then our eyes met. There was a shudder of recognition between us. Overwhelmed, I surrendered to this extraordinary moment. Remaining motionless and completely vulnerable, I felt a great power emanate from her body, a protective embrace, like an attuned mother. As we maintained steady eye contact, she not only evoked the sublime within me, but challenged me to re-evaluate my perception of intelligent, conscious life. Her wise, soulful, left eye held and contained me like none other for what felt like an eternity. My mystical encounter with Molly took me further; I felt reborn and resurrected by Molly and inspired to meditatively introspect and rekindle my creativity. In one instant, she taught me that I could surrender to my emotions to heal.

As a result of having gone through these mystical experiences, from my spiritual response to being poisoned with anthrax to my blissful encounter with Molly, I began to develop a deeper faith in a beyond I did not fully recognize. I felt it was closer and that one day, it would sweep me up into its majesty. Through daily meditation, I was further liberated from bounded self-states and released into the vastness of a more expansive numinous identity. I began to see my patients' suffering less as a form of psychopathology, and instead to view them as precious divine beings, engaged in a poignant struggle to grow and discover their own creativity. As I surrendered more to not knowing in the therapeutic relationship, I felt guided by a greater sense of connection and oneness. It felt that there was a divine purpose in the struggles my patients and I had in our daily lives. It took years of contemplating the meaning of my mystical experience to glimpse its spiritual lessons and gifts.

A distortion inevitably develops when attempting to define spiritual knowing, as it is ineffable. The vastness of the mystical experience refuses to be girdled by words. Despite this paradox, and the fact that my words will seem insufficient and didactic, I will describe how my mystical awakening altered not only my sense of self but my psychoanalytic relationship with Ben, a patient.

My spiritual awakening helped usher in a more spacious sense of the Third (Benjamin, 2007), in which Ben and I co-created a new relationship to explore the unknown and develop a sense that we were participating in something larger than ourselves. There evolved a new sense of a divine love permeating the transcendent Third (Starr, 2008) between us, which created a deeper faith to explore dissociated parts of ourselves, accept, and even change them. This newly co-created Third guided us to find new forms of relating, in which Ben and I could better come together as two separate, curious people who cared about each other and who could explore dissociated self-states, which previously had been impossible. After Ben unconsciously sensed and commented upon "my spiritual transformation," we became freer from our previous interlocking enactment. My becoming more infused with divine love allowed me to more readily accept my own vulnerabilities, which was unconsciously and nonverbally communicated to Ben.

Therapy with Ben prior to our transformative experience

Forty-seven-year-old Ben was a depressed, emotionally stilted overeater. Before my mystical experience, I experienced him as controlling, demanding, and emotionally suffocating, although he consistently thought of himself as being a "ray of sunshine" who constantly smiled and brought joy to others, despite acting in spiteful, self-destructive ways to enact and express his unprocessed anger. His dissociation owed much of its existence to surviving through submission to his mother's claustrophobic wishes.

Ben felt attacked by his own painful thoughts and avoided them at all costs. Initially, he refused to acknowledge he was overweight, as this was too upsetting. He insisted on thinking of himself as fit, despite being 90 pounds overweight. Ben shunned being known as he feared and associated relating with being shamed. While clothes shopping, he fooled himself into believing he could hide his large size by not asking for help. Feeling unknown by his mother, Ben clung to knowing himself in the only way his mother recognized him: as having unvaried and transparent goodness.

Ben related submissively to me as a constricted, rigid authority figure in order to avoid being responsible, and he tried to make me culpable for his well-being. Yet as a child, his mother's emotional needs eclipsed his own, and therefore he did not see me as a person whose thoughts and needs were separate from his own. In this way, Ben used our relationship to turn the tables, putting me in his place as little Ben. He attempted to overwhelm me with his unrecognized neediness and by playing his mother's role. Thus I was not allowed to have feelings, just as Ben was not allowed emotions that differed from those of his mother.

When Ben began analysis, he ate unhealthy foods high in cholesterol, salt, and sugar while remaining oblivious to the effects this diet had on his developing acid reflux and overall sluggishness. When we did discuss his diet's connection to his hypertension, he became enraged with me, as he insisted I was the all-knowing physician who should magically cure him. His mother had drowned him in her needs. She had expected him to save her. Now he expected me to save him. He became angry because I did not know the specific healthy foods uniquely suited to his physiology. I encouraged him to experiment with small amounts of healthy food to discover what felt beneficial.

After several months of interpreting his rage over my lack of omniscience, he confessed that after leaving my office, he went straight to McDonald's for a high-calorie, fatty feast. His mother's anger that Ben could not save her from herself became Ben's rage that I could not save him from himself.

I saw Ben's relationship with food—hurting himself and disavowing the cause-and-effect relationship between his diet and health—as masochistic, the giving up of agency. He engaged in negative surrender, a self-destructive submission. I use "surrender" in accordance with Emmanuel Ghent's (1990) reframing of the term in a spiritual and Eastern philosophic sense as an antithesis to the submission of classical masochism. It has nothing to do with hoisting a white flag. Rather than carrying a connotation of defeat, it enables a liberation of the self by lowering one's defensive barriers.

Therapy with Ben during and after our transformative experience

After my mystical encounter, part of my spiritual practice was to meditate prior to seeing patients. On a blistering August day, while I was meditating in my office with the door closed, Ben was early and sat in the waiting room. A feeling of rage and agitation crashed in on my peaceful and relaxed state of mind. I tried to breathe into the rage, but I felt suffocated and was overcome with waves of panic and the feeling of being out of control. When I opened the door to welcome Ben into my office, I asked him how he was feeling and he responded, "Good." Upon my pointing out that he seemed agitated, Ben stated that he resented waiting in my warm, unairconditioned waiting room, while he imagined that I sat comfortably in my air-conditioned office. We explored his transferential feeling of being a puppet to me, based on his earlier relationship to his mother.

When I shared my experience of feeling his suffocating anger while he sat in the waiting room, something shifted between us. While maintaining my sense as an analyst, I experienced Ben's rage as if I was inside his mind for a moment, as if I was a part of Ben himself. Feeling his rage from the inside was uncanny. I had gained access to his experience of feeling suffocated and with that a deep sense of being connected emerged. This superconscious experience (Suchet, 2016) of feeling Ben's rage while meditating struck me as an extraordinary way of knowing that began the process of creating more space to know parts of Ben that were previously inaccessible. This uncanny experience of knowing required a silence, a moment of not trying to understand in words that allowed for the experience to be felt and known from the inside.

After my mystical awakening, which encouraged his own burgeoning awareness, Ben became able to take into account my existence outside of my professional life. He nonverbally sensed and then commented on my spiritual awakening, saying I seemed "happier, serene, and peaceful." Before, when Ben occasionally sensed I was calm, he unconsciously resented it, as he had experienced my separateness as a loss of control and abandonment. Now he was able not only to become cognizant of my newfound equanimity but to find it comforting. He still at times regressed into defensiveness and feelings of shame, but he no longer thought of himself in reductive and purely positive terms, and became far less brittle. He also began to take initiative and risks, even though it petrified him, and to have more expansive experiences. Ben discovered joy in being a more involved grandparent and developed his significant artistic talent with less of the paralyzing fear of needing to be perfect.

Ben eventually surrendered his insistence on feeling like a puppet to his analyst and mother. He let go of his defensive relationship with food and began to take responsibility for what he ate. Radically changing his diet, he lost 90 pounds, which resolved his hypertension and need for medication. He transcended his need to be a victim, fulfilling what Winnicott (1960) described as the yearning to surrender the false self. In Ben's words, "I was fed up with being oppositional and butting heads. It did feel like a revelation, the shift in me, that I'm responsible for my own feelings. Although it felt sudden, it felt like a big container filling up with water but one drop makes a sudden difference and overflows." Then he added, "It had something to do with feeling less judgemental. I associate spirituality with being non-judgmental, not that you were particularly judgmental prior." He expressed his newfound need "to have a sense of community and belonging to something bigger than myself, like having a connection to my parent's religious practices of my past but with the new ability to take in the warmth and richness of the teachings, while leaving the exclusive, judgmental part."

Paradoxically, Ben and I had a meeting of our inner beings which allowed for a separation between us to grow and develop. Being allowed to become more separate freed us from being drowned in Ben's previously unknown, unprocessed anger. Ben began to experience a sense of authentic identity where he became more self-aware rather than reflexively allowing "the other" to define himself. He learned how to surrender to the analytic process, which did not constitute a submission to interpretation but rather a release of emotional bondage that obscured his subjectivity and a turn to a much fuller, more hopeful story about who he was and what he could do. As we learned to relate as a contemplative psychoanalytic couple, there evolved space for Ben to become self-reflective. His hostile dependency shifted to a more loving interdependency where we could be two different people with varying interests.

Ben's transformation came to be reflected in his personal life as well, becoming more thoughtful and connected with others. He became able to take the leap of faith to "confess," which was his word, to his wife that he was working on becoming responsible in his analysis, which freed him from his shackles of clinging to the need to appear perfect. He was forging a path to having a more empathic, loving, intimate marriage.

Another interaction that highlighted Ben's transformation occurred after he saw ants in my waiting room. He entered my office and stated, "I saw ants crawling from under the floorboard beneath the mirror in your waiting room. I felt a shift in me. Before I would have felt it's not my business and resisted feeling a personal connection with you by not telling you and not doing anything. But now I realized, this is Nina's place and she doesn't want to have ants in her office, so I took care of them and squashed them." Ben could think of me as not only a separate person from himself, but as someone who cared more about my environment. I interpreted his response with the ants as his evolving ability to relate to me as a more emphatic, whole other.

Discussion

One can learn about spiritual knowing, but it must be experienced and reflected upon to be fully understood. Even then, the experience is ineffable, revealing the limitation of words, as it is vast and limitless. Spiritual knowing can be seen from many different vantage points, but I will focus my discussion to this clinical case in terms of extraordinary knowing and the permeability of self-states.

Spiritual knowing as extraordinary knowing

Superconscious states of knowing reside at the far reaches of the continuum of empathy and intuition. They transcend space and time. They are associated with higher creativity and spiritual awareness that many of us have known, albeit fleetingly. Examples of transcendent states are heightened moments in the arts and sports, as well as in drug-induced, religious and meditative experiences. Superconsciousness involves knowing at the higher levels of consciousness called universal consciousness, in which we are all one and have access to all knowledge. More simply put, superconsciousness is the attempt of human beings to understand the numinous. Subtler states of consciousness (Suchet, 2016) emerge as we go beyond our ordinary senses and experience states of rapture, bliss, and equanimity. In these realms, subject and object dissolve and we experience states of grace and compassion that expand our ways of knowing.

My mystical and ecstatic moment with Molly gave me the sense of wholeness that characterizes spiritual knowing. Molly's soulful gaze welcomed me into an infinite, blissful universe, where my internal introject shifted from a disappointing, critical one to a more loving, benevolent, attuned one. In Molly's recognition, I felt known with a new sense of an empathic internal other (Laub & Podell, 1995) so that I became better able to glimpse a more attuned introject and articulate an inner empathic dialogue.

This process has been further explored by Elizabeth Lloyd Mayer (2007), a classical psychoanalyst, whose process shifted to incorporate the art of extra-ordinary knowing. When her daughter's rare harp was stolen and, despite all efforts, could not be located, she hired a dowser who located lost objects. From Arkansas, the dowser told her the exact street in California the harp was on, and Mayer was able to retrieve it. This uncanny experience changed how she worked as a psychoanalyst. Mayer writes about Grace, a patient who had unusual intuitive capacities to survive a traumatic childhood with a vio-lent alcoholic father. Grace suddenly knew, "by listening with my whole body, not my ears," that her father was 15 minutes away and driving home drunk. She would hustle her sister and herself into the closet to avoid his uncontrol-lable violence. She knew because she had to. Mayer describes patients similar to Grace, who developed extraordinary intuition through no known sensory means, in order to survive traumatic circumstances that required knowing more than people can usually perceive.

Cynthia Bourgeault (2003), a Christian mystic who teaches how to know through meditation and breath, refers to the ensuing wisdom as "seeing with the eye of the heart." By slowing down the breath, one may surrender into a deeper state of relaxation that allows for a spaciousness to open and for a deeper empathic intuitiveness to develop. Bourgeault's "wisdom way of knowing" goes beyond one's mind, the intellectual and rational way of thinking, to embody the entirety of the person: body, mind, and spirit. Through contem-plative practices and sitting still, one creates a safe place, apart from the chaos, to allow deeper insights to emerge. Tapping into one's "contemplative intel-ligence" is an authentic way of knowing, harnessing a deeper source of self.

While meditating prior to seeing Ben, I was close to being in Bion's "O" (1984), although I only realized that in retrospect. By suspending my ego, memory, and desire for future hopes for Ben, the space for something unknown and new emerged which enlivened the analysis. Bion felt that even the therapist's wish for the patient to heal must be abandoned so as not to interfere with evolving truths within the present moment. He referred to those moments as transformations in O, where O is the unified single source in which all consciousness—known and unknown—arises.

Spiritual knowing as permeability of self-states

Participating in a mystical experience involves not only a desire but also an ability to surrender. Ghent (1990) referred to surrender as "reflective of some 'force' towards growth, for which, interestingly, no English word exists" (p. 109). He reframed surrender as a desire to release ourselves from more rigid, bounded self-states; one's sense of wholeness is enhanced by the resulting sense of unity with other living beings.

Ghent's (1999) goal was not insight, but transformation, as patients come in contact with frozen parts of themselves that are aching to be known, examined, and understood. Surrender embodies the release of precious dissociated self-states (Ghent, 2001) that prior to falling ill had been inaccessible to me. Through my spiritual growth, anthrax poisoning ironically allowed me the space to begin to wrestle with previously frozen parts (Mitchell & Aron, 1999) of myself, and also of my patients, that were yearning to be known, and to come to peace with them. As a result of becoming ill, I learned to surrender, which required developing a certain pliability and lessening of my brittle defensiveness to have more faith to dive into the uncertainty of the unknown.

While the exact process in which Ben became able to examine unknown aspects of himself in a parallel process to my own remains somewhat mysterious, what follows are my hypotheses. As I developed more of an internalized sense of an empathic other, I became more willing to puncture and relinquish my grandiose self-states and become more acquainted with my vulnerabilities, with less fear of annihilation. Feeling inspired by Molly, my mystical experience lent me a greater flexibility to examine, understand, and integrate previously disavowed and unknown self-states. In parallel process, Ben seemed to begin to mirror a similar flexibility to articulate his authentic sense of self and unknown self-states.

As I became more aware and accepting of my different self-states and they were more permeable, my analytic relationship with Ben cascaded to become more open, fluid, and authentic. Before my spiritual awakening, my defensive stance of "warrior king" precluded me from having the fluidity of a full range of emotions. This may have been unconsciously and nonverbally communicated to Ben. Now having more permeability between my different self-states, I may have conveyed more empathy for myself and Ben. Loosening the rigidity of my dissociative truth about myself may have allowed Ben to see me more as a whole person and for him to become aware of his anger. Bromberg (2013) describes the patient/therapist relationship in the analytic treatment "as a journey in which two people must each loosen their rigidity of their dissociative 'truths' about self in order to allow 'imagination' to find its shared place. This creates a gradual greater communication of self-states both within each member of the analytic dyad and between them. As the self-states' permeability increases, so does openness to 'state-sharing.'"

Prior to my transformation, my grandiose self as "warrior-king" related to Ben' false sense of self as "a ray of sunshine." I was dissociated from my vulnerability and Ben was dissociated from his feelings of worthlessness and rage. These unknown aspects of ourselves kept us in an intersubjective dead-lock. My brittle sense of "warrior king" interfered with knowing my other self-states, and may have colluded with Ben's not wanting to take agency in his life. As I acquired more fluidity among my self-states, I had a greater faith and took less responsibility for Ben's life. In Bion's sense, I relinquished some of my desire to heal Ben. This yielding liberated me to hold Ben more responsible for his struggles and for Ben to begin to have more agency to change them. As we became able to examine Ben's profound and unknown feelings of worth-lessness, Ben became better able to glimpse his false sense of self. He began to have the courage to examine those unknown parts of himself, even though it terrified him, including his rigid defensiveness as a social Pollyanna persona (Jung, 1965/1966/2000) which emotionally crippled him both professionally and interpersonally. When I was more armored, Ben was more inclined to judge and disavow his dissociated anger. As I thawed with more pliability of self-states, Ben became more aware and able to articulate his anger. Before my transformation, Ben's desperate neediness was acted out unconsciously by overeating. Eventually, Ben became more aware of his neediness and was even able to verbalize and enact it less.

The loosening of rigidities within the therapeutic dyad allowed both Ben and me to tolerate uncertainty. Estelle Frankel (2017) writes of how sitting with uncertainty can create openness and curiosity. After my transform-ation, I surrendered to a greater receptivity to the unknown, which created an enhanced spaciousness in the analytic relationship to allow Ben's becoming. This practice of losing self to find self is expressive of the paradoxical opening that comes with letting go of usual mindsets (Marion Milner, 1934/2011). This paradoxical finding is expressed by Dogen (2011), a Japanese Buddhist priest, in the statement, "To study the Buddha Way is to study the self. To study the self is to lose the self. To forget the self is to be actualized by myriad things" (p. 24). By clinging less to what was already known, Ben and I created a deeper spaciousness where previously unknown dimensions of both of us were better understood and actualized.

Spiritual knowing borrows from many sources including extraordinary, uncanny knowing and enhanced permeability of self-states, the latter put forth by the relational psychoanalytic model. These avenues of spiritual knowing came together psychodynamically to play an intricate role in both my transformation and the creation of the transcendent Third in the analytic relationship. Ben and I became able to loosen our rigidities of dissociated self "truths," to have the faith to know previously unknown aspects of ourselves, and better sit with uncertainty. We were both freed from old mindsets and better able together to experience a far-reaching inclusiveness and greater sense of equanimity.

References

Benjamin, J. (2007). *Intersubjectivity, Thirdness and Mutual Recognition. Speech presented at the Institute for Contemporary Psychoanalysis.* Los Angeles, CA.

Bion, W.R. (1984). *Transformations.* London, UK: Karnac Books. (Original work published 1965).

Bourgeault, C. (2003). *The Wisdom Way of Knowing.* San Francisco, CA: Jossey-Bass.

Bromberg, P.M. (2013). Hidden in plain sight: Thoughts on imagination and the lived unconscious. *Psychoanalytic Dialogues, 23*(1): 1–14.

Cerfolio, N. (2016). Loss, surrender, spiritual awakening. *Palliative and Supportive Care, 14*(6): 1–2.

Cerfolio, N. (2017). My mystical encounter with a wild gray whale. *Psychoanalytic Perspectives 14*(2): 265–269.

Dogen, E. (2011). *Dogen's genjo koan: Three Commentaries* (B. Nishiari, S. Okamura, S. Suzuki, K. Uchiyama, S. M. Weitsman, K. Tanahashi, & D. M. Wenger, Trans. and Comm.). Berkeley, CA: Counterpoint Press.

Frankel, E. (2017). *The Wisdom of Not Knowing: Discovering a Life of Wonder by Embracing Uncertainty.* Boulder, CO: Shambhala Publications.

Ghent, E. (1990). Masochism, submission, surrender – Masochism as a perversion of surrender. *Contemporary Psychoanalysis, 26*: 108–136.

Ghent, E. (1999). Afterword to: Masochism, submission, surrender. In S.A. Mitchell & L. Aron (eds.), *Relational Psychoanalysis: The Emergence of a Tradition*, pp. 239–242. Hillsdale, NJ: Analytic Press.

Ghent, E. (2001). Need, paradox, and surrender. Commentary on paper by Adam Phillips. *Psychoanalytic Dialogues, 11*: 23–41.

Jung, C.G. (1965/1966/2000). *Collected Works* (Vols. 7 & 16). Princeton, NJ: Princeton University Press.

Laub, D., & Podell, D. (1995). Art and trauma. *International Journal of Psycho-Analysis, 76:* 991–1005.

Mayer, E.L. (2007). *Extraordinary Knowing: Science, Skepticism, and the Inexplicable Powers of the Human Mind.* New York: Bantam Books.

Milner, M. (1934/2011). *A Life of One's Own.* New York: Taylor & Francis.

Mitchell, S.A., & Aron, L. (1999). Editor's introduction to E. Ghent's "Masochism, submission, surrender" in S.A. Mitchell, & L. Aron (eds.) *Relational psychoanalysis: The Emergence of a Tradition*, pp. 211–242. Hillsdale, NJ: Analytic Press.

Starr, K. (2008). Faith as the fulcrum of psychic change: Metaphors of transformation in Jewish mysticism and psychoanalysis. *International Journal of Relational Perspectives, 18*(2): 203–229.

Suchet, M. (2016). Surrender, transformation, and transcendence. *Psychoanalytic Dialogues, 26*: 747–760.

Winnicott, D.W. (1960/1965). Ego distortion of true and false self. In D.W. Winnicott, *The Maturational Process and the Facilitating Environment: Studies in the Theory of Emotional Development*, pp. 140–152. New York: International Universities Press.

Knowing in the contemporary sociocultural context

Chapter 13

Income inequality and psychoanalytic practice

An unexamined juxtaposition

John O'Leary

There is a display board in the middle of Times Square that registers a steady stream of very high numbers—the national debt. Underneath that sign a second one tells us the portion that each taxpayer would owe if the debt were divided evenly. Clearly, the sign makers are trying to grab our attention but only once did I seriously engage it, and that was to count the number of digits the sign displayed—fourteen. These numbers are getting larger. The world has marched along steadfastly despite them. So it goes with income inequality, the size of the gap between rich and poor. Who really cares about the vastness of the numbers? Only in this past year has there been an outpouring of concern during the presidential election. Yet, the data of Income inequality is easily as abstract as the national debt. Reading that 92 percent of the new money generated in this country goes to the top one percent will move you (Stone, Trisi, Sherman, & Horton, 2016). What about the statistic that nearly 50 percent of this country's wealth belongs to the top 3 percent? Do you feel any consternation about an Oxfam report (Hardoon, Funetes-Nieva, & Ayele, 2016) that said the top one percent now owns more of the world's wealth than the rest of the world (7.2 billion people) combined?

Let us bring these statistics to specifics. I received an e-mail from a friend. This Upper West Side psychologist says his psychoanalytic practice is down, and he can't yet afford to retire in New York City with its extraordinary rents and cost of living. What allows him to keep going is that he has a few wealthy clients who are gradually leaving treatment. Some have moved into Medicare, paying substantially lower fees. He is sick with worry that one of them will quit, even his Medicare patients. Several of his psychologist friends are in the same boat. He also knows many who seem to be thriving. I am alarmed. I write back that he has always had a diverse group of patients. Where did they go? He says that the ordinary middle-class people he sees are no longer been able to pay his fees. Even at annual incomes of $80,000 a year they have dropped out. They cite rising health care and housing costs, lack of a substantial pay raise, and job insecurity.

I submit that these vignettes of national indebtedness and personal trauma are part of a single narrative. It is probably not on your radar yet, but soon will be. It may have been one of the determining factors in America's unprecedented 2016 presidential elections, i.e. how much the working class were suffering.

I realize that in focusing on New York City I may be choosing a place where income inequality is especially high, although not the highest. San Francisco and Wasington D.C. deserve that designation. Most analysts work in large metropolitan areas where income inequality is rapidly accelerating. We all need to be on alert.

My interest in inequality started with reading Thomas Piketty's (2014) *Capital in the 21st Century*. Piketty's seminal accomplishment is that he tracked income and wealth in four different countries over the last few centuries and showed how wealth differentials are growing at a vastly accelerated pace, especially in the United States. Since the end of the 1970s we have been rapidly approaching a "gilded age" of income inequality. The only time we saw this much inequality was just before the Great Depression of 1929.

I am not unique in being taken off guard. Most Americans have no idea of the breadth and sweep of economic disparity in our country. They do know that something is terribly wrong (Norton & Ariely, 2011). The working class and even the so-called middle class are being pressed in America, the richest of countries.

My contention is that psychoanalysts are both victims and perpetrators in this new world of inequality. First, let's look at the victim side. The shrinking middle class (Alpert, 2012) has adversely affected patient hours and our pocketbooks—especially for more recent graduates. Second, our country is overwhelmed by the sheer number of mentally ill because of the significant correlations obtaining between mental illness and degree of inequality (Wilkinson & Pickett, 2009). Third, we are especially unable to reach the millions of people of color in the United States who need our help more than ever. Unfortunately they do not seem interested in reaching back to us—so deep is the divide between rich and poor. Finally, because psychoanalysts stay in school longer (for a PhD, an average of 27 years) we are more affected by the cost of higher education. Going forward, how many of us will be able to afford the long years of training?

How are we perpetrators? With fees in NYC averaging between $200 and $300 a session, we are running the risk of becoming a therapy for the rich. Income inequality has taken this trend to new levels. Also, these troubled times create countertransferential pulls, for example, to keep people of means in therapy longer than necessary. News media have been quick to seize upon this accusation (*New York Times*, 2012; *Psychology Today*, 2014). Have we become a highly skilled professional elite who have near-zero interest in lifting the masses? And why are there so few people of color in our profession? They are not our patients, nor are they our colleagues.

On a more personal level, several years ago I became aware that something troublesome was happening in New York. Friends were forced to take jobs below their potential. Some couples had to maintain three jobs to keep things afloat. I found myself financially unable to retire if I had so desired. I saw the neighborhood I so cherished invaded by dozens of new high rises with apartment prices in the several million dollar range. My own daughter who does well in corporate America could not afford to move into our neighborhood. That same neighborhood is changing in myriad ways. Old stores are closing; new, more pricey, chain stores are opening. Much of the old charm is gone.

I fully realize I am treading in dangerous waters with this theme. As some analyst colleagues have said, "John, you have chosen a topic that is more about politics and economics than psychoanalysis." I have always found it difficult to separate these disciplines. Fortunately, some of our more foundational predecessors like Erich Fromm, Wilhelm Reich, and Harry Stack Sullivan have felt similarly. They charted these same territories, finding much to be gained for psychoanalysis. As students of culture how can we avoid it? Income inequality is in the air we breathe.

Why is there such a cavalier attitude among analysts regarding this issue? Are we not concerned because it has not touched us in ways that count? Insurance companies and managed care have always been around to give focus to any complaints about remuneration. Admittingly, there are compelling reasons for that. For example, parity for mental health (equal coverage for physical and mental health costs) was passed by Congress in 2008. It has yet to be implemented. It is the law of the land, with no teeth. Insurance companies have provided the greatest resistance to its implementation. It has been futile to fight those monolithic agencies.

I suspect deeper levels of resistance. For one, I think we may as a profession identify with the "one percent." Many of them came from lesser means and earned their way to the top—as was the case for many psychoanalysts. The one percent supports institutes of higher learning, museums, theatres, and art galleries we so enjoy. They are often in seats of power that affect our daily lives. We are sometimes recipients of their grants. In short, we make use of their largesse. Although psychoanalysts are not true members of the financial elite, we do as a rule consider ourselves among the cultural elite with high levels of education and sophistication. Furthermore, the one percent have many admirable qualities, including a penchant for savings and investment which at least in part fuels the economy. And look what they have done for charity. Bill Gates, who vies for the richest man in the world, is a prime example. Many of us believe we have benefited from the meritocracy that appears to embrace and reward the best players. Why should we criticize it? Why resent the blessings of the one percent? If you earn over \$500,000 a year you probably qualify as a member. Besides, if they are the people most likely to use our services, there is a net good that comes to all of us. Even they have "problems" we are trained to heal.

Meritocracy refers to the notion that society should award people according to the demanding work they do, their innovation, and level of education. This belief has worked in tandem with the view of ourselves as a classless society. Has our embrace of meritocracy been accompanied by a sort of hyper individualism militating against any expression of being needy or dependent? Lynn Layton (2009) argues that the prevalence of "neoliberal subjectivity," initially ignited during the politics and policies of the 1980s, requires a renunciation of vulnerability in ourselves and others. According to Layton, the legacy of this thinking is still with us. We distance rather than empathize with the less fortunate. Worrying about yourself and those closest to you can seem like the most robust and tough way to be in a highly competitive, global world. The poor, uneducated, and the working class have only themselves to blame for their plight. These beliefs are infusing our current political scene at elevated levels.

In like vein, the movement towards privatization requires a shift in thinking about how much the government can do for someone. In privatization, government hands over an important function, like the prison system, to private entrepreneurs, believing they can do it better, cheaper, and more efficiently. Many social services have become privatized (Graybow, Eighmey, & Fader, 2015) with the consequence that a lot of us no longer see the most vulnerable as "our" problem.

Others have argued that psychoanalysis has lost its way—at least in comparison to the ideologies of our founders (Altman, 2010; Graybow et al., 2015). We seem to have moved away from a socialist bent that was distinctively European, beginning with Freud. He and several other prominent European analysts sponsored the creation of free clinics (in Vienna, Budapest, and Berlin). Their growth came largely from the notion that we had a duty to the poor and disenfranchised (Danto, 2005; Aron & Starr, 2012). These clinics were decimated by the Nazis. Several European Jews who immigrated to the United States maintained their Marxist bent, but that never translated into a large-scale effort to recreate the European model. I will grant that some institutes have low-cost clinics, usually for providing their trainees experience and supervision but, Richards (2016) argues, the lucrative nature of private practice got in the way. Also, there is the near total capitalist orientation of America as opposed to many countries with European social structures.

Couple all this with a conspiracy of silence in psychoanalytic practice about fees (Dimen, 2006). This silence should surprise no one. We simply do not know what each of us is charging. For example, try and find a decent article on analytic fees that offers actual numbers. Like you, I refer prospective patients to certain therapists more often than to others. I have little idea what these preferred therapists charge and rarely ask. Neither do they ask me. Granted, this taboo is a characteristic of the larger society where it is impolite to talk about money. During my tenure at the White Institute, there was never a single discussion about setting fees. Many of us have gone through as many as 10 supervisors without the topic coming up once.

Part of the reason money is so difficult to discuss is there are unacknowledged status differences between those who charge more and those who charge less. Commanding a high fee tells something about your assessment of competence and confidence—that largely goes unspoken. Our fees also distinguish us from lesser trained professionals. Length and diversity of experience can also be a factor. Many of us believe, albeit mistakenly, like Freud, that patients will improve more if it hurts.

My own belief is that there are two distributions of analysts in New York. One group that accepts most insurance, has moderate fees ($150 range) and a sliding scale. A second group's fees are in the $250 range and do not accept insurance, especially if the latter have a forced co-payment system. This second group only accepts insurance if it is of the type executives can obtain where there are no constraints on fee. They generally have a more restricted sliding scale.

Another dimension of our ease of denial comes from a peculiarity within the terms of the inequality debate itself. Much of that debate is framed around the "One Percent" vs. the 99 percent (the rest of us). This divide seems so large that it allows many of us in the 99 percent to be cavalier about our own responsibility for inequality. It can feel like unless you earn close to $500,000 or a million dollars in New York, you are not part of the problem. If, instead of the one percent we used the top 20 percent, as Richard Reeves (2017) argues, an appreciably different picture emerges. This group begins at $112,000. It includes most professionals, middle managers, college professors, and psychoanalysts. We are now talking about being part of a group made up of tens of millions who wield a great deal of power. Reeves describes many of the advantages that accrue to us 20 percenters and how hard we work to keep others out of our ranks. "Hoarding the American Dream," he calls it. Some examples of that exclusion are the restrictive zoning of school districts that end up keeping the poor and working class out. We get tremendous tax advantages from carrying large mortgages on our homes, plus write offs for putting money in college savings plans, a widely used tool that the working class and poor can ill afford. Interestingly, intermarriage rates are also higher among this better-off group, keeping the wealth within the family. Far larger numbers of people have benefitted from inequality than is generally recognized—even by experts. It is easy to see this as "not my problem." It is a very small calculation that allows one to move from what is in our best interest to what is in the interest of the one percent.

Reeves' argument can elude us for another reason. It is very close to suggesting that at the heart of things sits a fairly rigidified social class system—almost as bad as that of his birthplace, England. He uses terms like "upper middle class" to describe the upper 20 percent. There has always been a resistance in American culture to class notions. Most describe themselves as part of the great middle class. According to Joanna Ryan (2017) this resistance has also been a hallmark of psychoanalysis beginning with Freud, despite Freud's concerns about money and commitment to clinics for the poor. Ryan also argues that in more recent times, "The demise of Marxist thinking, the influence of postmodernism, and the privileging of identity politics, all led to a focus on other forms of difference while generally ignoring class" (p. 6).

The larger point is that we as psychoanalysts are enmeshed in the very system we would wish to correct—if only we could see it. I postulate that we are blind to our participation in this social system because of our proximity, gratitude, and similarity to the wealthy. The perception is we have a great deal of common ground with the wealthy. The exclusionary consequences of our behavior remain invisible to most of us. For example, it is hard to see the racism indicated by the dwindling numbers of minority patients we service or the relative absence of non-white colleagues. After all, no one is standing at the door preventing them from entering. It may be especially hard to see how our fees may drive many middle and working-class people to other forms of treatment, especially when there appears to be a conspiracy of silence in our halls of learning about how to set fees.

Likewise, it is hard to see the insidious ways that this 20 percent posture leaks into treatment. How do we find a language for the increasing polarization this issue leaves in its wake? Do we locate the turmoil as inside the individual and miss powerful outside forces at play? Are we more motivated to push along a capitalist system that agrees with our private chosen pathways, one that subtly undercuts different views of money, education, and meritocracy.

How informed is the average citizen about income inequality?

With all the publicity of late, we should know something substantial about income inequality. Most educated Americans do know that the greater part of new wealth generated in this country goes to the top one percent. Many also know that the United States has the worst inequality of the 23 most industrialized nations. They know some of the biggest effects of these numbers, like how difficult it is to climb the economic ladder. The saying goes: "If you want to live the American dream, move to Denmark." Many know how corrupted our political system has become by moneyed interests.

Research by Norton and Ariely (2011) done at Duke with thousands of subjects nonetheless underscores that we only know a fraction of the story. When asked to draw graphs that portray how wealth is distributed in the United States, most Americans, Republicans and Democrats alike, underestimate the amount of inequality by multiples. They show very good agreement about what the ideal distribution should look like. Most Americans believe those in the top 5 percent should earn about 20 times more than those in the bottom 5 percent. This is not exactly a socialist economy they are endorsing. Sadly, their estimates of wealth inequality in America yield only the tiniest resemblance to what is happening. It is so much worse than what they think.

One of the most disturbing things about income inequality is what accompanies it. The countries that are the most unequal, like the United States, Brazil, Great Britain, and Israel are also the countries with the greatest social problems, such as low longevity, high infant mortality rates, high rates of incarceration, and high rates of mental illness. (Asafu-Adjaye, 2004; Wilkinson & Pickett, 2009).

This readership might ask why would there be more mental illness. Remember we are not talking about poor countries but countries with extraordinary gaps between rich and poor. The main argument here is that people can see the gaps between themselves and others. This gap can lead to increased isolation, a deeper sense of shame, frustration, anger—and a sense of injustice. Finally, I think it is likely to yield diminished trust in others (Wilkinson & Pickett, 2009)

A large survey conducted by the American Psychological Association (2016) queried ordinary citizens on what issues they were most stressed out about. Seventy-two percent mentioned money—much higher than in previous surveys. It was more of a concern for poor people, parents, and the young. Anyone who doesn't know that people are more worried about money than in times past is living with blinders on.

How is this likely to affect us as professionals? Concerns might include the following: will building a practice be harder because fewer people can afford our fees? This seems true for the working and middle-class patient and a significant portion of the upper middle class. We have always been out of reach for the poor. I don't want to make too broad a critique. I know there are many analysts who see the poor pro bono or at very low fees.

Countertransference

To concretize this argument, I will present case material from my practice pertinent to inequality. There is an important caveat. Nothing that I am about to discuss is exclusive to income inequality. These case scenarios could have occurred before any significant inequality was noted. I believe, however, these situations are more likely to arise in a time when inequality is such a powerful force.

Case 1: Envy of the patient

My 50-year-old patient's name is so prominent he would be immediately recognizable. He comes from a family that has had great wealth for a long time. As an executive in a large firm, he travels a great deal for the company. He is encouraged to fly first class. In a recent session, he expressed great annoyance because the accountant at his firm wanted his flight receipts for the past year. Seems like a simple enough request! My client could never supply these receipts because he doesn't use the first-class ticket. He uses his private plane. He does not want his colleagues to know this. He believes they will see him as spoiled and entitled. He is mad at the accountant for his persistence. Put yourself in my place as I listen to this complaint. Suffice it to say I am not sympathetic.

Case 2: Rich patients terminating

A 45-year-old hedge fund manager announced he was terminating his twice per week therapy. He is extremely reliable and pays better than my top fee. He had been in treatment for about three years. He said he knew the procedure of terminating would involve a few weeks. After I came out of my initial shock I immediately went into overdrive about the many reasons he should stay longer. What about this and that issue? I probed. I had three years to compile issues. Somewhere in the middle of this, the better angels of my nature took over and I realized what I was doing. I knew I was going to miss him—not just for the money. I was finally able to talk to that loss.

Case 3: Soft pedaling therapy to rich patients

I have been seeing a 42-year-old patient twice per week for marital issues. Partly because of work (he is COO of a midsize firm) he misses about 30 percent of our sessions. He often calls to cancel on the day of his appointment. When I raise this issue, he replies with impatience, "Look I cannot avoid certain business engagements, and don't I pay you for my missed sessions? What is your problem?" Besides the obvious disrespect for the analytic process and a certain self-sabotage, I have other problems with this behavior. The biggest is that he is doing in his life what he is doing in the therapy. He goes missing from his wife and children for extended periods of time—physically and psychologically. He is extremely sensitive to this criticism. The question for us (you and me) is how much do I push it? I do not want to lose this high-fee patient. Is there a temptation to soft sell my interpretations? I am cautious.

Case 4: How do we remain analytic in the face of suffering?

On the non-wealthy side of my practice, I have been seeing a woman for over 20 years. When we first started, she was a member of an order of nuns that did a lot of charity work. The precipitant for seeking treatment was her sexual abuse at the hands of a priest who was supposed to be spiritually ministering to her. While in treatment, she left the order, obtained her PhD, and the last 10 years of her working life was as a college professor. She is now retired, living off a small teacher's pension and a little social security. She receives no money from the Order of Sisters despite 30 years' service to them. She gets by on $2400 a month, paying me through Medicare. She is on a strict budget. Most of her bills have increased and her resources are being spent at an alarming rate.

Recently she called to tell me she just "killed her dog." She took her five-year-old pet to the veterinarian because of extreme lethargy. He told her they would have to do an MRI and needed to keep the dog overnight. The cost would be $1200. My patient could not afford this fee. They put the dog down. She feels responsible: "I murdered my dog." In such instances, how do we bear the unbearable? I felt frozen in face of the calamity of her losing her pet because she could not afford the medical expenses. I did not know how to soothe her. It is painful to witness the steady decline of her situation, especially in view of all she has contributed. My fee has remained constant for years. I would even see her pro bono if that were required. Some therapeutic transactions have nothing to do with money.

Each of these cases has a countertransference tug, a pull to do less than optimal therapy. I plead guilty in all four examples. Many similar countertransference tugs are put forward by Irwin Hirsch (2008) in a remarkable contribution to the literature. Added pressures about money are going to amplify this situation for most of us. That added pressure is coming with unrelenting force by way of income inequality.

I have tried to highlight certain trends that are adversely effecting how therapy is conducted. These trends are manifest in subtle ways. The magnitude of economic data on inequality is often obscured. Confusion about

140 John O'Leary

our fees and failures to be more open with each other prevent us from scrutinizing our own profession. We do not sufficiently address the paucity of minority patients that we see. There will be major consequences if we maintain a "head in the sand" attitude. I have outlined some of these in the way of countertransference pulls.

In the end we must ask ourselves, do we have a moral obligation to patients we see? Does that obligation include an awareness of economic forces bearing down on so many of them in horrific ways? What type of patients do we want to serve? Are they the neediest, the most diverse, those who can pay, those who can commit to long-term analysis? What is our purpose? What are our personal goals and personal limits? And how can we expand this conversation? The above inquiries are in for testier times over the next four years. Since we are a compassionate profession, it will not happen without pain. Keep in mind that these problems have been around 40 years or more. Thinking about them, gathering data, bearing witness, and remaining open to political engagement may, in the end, be our best tools.

References

American Psychological Association (2016). *Stress in America. The Impact of Discrimination. Stress in America Survey.*
Alpert, J. (2012). Is therapy forever? Enough already. *New York Times Sunday Review*, April 21.
Altman, N. (2010). *The Analyst in the Inner City: Race, Class and Culture Through a Psychoanalytic Lens* (2nd ed.). New York: Routledge.
Aron, L., & Starr, S. (2012). *A Psychotherapy for the People: Towards a Progressive Psychoanalysis.* New York: Routledge.
Asafu-Adjaye, J. (2004). Income inequality and health: A multi country analysis. *International Journal of Social Economics,* 31(1/2), 195–207.
Danto, E. (2005). *Freud's Free Clinics: Psychoanalysis and Social Justice, 1918–1938.* New York: Columbia.
Dimen, M. (2006) Money, love, and hate: Contradiction and paradox in psychoanalysis. In L. Layton, N. Hollander, & S. Gutwell (eds.), *Psychoanalysis, Class and Politics*, pp. 29–50. New York: Routledge.
Graybow, S., Eighmey, J., & Fader, S. (2015) Privatization of psychoanalysis: The impact of neo-liberalism on Freud's tool of social justice. *Journal of Psychohistory*, 42(4): 280–284.
Hardoon, D., Funetes-Nieva, R. and Ayele, S. (2016) An Economy For the 1%: How privilege and power in the economy drive extreme inequality and how this can be stopped. Oxfam Briefing Paper, January 18. Available from: https://policy-practice.oxfam.org.uk/publications/an-economy-for-the-1-how-privilege-and-power-in-the-economy-drive-extreme-inequ-592643 (accessed December 17, 2018).
Hirsch, I. (2008). *Coasting in the Countertransference: Conflicts of Self-Interest Between Analysts and Patients.* New York: Routledge.

Layton, L. (2009). Who's responsible: Our mutual implication in each other's suffering. *Psychoanalytic Dialogues*, 19: 105–120.

Norton, M., & Ariely, D. (2011). Building a better America—One wealth quintile at a time. *Perspectives in Psychological Sciences*, 6(9): 9–12.

Piketty, T. (2014) *Capital in the Twenty-First Century*, Cambridge, MA: Harvard University Press.

Reeves, R. (2017). *Hoarding the American Dream*. Washington DC: Brookings Institute Press.

Richards, A. (2016). The left and far left in American psychoanalysis: Psychoanalysis as a subversive discipline. *Contemporary Psychoanalysis*, 52: 111–129.

Ryan, J. (2017). *Class and Psychoanalysis; Class and Psychoanalysis*. Routledge: New York.

Stone, C., Trisi, D., Sherman, A., & Horton, E. (2016). A guide to statistics on historical trends in income inequality. *Center for Budget and Policy Priorities*. Available from: www.cbpp.org/research/poverty-and-inequality/a-guide-to-statistics-on-historical-trends-in-income-inequality.

Wilkinson, R., & Pickett, K. (2009) *The Spirit Level: Why Greater Equality Makes Societies Stronger*. Bloomsbury: New York.

Chapter 14

Invisible immigration
Family building across borders and bodies

Anne Malavé

"How could she?" said Dr. I, referring to her patient Michele's decision to have a baby on her own. "It's selfish," she added. "Why doesn't she adopt, or at least use a friend's sperm so the child can have a *real father*, instead of just some random sperm donor guy." Neither Michele nor Dr. I is alone. Michele is one of many people deciding to have children in ways that would have been almost unimaginable when Freud created psychoanalysis. Dr. I is experiencing a common countertransference to Michele's choice. This chapter aims to help with these new realities.

These new families are changing society and being negatively impacted by antiquated societal beliefs about *what it means to be family* that leaves them on the *outside*. Psychoanalysts need to become familiar with these rapidly expanding family building possibilities in order to fulfill our responsibilities for promoting social, family, and individual healthy mental health functioning and well-being.

The quest to have a child is profound, propelling people with fertility barriers across borders and bodies to build families in territory dominated by issues of not knowing or being known in what I am calling *invisible immigration*. *Invisible* because personal identity may not be apparent—origins may be hidden, inaccessible, or unknown to others as well as to the individuals themselves. *Immigration* because of the impact of this local and international movement of people and parts of people on personal, familial, social, and global identity and belonging.

In adoption and third-party reproduction, *knowing* and *being known* are most closely associated with open and closed adoptions; known or anonymous arrangements of sperm, egg, embryo donation, and gestational surrogates; disclosure versus non-disclosure of origins. Individuals created through or impacted by these new family-building options may learn details or origins accidentally or later in life, which can be traumatic.

As a clinical psychologist-psychoanalyst working directly with all participants in these family-building variations, I hope this chapter will achieve the following goals: *provide information* about modern families struggling for recognition in a heteronormative, pronatalist world that privileges traditional family-building and biogenetic connection; *address* the increasing complexity of identity and the possibilities for belonging and being outcast that already do and will increasingly enter our consulting rooms; *advocate* for an expanded awareness of what it means *to be family; emphasize* how psychoanalysis can both contribute to and benefit from a deeper understanding of the complexities these families face.

Voices

"How can I bear it when she tells me I am not her real mother!" said Elaine, a mother through egg donation.

"I cannot tell her because then she will see herself as being more connected to my child than I am," said Eliza, talking about her fears of telling her mother-in-law about using donor eggs because her mother-in-law has the genetic connection, whereas she does not.

"This is like adoption," said Jennifer, who used donor eggs and sperm.

"This is much better than adoption," said Rose, "because in adoption you don't know where the child comes from."

" 'Why don't you just adopt?' she said. I was so upset. I felt like saying, 'If you think adoption is so great then why did you have your biological kids?' I don't want someone else's child. I want my own!" said Gloria, a woman suffering from infertility.

"Who is your real father?" (question asked of 10-year-old Gabe, son of two fathers).

"What do you mean there is no father," she said. "Everyone has a father." Luke, son of a single mother, replied, "Well I don't."

"She is having the baby I was meant to have!" said Isabelle, whose sister-in-law was about to give birth to a child created with Isabelle's husband's sperm. Isabelle, also experiencing infertility, had just been told she needed to use donor eggs to have a child.

"It's nobody's business. It's my body, my blood. We're not going to let our child become stigmatized," declared Patricia and Sam, defending their plan to tell *no one*, including their child, about their egg and sperm donor origins.

While many of these participants are adapting well, some may seek help with psychoanalytic professionals unfamiliar with both this rapidly expanding territory and their own pre-existing beliefs about what constitutes *proper* families (Nordqvist & Smart, 2014a).

Background

In recent history there have been radical changes in family structures. *Parents* now include people with infertility; age, social/elective, and cancer-related fertility preservation; other medical and genetic problems; and heterosexual and LGBTQ singles and couples (Mamo, 2007; Brodzinsky & Pertman, 2012). *Children's* origins encompass domestic and intercountry adoption; third-party reproduction with partial or no genetic connection in sperm, egg, and embryo donation; and gestational surrogacy. Future reproductive possibilities include artificial gametes and wombs, and cloning (Gosden, 2000; Hayashi, Ohta, Kurimoto, Aramaki, & Saitou, 2011; Gurdon, 2012).

Adoption—the oldest solution for people needing children—now involves all possible parents, older children, sibling groups, children from the public foster-care system, children with special needs, and more transracial adoptions. While most adoptions are kinship based, this chapter focuses on those between strangers who have no pre-existing genetic/familial connection. Past secrecy has been replaced with *open adoption*—ongoing contact between birth parents and adoptive families—and openness in adoption (Siegel & Smith, 2012). Parents and children were previously *matched* for sameness in order to replicate the traditional family. Currently, prospective parents identify which kinds of children they would be comfortable parenting, including characteristics like race and age.

Adoption theories have historically emphasized the need to help individuals and their adoptive families integrate similarities and differences (Kirk, 1984; Brodzinsky, 1990). Recent theoretical developments look at cultural (e.g. transracial adoptive families' experience can be dramatically different in countries with little versus much racial diversity) and protective factors, including the development of resilience and pride (Daniluk & Hurtig-Mitchell, 2003; Palacios, 2009).

As the availability of desirable children (i.e. infants) dropped domestically, other options were pursued. Intercountry adoption began last century and rapidly expanded. Nearly one million children changed countries between 1948 and 2010 (Selman, 2009). Many were transracial; most were closed. After a 1993 international treaty (Hague, 2016) responding to abuses, corruption, and child trafficking, incoming US adoptions decreased from approximately 23,000 in 2004 to 5,500 in 2015 (US Department of State, 2016). Decreasing availability of overseas children resulted in more adoptions from the (public) foster-care system (AFCARS, 2013), transracial adoptions, and alternative reproductive forms.

In third-party reproduction, family-building options have grown considerably. Attempts at sperm donation began in the 1700s. In 1884, donated sperm was first reported in the medical literature (Hard, 1909). In the 1970s, US sperm banks opened. Originally, most donors were *anonymous*. Clients were heterosexual couples who were advised to keep the donation secret. Recently clients have expanded and now include more *same sex female couples* and *single mothers by choice than heterosexual couples*. Donors increasingly agree to make themselves available to answer offspring's questions and curiosity when offspring turn 18 years old.

The creation of in vitro fertilization (IVF) (Steptoe & Edwards, 1978) separated sexuality from reproduction, genetics from gestation. IVF introduced an ever-expanding number of reproductive options including egg, sperm, and embryo donation, surrogacy, and combinations such as lesbian mothers choosing the egg of one mother to be gestated by the other, so both women can share in the creation of the child (Vaughn, 2007). Heretofore unthinkable arrangements became possible, such as a grandmother gestating her grandchildren (Miller, 2013) and posthumous reproduction. Freezing added the egg bank option to the original fertility clinic recruitment of egg donors and subsequent donor egg agencies. It can take up to five people to create one baby: sperm and egg donors; gestational carrier/surrogate; two intended parents. Embryos can now contain DNA from three people (Human Fertilisation and Embryology Authority, 2016).

People travel increasingly for *cross-border reproductive care*, aka *reproductive exile* (Inhorn & Patrizio, 2009), for less costly or improved care; circumnavigating local laws and other (e.g. religious) prohibitions; and privacy, since some countries have removed donor anonymity. Sperm has been traveling around the world for several decades. More recently, embryos, egg donors, and people seeking gestational surrogates cross borders. Egg banks are becoming globalized. There is movement towards openness in egg donation.

Laws are changing from unknown to known donor gametes. Some countries (e.g. Italy) prohibit openness. Others forbid anonymity (e.g. Australia, Canada, the UK). A UK national registry allows donor-conceived people conceived on or after April 1, 2005 to locate their gamete donors at the age of 18 years old (Human Fertilisation and Embryology Authority, 2016). There is no central donor registry in the United States, although an informal website, the Donor Sibling Registry, exists (Kramer, 2016). Guidelines developed by the American Society for Reproductive Medicine (ASRM, 2016) recommend knowledge of origins. *No country mandates that parents tell their children about their donor-conceived origins.*

In adoption, *the best interests of the child* policy prevails. In US private adoptions, adoptive *parents are chosen* by birth mothers. In contrast, in third-party reproduction, parents choose *donors and gestational surrogates*. Egg donation programs *match* recipient/s and donor, usually based, at least partially, on *resemblance,* which is seen as a vital criterion by many for belonging (Witt, 2005). For some, resemblance promotes *privacy*; for others, *secrecy (passing* as a traditional family).

Many professionals see third-party family-building options following adoption history: becoming increasingly open; helping parents *claim* and *feel entitled* to parent; promoting early, age-appropriate disclosure to children as a process helping them integrate details about their origins into their identities; recognizing that offspring will be curious about progenitors and other third parties and that genetic connections matter; assisting children and families with being different; helping parents become comfortable with donors and other individuals sharing genetics with their children; assisting children with potential loyalty conflicts between families and genetic origins; recognizing the ongoing *psychological presence* of third party/ies in the new family's life as well as the parallel impact on third party/ies and their families (Freundlich, 2001; Crawshaw, 2002; Feast, 2003; Cahn, 2009).

The exact number of these new families is unknown. Approximately 2 percent of US children have been adopted. Precise statistics are not possible because records of private adoptions are not kept. Records have not been kept for most children created through sperm donation, the most common form of third-party reproduction (with a past history of secrecy and accessible outside the fertility clinic system). Records of individuals created by egg and embryo donation are incomplete. Perhaps over a million people have been created through sperm donation, tens of thousands through donor eggs, and thousands through donor embryos (Kramer & Cahn, 2013).

Voluminous research on these families is beyond the scope of this chapter. For reviews on adoption see Juffer and van IJzendoorn, 2005, 2007; Palacios and Brodzinsky, 2010. For research on families created through third-party reproduction see Nordqvist and Smart, 2014a; Golombok, 2015. These investigations indicate that most of these families do well.

Most third-party reproduction research focused on comparisons with traditional families to see if there are deficits. It appears what matters most for the development and well-being of children and families is not the presence of traditional family structure or genetic connection but rather the quality of family relationships, being told early about origins, and an accepting, supportive environment (Howe & Feast, 2000; Brodzinsky, 2006, 2011; Golombok, 2015). There is even some evidence of gains in these new formations. Children of same-sex parents demonstrate greater tolerance for diversity (Stacey & Biblarz, 2001; Fulcher, Sutfin, & Patterson, 2008). Through expanded identity as world citizens, there may be increased possibilities of promoting global integration. *Reproductive Pioneers* (Malavé, 2013) who have *adapted* may provide us with opportunities for learning more about growth and resilience.

Challenges

These parents find themselves at the epicenter of a worldwide maelstrom of ethical, psychosocial, legal, and philosophical controversies (Spar, 2006; Gentile, 2016) at a time when genetic determinism has captured the public imagination, causing a geneticization of our society (Jones, 1993, 1996; Carey, 2012). LGBTQ families are becoming *more similar* to mainstream families through the act of having children. Heterosexual couples are becoming *more different from* mainstream families by having children through *untraditional* pathways. For some, these new family formations represent an *opportunity.* Others perceive these pathways as *inferior.* Sperm donors see themselves as *fathers*, consistent with social identification of genetics with parenthood. Egg donors identify themselves as *not mothers*, separating genetics from gestation (Almeling, 2011). Male and female donors have equal concern about impacts on their future families (Almeling, 2011).

These families share a common need for *assimilation*, to be accepted, to *feel real and "proper"* (Nordqvist & Smart, 2014a). They may be seen as—and feel—second-class, *fraudulent or fake*. Pronatalist, heteronormative beliefs threaten their healthy development. Even in adoption, discrimination still exists. Adoption seems "a good idea … for someone else" (Palacios, 2009) and is "not quite as good as having your own" (Fisher, 2003). Internalized reflected appraisals that one's family is *less than* lead to feelings of inferiority and shame.

Whether *conspicuously different*, as in transracial adoption, or *matching* in *resemblance*, these families commonly fear *stigmatization*. Even when parents choose to be open, or do not have a choice, as in transracial adoption and same-sex parenting, these families face common questions. With transracial adoption: *Where are her/his/your real parents?* and *Do you have any children of your own*? For same-sex couples: *Who is the mother?* or *Which one is the father?*

There are common fears of birth parents or donors returning to claim children or rejection *by* their children. There are conflicts about telling or not telling children and others about their children's origins—knowing and not knowing, being known and unknown. There is *hypervigilant surveillance* about potential breaches of *anonymous* arrangements. Surveillance operates in both directions, with *scrutiny towards others* to determine if origins have been discovered, as well as *scrutiny by others* who already know and may be scanning and searching for differences in family functioning. In blended families, scrutiny may involve examining to see if one child's origins are favored over another's.

Mental health professionals working with these alternative families (e.g. the Mental Health Professional Group of the American Society for Reproductive

Medicine) look to adoption for guidance, following the *always have known model* so children can integrate the complexities of their origins over time within the safety of their families. Parents who delay telling their children about origins often find it increasingly difficult to do so (Isaksson, Sydsjo, Skoog-Svanberg, & Lampic, 2012; Applegarth, Kaufman, Josephs-Sohan, Christos, & Rosenwaks, 2016).

Families where only one parent is genetically related struggle to simultaneously communicate that *genetics do and do not matter*. There are challenges in conceptualizing relationships with offspring who have been created by the same donor or birthparent/s who are part of other families. In an age where *people finding* is increasingly accessible, searches to find genetic relationships are ongoing (Hertz, 2009; Kramer & Cahn, 2013; Cahn, 2014).

Many parents address concerns about attachment, family integrity, and social media exposure by choosing an arrangement that feels securely disconnected from their children's origins. Others are constricted if their fertility clinic only uses anonymous donors. Where parents hide their reproductive histories, questions of *Is a secret always harmful?* and *Who has the right to know?* permeate experience. *Topic avoidance* negatively impacts family relationships (Paul & Berger, 2007; Berger & Paul, 2008). Fears and secrets may form a kind of *shadow* (Malavé, 2006) that may be benign or become persecutory, presenting potential for shame and trauma (Rose, 2015).

Many individuals do not know their origins. Others seek genetic connections (Volkman, 2009) or breach anonymous arrangements via genetic testing and databases, facial recognition software, online people searching companies, and other Internet resources (Evers, 2016). Still others discover accidentally or via *late telling*. Families of third parties may find out they have genetic connections to people they have never met (Nordqvist & Smart, 2014b). There are threats of *consanguinity* (aka *incest*). These issues pertaining to knowing and being known are important for the development of identity and belonging.

Psychoanalysis

Psychoanalysis can do much to help. We can expand our awareness of the interpersonal and intrapersonal struggles of these individuals for recognition in a world that privileges traditional family building. We must *learn for* and *from* these patients, as well as the larger society. We need to *make room* for the existence of these family builders, and for related people affected by these arrangements. We need to allow for the challenges and advantages of diversity. We need to be aware that patients may need our *blessing* for their wish to pursue options for themselves or their children (e.g. in Transgender

Reproductive Health where parent/s help their child/ren by freezing their genetic material in fertility preservation for future family building before transition). We need to refrain from using terms like *real mother*, *real father*, or their *own child*. We can be leaders, changing the reflected social appraisals these families will internalize.

Patient/s who may *have helped create* or *have been created by* one of these new family formations may be reluctant to share this information for fear of being judged. Others may *not* know *they do not know* their origins. There may be present absences that will *not* appear in the room.

Psychoanalysis can strengthen these families. It has always valued complexity and therefore can be invaluable for promoting attachment, belonging, and the development of secure individual and social identities. We know how difficult it can feel to be on the *outside* or *closeted* in stigmatized, disempowered positions. We understand the co-habitation of dialectical experience. We can help people recognize their mixed and contradictory feelings and allegiances, accept paradoxical experience and polarizations, and challenge their fears. Valuing fantasy and reality, we can help parents realize that a third party, such as a gamete donor, remains psychologically alive within the family system over the course of a lifetime and has implications for future intergenerational transmission.

Psychoanalysis respects that which we do not yet, perhaps cannot *ever* know. We make room for the *unthought known* (Bollas, 1987), for unformulated and dissociated experience to emerge (Stern, 1997). We can give voice to the concurrent deep love for one's *actual* child while simultaneously longing for the one that *could not* be born. We can empathize with the mystification of a secret hiding in plain sight, and with loyalty conflicts between curiosity and belonging for both parents and children. We can help people find the strength to risk rejection, exposure, and hurts. We can assist with tolerating uncertainties. We can hold a potential space for positive aspects of these diverse families to emerge. All this and more we have to offer.

To accomplish these goals we need to modify and expand our theories. We must reflect on how psychoanalysis has caused harm to individuals and society through homophobia and a deterministic reproductive rigidity that led to women being blamed for infertility caused by theorized, but since refuted, maternal conflicts (Rosen, 2002; Apfel & Keylor, 2015). The existence of these families challenges some aspects of psychoanalytic bedrock, such as the inevitable primacy of the mother, sexual reproduction, and the Oedipus complex. In these families, early parental experience is never quite so dyadic as has hitherto been theorized. We must make room for other participants (Malavé, 2006; Ehrensaft 2008, 2016); for the reality that technology outpaces our capacity to integrate changes; be on guard against our *pronatalist* and *heteronormative* biases and *reproductive technophobia* (Ehrensaft, 2014); and provide a more pliable, relational approach (Nordqvist & Smart, 2014a, 2014b) to theory that allows for constant change. In this endeavor, *we too* must adapt, relinquish our symbolic genetic attachments to our past and our psychoanalytic ancestors, expand our conceptualizations of *what is family*, and *evolve*. Our collective future depends upon it.

Psychoanalysis can help the world integrate these new families, to recognize that "everyone is much more simply human than otherwise" (Sullivan, 1953), that we are all different and similar. Everyone needs to know and be known in these ways.

References

AFCARS (2013). Adoption and Foster Care Analysis and Reporting System Federal Fiscal year 2013 data. Available from: www.acf.hhs.gov/programs/cb/resource-library/search?keyword=AFCARS%20report%202013 (accessed December 16, 2016).

Almeling, R. (2011). *Sex Cells: The Medical Market for Eggs and Sperm.* Berkeley, CA: University of California Press.

Apfel, R.J., & Keylor, R.G. (2015). Psychoanalysis and infertility: Myths and realities. In K. Fine. (ed.), *Donor Conception for Life: Psychoanalytic Reflections on New Ways of Conceiving the Family*, pp. 19–48. London: Karnac.

Applegarth, L.A., Kaufman, N.L., Josephs-Sohan, M. Christos, P.J., & Rosenwaks, Z. (2016). Parental disclosure to offspring created with oocyte donation: intentions versus reality. *Human Reproduction*, 31: 1809–1815.

ASRM (2016). Guidelines for Practice. Available from: www.asrm.org/Guidelines_for_Practice/ (accessed December 16, 2016).

Berger, R., & Paul, M. (2008). Family secrets and family functioning: The case of donor assistance. *Family Process*, 47: 553–566.

Bollas, C. (1987). *The Shadow of the Object.* London: Free Association.

Brodzinsky, D. (1990). Stress and Coping Model of Adoption Adjustment. In D. Brodzinsky, & D.M. Schechter (eds.), *The Psychology of Adoption*, pp. 3–24. New York: Oxford University Press.

Brodzinsky, D.M. (2006). Family structural openness and communication openness as predictors in the adjustment of adopted children. *Adoption Quarterly*, 9(40): 1–18.

Brodzinsky D.M. (2011). Children's understanding of adoption: Developmental and clinical implications. *Professional Psychology: Research and Practice*, 42(2): 200–207.

Brodzinsky, D.M., & Pertman, A. (eds.) (2012). *Adoption by Lesbians and Gay Men.* Oxford: Oxford University Press.

Cahn, N. (2009). *Old Lessons For a New World: Applying Adoption Research and Experience to Assisted Reproductive Technology.* New York: Evan B. Donaldson Adoption Institute. Available from: www.adoptioninstitute.org (accessed November 19, 2018).

Cahn, N. (2014). Legal kinship and connection in US donor families. In T. Freeman, S. Graham, F. Ebtehaj, & M. Richards (eds.), *Relatedness in Assisted*

Reproduction: Families, Origins, and Identities, pp. 113–128. Cambridge: Cambridge University Press.

Carey, N. (2012). *The Epigenetics Revolution*. London: Faber & Faber.

Crawshaw, M. (2002). Lessons from a recent adoption study to identify some of the service needs, and issues for, donor offspring wanting to know about their donors. *Human Fertility*, 5: 16–21.

Daniluk J.C., & Hurtig-Mitchell, J. (2003). Themes of hope and healing: Infertile couples' experiences of adoption. *Journal of Counseling and Development*, 81: 389–399.

Ehrensaft, D. (2008). When baby makes three, four, or more: Attachment, individuation, and identity in donor-assisted families. *Psychoanalytic Study of the Child*, 63: 3–23.

Ehrensaft, D. (2014). Family complexes and oedipal circles: Mothers, fathers, babies, donors, and surrogates. In M. Mann (ed.), *Psychoanalytic Aspects of Assisted Reproductive Technology*, pp. 19–43. London: Karnac.

Ehrensaft, D. (2016). Baby making: It takes an egg and sperm and a rainbow of genders. In K. Gentile (ed.), *The Business of Being Made: The Temporalities of Reproductive Technologies, in Psychoanalysis and Culture*, pp. 113–134. New York: Routledge.

Evers, J.L.H. (2016). Due to genetic testing donor anonymity does no longer exist [Forum post]. *The Men's Fertility Forum*. Available from: http://www.mensfe.net/forum/index.php?topic=273.0 (accessed December 18, 2018).

Feast, J. (2003). Using and not losing the messages from the adoption experience for donor-assisted conception. *Human Fertility*, 6(1): 41–45.

Fisher A.P. (2003). "Not Quite As Good As Having Your Own"? Towards a Sociology of Adoption. *Annual Reviews of Sociology*, 29: 335–361.

Freundlich, M. (2001). *Adoption and Ethics: Adoption and Assisted Reproduction*. Washington, DC: Child Welfare League of America.

Fulcher, M., Sutfin, E.L., & Patterson, C.J. (2008). Individual differences in gender development: Associations with parental sexual orientation, attitudes, and division of labor. *Sex Roles*, 58: 330–341.

Gentile, K. (ed.) (2016). *The Business of Being Made: The Temporalities of Reproductive Technologies, in Psychoanalysis and Culture*. New York: Routledge.

Golombok, S. (2015). *Modern Families: Parents and Children in New Family Forms*. Cambridge: Cambridge University Press.

Gosden, R. (2000). *Designing Babies: The Brave New World of Reproductive Technology*. New York: Freeman.

Gurdon, J.B.G. (2012). Human cloning could start within 50 years. *The Life Scientific*, BBC Radio 4.

Hague Adoption Convention on Protection of Children and Co-operation in Respect of Inter-Country Adoption. (2016). Available from: www.hcch.net (accessed April 26, 2016).

Hard, A. (1909). Artificial Impregnation. *The Medical World*, April, pp. 163–164. Letter to the Editor: Artificial Impregnation.

Hayashi, K., Ohta, H., Kurimoto, K., Aramaki, S., & Saitou, M. (2011). Reconstitution of the mouse cell specificiation pathway in culture by pluripotent stem cells. *Cell*, 146(4): 519–532.

Hertz, R. (2009). Turning Strangers into Kin: Half Siblings and Anonymous Donors. In M.F. Nelson, & A.I. Garey (eds.), *Who's Watching? Daily Practices of Surveillance among Contemporary Families*, pp. 156–174. Nashville, TN: Vanderbilt University Press.

Howe, D., & Feast, J. (2000). *Adoption, Search and Reunion*. London: British Association for Adoption and Fostering.

Human Fertilisation and Embryology Authority (HFEA). (2016). UK's independent expert panel recommends "cautious adoption" of mitochondrial donation in treatment. November 30. Available from: www.hfea.gov.uk/10559.html (accessed December 11, 2016).

Inhorn, M.C., & Patrizio, P. (2009). "Rethinking Reproductive 'Tourism' as Reproductive 'Exile'". *Fertility and Sterility*, 92(3): 904–906.

Isaksson, S., Sydsjo, G., Skoog-Svanberg, A., & Lampic, C. (2012). Disclosure behavior and intentions among 111 couples following treatment with oocyte or sperm from identity-release donors: Follow-up at offspring age 1–4 years. *Human Reproduction*, 27: 2998–3007.

Jones, S. (1993). *The Language of the Genes*. London: Flamingo.

Jones, S. (1996). *In the Blood: God, Genes, and Destiny*. London: Flamingo.

Juffer, F. &van IJzendoorn, M.H. (2005). Behavior problems and mental health referrals of international adoptees: A meta-analysis. *Journal of the American Medical Association*, 293(20): 2501–2505.

Juffer, F., & M.H. van IJzendoorn (2007). Adoptees do not lack self-esteem: A meta-analysis of studies on self-esteem of transracial, international, and domestic adoptees. *Psychological Bulletin*, 133(6): 1067–1083.

Kirk, H.D. (1984). *Shared Fate*. Originally published in 1964. New York: Free Press.

Kramer, W. (2016). *Donor Sibling Registry (DSR)*. Available from: www.donorsiblingregistry.com (accessed November 19, 2018).

Kramer, W., & Cahn, N. (2013). *Finding Our Families: A First-of Its-Kind Book for Door-Conceived people and Their Families*. New York: Avery.

Malavé, A.F. (2006). *The Shadow Within*. Mental Health Professional Group of the American Society for Reproductive Medicine Newsletter, March 16.

Malavé, A.F. (2013). *Reproductive Pioneers*, July 1. Available from: www.reproductivepsych.org (accessed November 19, 2018).

Mamo, L. (2007). *Queering Reproduction: Achieving Pregnancy in the Age of Technoscience*. Durham, NC: Duke University Press.

Miller, T. (2013). Grandmother, 53, gives birth to her own twin granddaughters. *New York Daily News*, August 15.

Nordqvist, P., & Smart, C. (2014a). *Relative Strangers: Family Life, Genes, and Donor Conception*. Basingstoke, UK: Palgrave Macmillan.

Nordqvist, P., & Smart, C. (2014b). Relational lives, relational selves: Assisted reproduction and the impact on grandparents. In T. Freeman, S. Graham, F. Ebtehaj, & M. Richards (eds.), *Relatedness in Assisted Reproduction: Families, Origins, and Identities*, pp. 296–311. Cambridge: Cambridge University Press.

Palacios, J. (2009). The Ecology of Adoption. In G.M. Wrobel, & E. Neil (eds.), *International Advances in Adoption Research for Practice*, pp. 71–94. London: Wiley-Blackwell.

Palacios, J., & Brodzinsky, D.M. (2010). 'Review: Adoption research. Trends, topics, outcomes'. *International Journal of Behavioral Development*, 34(3): 270–84.

Paul, M., & Berger, R. (2007). Topic avoidance and family functioning in families conceived with donor insemination. *Human Reproduction*, 22(9): 2566–2571.

Rose, J. (2015). Donor conception and the loss of old certainties. In K. Fine (ed.), *Donor Conception for Life: Psychoanalytic Reflections on New Ways of Conceiving the Family*, pp. 211–223. London: Karnac.

Rosen, A. (2002). Binewski's Family: A Primer for the Psychoanalytic Treatment of Infertility Patients. *Contemporary Psychoanalysis*, 38(2): 345–370.

Selman, P. (2009). From Bucharest to Beijing: Changes in countries sending children for international adoption 1990 to 2006. In G. M. Wrobel & E. Neil (eds.), *International Advances in Adoption Research for Practice*, pp. 41–69. New York: Wiley.

Siegel, D.H., & Smith, S.L. (2012). "Openness in Adoption: From Secrecy and Stigma to Knowledge and Connections," *Evan B. Donaldson Adoption Institute*, March 2012. Available from: www.adoptioninstitute.org (accessed November 19, 2018).

Spar, D. (2006). *The Baby Business: How Money, Science, and Politics Drive the Commerce of Conception*. Boston, MA: Harvard Business School Press.

Stacey, J., & Biblarz, T. (2001). (How) does the sexual orientation of parents matter? *American Sociological Review*, 66(2): 159.

Steptoe, P.C., & Edwards, R.G. (1978). Birth after the reimplantation of a human embryo. *Lancet*, 2(8085): 366.

Stern, D. (1997). *Unformulated Experience: From Dissociation to Imagination in Psychoanalysis*. Hillsdale, NJ: Analytic Press.

Sullivan, H.S. (1953). *The Interpersonal Theory of Psychiatry*, p. 32. New York: Norton.

US Department of State (2016). Intercountry Adoption. https://travel.state.gov/content/adoptionsabroad/en/about-us/statistics.html. (accessed April 24, 2016).

Vaughn, S.C. (2007). Scrambled eggs: Psychological meanings of new reproductive choices for lesbians. *Journal of Infant, Child, and Adolescent Psychotherapy*, 6: 141–155.

Volkman, T.A. (2009). Seeking sisters: Twinship and kinship in an age of internet miracles and DNA technologies. In D. Marre & L. Briggs (eds.), *International Adoption: Global Inequalities and the Circulation of Children*, pp. 283–310. New York: New York University Press.

Witt, C. (2005). Family resemblances: Adoption, personal identity, and genetic essentialism. In C. Witt & S. Haslanger (eds.). *Adoption Matters: Philosophical and Feminist Essays*, pp. 135–145. London: Cornell University Press.

Chapter 15

If the sons didn't know
Madoff's family business and financial fraud

Claudia Diez

In December 2008, Bernie Madoff, responsible for the largest and most protracted Ponzi scheme in history, was arrested by the FBI for the self-confessed commission of a $65,000,000,000 securities fraud. This gargantuan swindle had been sponsored for decades by the sustained oversight of multiple players, from family employees to investors and federal security regulators. Close aides and family members claimed not to know about Madoff's Ponzi scheme prior to its official discovery. The victims (thousands, among them Elie Wiesel, Stephen Spielberg, Eliot Spitzer, Larry King), the public and the media roared with indignation and contended with one question: Did the sons know? How could they not have known?

Greed has often been the obvious explanation for financial fraud, and it has been the motive ascribed to the Madoff family for this particular crime. However, recent work in behavioral forensics has overcome the simplicity of this assumption. Ramamoorti, Morrison, & Koletar (2014), bringing to the foreground the role of emotions in the commission of fraud, relegate greed to a symptom. They bring shame to the foreground as a critical emotion—if not *the* critical emotion—disrupting the workplace. Shame, a kaleidoscopic emotion that shifts and mutates into different experiences—defeat, inferiority, sense of failure, shyness, lack of self-worth, mortification, envy, greed—alerts the self to a disadvantage in social standing.

I believe shame (and its permutations into greed and envy), present and transmitted for at least three generations, was the operative emotion in the tragic history of Bernie Madoff's family. It is my claim that the Ponzi scheme was his attempt at mastering his shame, and his revenge against whatever, and whoever, he perceived had caused it. The following is a hypothetical construction of the psychodynamic forces that may have underlined the largest Ponzi scheme in history.

Family business, business of the family

Madoff's operation had two branches: a trading house and an investment advisory firm, the latter being the operation responsible for the Ponzi scheme. His wife Ruth acted, on occasion, as Bernie's assistant and bookkeeper. The trading house employed his two sons, Mark and Andrew. They were both experienced traders, and financially savvy, astute individuals. Office space and resources, financial transactions and funds were routinely shared, and collaboration was common between the two firms. Millions were funneled from Madoff's investment management company to his sons' trading operations and their personal accounts, and to his wife's account, even just a few days before the crime was officially discovered. A large portion of the sons' wealth was derived from funds that originated in their father's business operation.

The physical, emotional, and functional proximity between father and sons was such that, upon the collapse of the scheme, the sons became natural suspects of complicity in the father's crime in the eyes of the public and investigators. Picard, the trustee for the Madoff's victims, claims that Bernie's firm "operated as if it were the family piggy bank" (USBC, 2010). The family adamantly denied any knowledge of the scheme. The sons claimed innocence until their deaths. The investigations that followed did not turn up any evidence of their direct involvement, so the legal complaint filed by Picard against the family defendants seeking recovery of assets does not accuse the defendants of knowing, but rather it states, "The Family Members were completely derelict in their duties and responsibilities. As a result, they either failed to detect or failed to stop the fraud, thereby enabling and facilitating the Ponzi scheme … Simply put, if the Family Members had been doing their jobs—honestly and faithfully—the Madoff Ponzi scheme might never have succeeded" (USBC, 2010). Dereliction of duty is not a confirmation of knowing. Yet the lack of evidence of family involvement in the father's fraudulent operations does not resolve the fundamental question, "Did the sons know"? If in fact they didn't know, how could they not have known, given their close involvement with their father?

The Madoff family

Bernie Madoff's roots go back to Eastern Europe. His grandparents migrated in the early twentieth century, leaving behind the ghettos and shtetls to settle in New York City's Lower East Side (Oppenheimer, 2009). Bernie grew up in a predominantly Jewish and Italian, middle class, small community of Laurelton, Queens, New York. Oppenheimer, who extensively researched the

Madoff family, chronicled that Bernie's father, a plumber in a pinstriped suit turned stockbroker, was a quintessential Jewish tough guy, a rather aggressive, intense individual who put a premium on winning. The family, he wrote, had a record and reputation for dubious and illicit financial activities and was generally distrusted and disliked in Laurelton.

As a child, Bernie was allegedly embarrassed by the way his parents lived and acted. He rarely invited friends into his home. He was "a fairly popular kid, but an average to poor student" (Kirtzman, 2010, p. 20), a social disadvantage in the upward mobility-driven Laurelton town. He was "the only kid who didn't have Keds on his feet, which embarrassed him to no end" (Oppenheimer, 2009, p. 25). He was rejected by girls who deemed him mediocre, and lived in the shadows of his best friend and his younger brother. Bernie "developed an inferiority complex," a childhood friend recalled (Kirtzman, 2010, p. 22). Academically challenged but street smart, Bernie showed financial prowess from an early age. By high school he was making a nice income by installing lawn sprinklers and working as a lifeguard. He had two short-lived stints at the University of Alabama and Hofstra before he started transitioning into trading, following his father's footsteps in the financial industry.

As an adult, Bernie Madoff became a dangerously charming man at times, yet despotic and intimidating to those close to him. Considered a "control freak," screaming, shaming, and threats were everyday occurrences at the office and, likely, at home. Unwanted sexual conduct toward his female employees was common (Seal & Squillari, 2009). He was deeply preoccupied with the trappings of power and wealth. Allegedly he developed an obsessional concern with tidiness, appearance, order and controls over his environment, business operations and others.

Ruth and Bernie's sons, Mark and Andrew, grew up under the stardom and frightening shadow of Bernie. Like most of Bernie's extended family, they built their semi-independent business branches under their father's sponsorship. The lack of evidence of complicity in the scheme built by Bernie suggests that the sons—and wife— did not question or investigate their father's secretive operation, despite Barron's publication of an accusatory article (Arvedlund, 2001) and whistleblower Harry Markopolos' exposé of the operation as fraudulent (Markopolos, 2010), both around the same time.

A history of shame

In the beginning it was Bernie's shame over his precarious social standing in his community that propelled him to the hunger for upward mobility acquired from his parents. The deflection of shame necessitated a tremendous control apparatus, both logistic and emotional. The defense operations mounted against "shame anxiety" may have led to what appeared to be an obsessional disposition in Bernie, originally directed to perfecting the trappings of his new wealth. (He was known for being excessively punctilious in matters of style and appearance.) This ploy was likely intended to master the humiliation inflicted on him by his perceived substandard childhood social status. Bernie turned shame into an instrument of emotional control by injecting it into those around him—specifically his offspring, from their most tender years. The social awkwardness or "inferiority complex" permuted into a grandiose sense of self and into the active, hostile demeaning of others, directly or surreptitiously. Anecdotally, Bernie kept a giant erect plastic screw in his office, and called his boats "Bull," for bull market, or bullshit. Over time, obsessional controls on matters of style and relationships turned into frantic, anguished attempts to gain control over the unraveling catastrophe he had created (Seal & Squillari, 2009).

Unknowing: emotional and cognitive underpinnings

As an emotion communicating threat of social annihilation, shame avoidance may become a matter of psychological survival. In turn, the defense against this anxiety may foreclose access to reality in ways that can threaten survival. Avoidance of shame may have been the main motive for the family's subjugation to Bernie's patriarchal might, and for their oversight in detecting his criminal maneuvers. Avoidance of curiosity, instrumental in this concerted familial not-knowing, was cultivated by his notorious use of shaming as a tactic of control deployed with his family and outsiders. He was known for forcefully discouraging curiosity or examination via cruel berating, ridiculing, and bulldozing—treatments applied equally to family members, employees, investors and to naïve SEC auditors assigned the task of inspecting his operation prior to the discovery of the Ponzi scheme.

Relentless curiosity and potential professional rewards motivated Harry Markopolos—the forensic accounting investigator who first discovered the fraud. Inversely, a colossal avoidance of curiosity, fueled by the fear of a catastrophically shaming discovery, may have sustained the family members' ignorance. Not knowing was crucial for sustaining their identity and sense of themselves as the wealthy, powerful and respectable high-profile family of a former NASDAQ chairman who had presumably achieved their prominent social stature and fortune by legitimate means. If we think of the capacity for shame as social competence, we may also speculate that the unquestioned avoidance of shame taught in the family by Bernie, with Ruth as a complicit bystander in this emotional "security operation," led to his children's diminished capacity to tolerate it and, thus, to know about their father's scheme, or to survive in the aftermath of knowing about it.

If there was something to avoid knowing, then there was also something known about it. What was known by the sons, and in which form?

We may think of knowing and not-knowing more than in binary terms, on a continuum, with "grades" of differentiation in the symbolization of the subject matter. The sons knew about Barron's article and Markopolos' claims about the fraudulent nature of their father's operation. The family is also said to have practiced tax evasion (Ross, 2009) and received sham loans from Bernie. Disbelief and fear of discovery may have induced a dampening of investigative curiosity regarding the origination of the funds, and various cognitive maneuverings would have been set in motion: minimization of the fraud, rationalization of well-known partial aspects of it; suppression from awareness and eventual forgetting of facts, all conflating to keep potentially painful experiences out of full consciousness. The claims made by whistleblowers would have turned into muddled, unformulated knowledge displaced from awareness by never becoming the focus of attention. The analytic reconstruction of the Ponzi scheme may have never taken place in the sons' minds; never given thought, never talked about, kept in the shadows of knowing.

We can describe the above processes as unconscious intentional unknowing, which is a defensively motivated unformulated knowledge, characterized by lack of cognitive clarity or differentiation affecting material which in a more complete form would be noxious to the self (Stern, 1983). Harry Stack Sullivan (1940) stated that one "has information about one's experience only to the extent that one has tended to communicate it to another or thought about it in the manner of communicative speech." For Sullivan, "not thinking about it" is one of the primary defenses, facilitated by the mechanism of selective inattention, at the service of keeping out of awareness material that can disrupt the equilibrium of the self. Selective inattention and avoidance of formulation can successfully avert anxiety, while giving rise to the "not-me," a representation of unacknowledged aspects of ourselves. This "not me" hampers the learning of and reflecting on that particular material. To the question, "What were they thinking?" we may thus answer, "They weren't." In Ruth Madoff's interview with the *New York Times* (Henriques, 2011) she speaks of this process:

> I simply didn't know. He didn't tell me. I would have no way of knowing. The boys didn't know. Peter didn't know. And he just kept it from all of us. None of them thought that anybody knew. The boys didn't think

I knew, Peter [Bernie's brother] didn't think I knew, I didn't think they knew ... It was very hard to imagine the Bernie they knew to be the Bernie that did this. It was a huge conflict. Everybody felt it. I mean, even the people who lost everything. You know, he was a guy that everybody loved. And he seemed to like them. It seemed unthinkable that he could do this to people.

While the family rested in the complacency of not knowing, the one who knew, Harry Markopolos, who had denounced the scheme years before its collapse, was in turn ridden by persecutory anxiety, haunted by his knowledge of an extraordinary crime. The angst of the whistleblower was the mirror image of the bystanders' gleeful unawareness.

The cost and burden of knowing—and being known

When the Ponzi edifice crashed, the shame the family experienced was of catastrophic, tragic magnitude. Their identities and lives, both public and private, were profoundly and indelibly shattered. The sons were made to bear the sins of the father: Mark, the elder, hung himself at age 46, on the anniversary of his father's arrest (December 11, 2010). Andrew, the youngest, who died at age 48, attributed the fatal recurrence of mantle cell lymphoma to the massive stress suffered following the discovery of fraud (Aleccia, 2014.) Ruth experienced the tragic loss of her husband (as she knew him) and her sons, as well as the loss of her privilege as a socialite, becoming ostracized by her social circle and falling into what may have felt like the abyss of a lower socioeconomic status.

Remarkably, the family held on, at least publicly, to the "not-knowing" defense (psychologically and legally). At no point did they acknowledge they "should have known" or "could have known," nor did they express remorse for having ignored or overlooked the facts, or for having failed in their legal duties toward the affected investors. Guilt, remorse or shame around their bystander role was never acknowledged to others, or perhaps to themselves. Not-knowing, a basic and universal defense, once established as a fundamental way of confronting the world, seems to contribute to character formation, if only in regards to specific pockets of experience. The endurance and reach of this stance suggest it was part of a transmitted characterological makeup in the Madoff family.

In conclusion, it is my opinion that the sons knew something, and didn't want to know something else, even though they could have, if a massive defensive operation designed to stall the knowing had not been put in place.

References

Aleccia, J. (2014). A final interview with Andrew Madoff. *Hutch News*, September 3. Available from: www.fredhutch.org/en/news/center-news/2014/09/Fred-Hutch-transplant-helped-Andrew-Madoff-battle-cancer.html (accessed November 19, 2018).

Arvedlund, E. (2001). Don't ask don't tell: Bernie Madoff attracts skeptics in 2001. *Barron's*, May 7. Available from: www.barrons.com/articles/SB98901966 7829349012 (accessed November 19, 2018).

Henriques, D.B. (2011). Interview: Ruth Madoff. *The New York Times*, October 31. Available from: www.nytimes.com/interactive/2011/10/31/business/ interview-ruth-madoff.html?_r=0 (accessed November 19, 2018).

Kirtzman, A. (2010). *Betrayal: The Life and Lies of Bernie Madoff*. New York: HarperCollins.

Markopolos, H. (2010). *No One Would Listen: A True Financial Thriller*. Hoboken, NJ: John Wiley & Sons.

Oppenheimer, J. (2009). *Madoff with the Money*. Hoboken, NJ: John Wiley & Sons.

Ramamoorti, S., Morrison, D.E., & Koletar, J.W. (2014). Bringing Freud to fraud: Understanding the state-of-mind of the c-level suite/white collar offender through "A-B-C" analysis. *Journal of Forensic and Investigative Accounting*, 6(1): 47–81.

Ross, B. (2009). *The Madoff Chronicles: Inside the Secret World of Bernie and Ruth*. New York: Hyperion.

Seal, M., & Squillari, E. (2009). "Hello, Madoff!" *Vanity Fair*, June. Available from: www.vanityfair.com/news/2009/06/bernie-madoff-secretary-reveals-secrets (accessed November 19, 2018).

Stern, D.B. (1983). Unformulated experience: From familiar chaos to creative disorder. *Contemporary Psychoanalysis*, 19(1): 71–99.

Sullivan, H.S. (1940). Conceptions of modern psychiatry: The first William Alanson White memorial lectures. *Psychiatry*, 3(1): 1–117.

USBC (United States Bankruptcy Court) (2010). *SIPA Liquidation*, August 3. Available from: www.nysb.uscourts.gov/sites/default/files/opinions/195578_49_opinion.pdf (accessed November 19, 2018).

Chapter 16

Catfishing

The new impostor

Danielle Knafo

As we welcome technology into our homes, offices, and even our bodies, we find technological expansion is a double-edged sword. Many benefits are obvious. Limitless information is just keystrokes away. The ability to connect in cyberspace facilitates many kinds of conversations. People all over the world can collaborate for artistic, professional, or political purposes. Friends and family members who live half a world away from each other can keep in touch through email, Skype, and social media. On the other hand, new technology has opened a Pandora's box of novel problems. People use the Internet to act out. A virtual universe of ghost worlds exists where bodiless meetings take place and dark secrets are exchanged without the intervening presence of a human face. Normal requirements of social convention are suspended in a space without horizons, where anything goes, and the private self can hide behind a code name and let its id play freely. Cyberspace is extremely public and exceedingly private—a world of both connection and disconnection in which the mask of civility may be dropped, along with restraints that keep nefarious desires in check. All people need do is open an electronic window and send a message through the world's new nervous system.

Catfish

In addition to providing the means to trawl for sex and pornographic images, the Internet allows people to misrepresent themselves. Ahmed, a dark, handsome, gay male in his 20s, was extremely self-conscious about his appearance when he decided to begin digital dating. He hated his looks, complained he was overweight, not toned enough, and too ethnic looking. He was also coming to terms with his attraction to males, something that made him feel guilty and ashamed, particularly since his Muslim family and community forbade homosexuality. All this contributed to self-loathing that culminated in a particular perverse enactment he eventually described to me.

Ahmed was recounting his experience with Grindr, a popular app for gay men wanting to hook up. The previous night he had tried to connect with several men, none of whom responded with a consenting swipe. He especially wanted a man named Bob to respond but had no luck. Ahmed's self-hatred surfaced and expressed itself as rage. He created a new profile. This time, he replaced his photo with a photo of Dave, a male acquaintance he considered more handsome and popular. "Borrowing" Dave's Facebook photo, he would become the man he desired and desired to be. He would also take revenge on two men—one for rejecting him, the other for being more attractive than he. Now looking quite buff, Ahmed again let Bob know that he was interested, and Bob agreed to hook up. Ahmed found himself in a bind. On the one hand, he had won: he felt vindicated for having tricked Bob into desiring him. On the other hand, he couldn't take the game any further because he'd have to present himself as himself.

As Ahmed guiltlessly narrated his evening's deceitful enactments, I wondered about my ethical responsibility, believing what he had done might be unlawful. Even if it weren't, he had crossed a line. I imagined the man whose photo was being used without his knowledge or consent. This could happen to anyone! I didn't know this type of masquerade—known as "catfishing"—has become increasingly common on the digital dating scene. A "catfish" refers to a person who creates a fictional profile to lure someone into a relationship. Interestingly, Ahmed had created an Oedipal triangle in which he was the chosen one. His deceitful theater (Stoller, 1985) excited him and placed him in a superior position, helping to restore narcissistic equilibrium.

We spoke of growing to tolerate painful feelings and understand their origin. Analysis centered around the identities he was conflicted about: Muslim, gay. His catfishing was an attempt to shed his dark skin and marginal social position, replacing them with one he was convinced would grant him greater acceptance and confidence. Magically, Bob and Dave—two white American names— would substitute for Ahmed, himself a giveaway of ethnic marginalization. Ahmed recalled his father's abuse as well as the abuse by children who bullied him and called him names, making him feel small and inadequate, the object of hatred and rage.

Our work around this incident aimed at helping Ahmed understand how he had fashioned a situation in which he felt in control to replace situations in which he had felt rejected, inferior, and humiliated. His was an attempt to bridge the gap between his real and ideal self. Understanding Ahmed's narcissistic vulnerability, as well as the mechanisms he enlisted in its defense, helped me to empathize with him rather than judge his behavior as ethically compromised.

Eighty-one percent of online daters misrepresent some aspects of themselves. Men lie about their height and income; women lie about their age and weight; both genders post pictures that are not recent (Rudder, 2010;

Rosenbloom, 2011; Dosh, 2012). Catfishing goes far beyond this misrepresentation. Like Ahmed, catfish try to trick another person into desiring them by adopting or creating a different identity. Some people feel insecure about their appearance and therefore "borrow" someone else's. Others want to enact revenge on an ex or on someone who has rebuffed them. Still others lie to sadistically humiliate and control. Trauma, insecurity, envy, and hostility combine to create an illusion that results in betrayal, cruelty, and harm that can be delivered only via the Internet. Betrayal seems to be an integral part of today's Internet dating scene. Some people state it simply goes with the territory. The degree to which catfishing is conscious and manipulative versus unconscious and defensive is only determinable on a case-by-case basis. I suggest a continuum of catfishing behaviors that begins with harmless self-deception (that always involves the deception of an other) moving all the way to psychopathic and callous trickery.

Notre Dame football player, Manti Te'o (Zeman, 2013) developed a publicized romance with a woman he thought was a Stanford student but who was later revealed to be fictitious. He had never met her. She apparently was ill and died of leukemia. Ronaiah Tuiasosopo, a former high school quarterback conflicted about his homosexuality, created the fictitious person and used the photo of a high school acquaintance to lure Te'o into a romantic relationship. Speculation still exists about whether Te'o participated in making up the story about the girl's death in order to lessen the shame at having been catfished.

A 2010 film, *Catfish* (Jarecki et al., 2010), inspired the MTV reality show of the same name. In this critically acclaimed documentary, Nev is a young man being filmed by his brother and a friend as he becomes Facebook friends with Abby Pierce, an 8-year-old Midwestern child prodigy who sends him her artwork. Through Abby, Nev connects with Abby's mother, Angela, and her sister, Megan, with whom he develops a passionate online romance. Nev and Megan exchange pictures and 1500 messages over nine months before Nev begins to suspect Megan is not telling the truth. The brothers decide to travel from New York to Michigan to make a surprise visit to the Pierce home. They find Angela and her husband, Vince, with his severely mentally challenged twin sons. Angela tells Nev she is undergoing chemotherapy for uterine cancer. Nev insists on meeting his love interest, Megan. Angela tells him she'll come the following day. The next day she says Megan has checked into drug rehab. In the meantime, Vince tells a story about cod being shipped from Alaska to Asia. The fish are inactive and turn to mush unless catfish are placed in the tanks. The catfish nip the tails of the cod, keeping them active so they arrive fresh and healthy. The message of Vince's story is that we all need catfish in our lives to keep us on our toes.

Angela turns out to be the catfish. She confesses to having made up multiple stories and numerous online profiles. She is the one who has been sending Nev her artwork. She is also Megan. Angela does have a daughter, but the pictures she posted are of a young Canadian model, Aimee Gonzales. Angela is not suffering from cancer. Surprisingly, Nev forgives Angela. They continue as Facebook friends. If Nev is angry, he sublimates it by transforming it into a creative production, *Catfish: The TV Show*.

Interestingly, Angela forms two discrete online relationships with Nev: one as a gifted child; the other a young, passionate beauty hungry for love. She employs two different seductions and creates two illusions, enlisting Nev to help create them. She callously uses him as the consciousness that experiences these illusions as real. Through Nev she experiences their projected reality. He becomes the interactive mirror that reflects back to Angela the magic of her creations—herself as a gifted child and a beautiful, desirable woman—two fantasies that empower her while masking her limitations. This perverse scenario would not be possible without today's technology that invites the expansive play of a subject who is defined as much by lack as by being, who longs to realize possibilities that challenge personal and existential limitation, and who can engage in such play with relative anonymity and freedom from the law. Is it any surprise that users find victims on whom to work this magic? Nev is duped and dehumanized, though at a distance, once removed from actual contact, which makes the egregiousness of Angela's action seem less severe. Perversion is rampant in this kind of dark, creative theatre. The actor steals another's identity, schemes, lies, tricks, seduces under false pretense, and uses the other as a self-object without regard to the consequences. The space of encounter is violated, mocking the social bond, creating a standard of inauthenticity.

Also interesting about this particular Internet seduction is the Oedipal triangle it expresses. Two creations of the perpetrator, child and beauty, occlude her presence as a real person. She is excluded from the triangle she creates, filling her absence with the man who loves the two figures of her imagination. She enjoys the entire production as the puppet master behind the scenes. In this way she becomes the Oedipal winner who not only witnesses the primal scene but also creates it for her own enjoyment.

The stated mission of the *Catfish* TV show (Jarecki et al., 2012–2015) which has had six seasons, is to help those who have become emotionally involved with questionable people on the Internet. Some couples have been communicating for months or years. The show follows both sides of the "relationship," trying to understand motives behind the catfishing as well as the impact on the person who has been duped. Normalization of catfishing is evident in an article on the trend that claims couples who come together by accurately representing themselves are boring, and that such a pedestrian approach to romance is passé (Weber and Moses, 2013). While the authors were being ironic, the humor and lighthearted nature of their piece indicate the level of acceptance that has been attained by online betrayal and the upending of conventional social bonding. In some cases, those who catfish discover they too have been catfished. Some even forgive the misrepresentation and end up together.

Others are not so forgiving. Artist and writer Dori Hartley (2011) publicly confessed to having been catfished. Enthralled by "the epic romance of [my] life," Hartley embarked on a five-year relationship with a man she never met, never even glimpsed a picture of. She admitted her vulnerability as a "lonely woman sitting at her computer, waiting for someone special to pay attention to her." Dimitri described himself as 6' 7" with long black hair. His phone voice was soft, with a southern accent. He refused to send a picture because he maintained he was dying of cancer and the disease had distorted his looks. Hartley was a cancer survivor herself and implicitly understood the importance of having love and support during such a challenging time. As years went on, Hartley was "finally fixated on seeing the person [I] loved." She insisted he show his face. Finally Alex Lee, the real person behind Dimitri, got on a webcam. Alex was a woman with three grown daughters and two grandchildren. Hartley was heartbroken: "There will never be any words to adequately describe my shock and disgust. It never occurred to me that the man I came to adore would turn out to be someone so utterly devoid of conscience, so thoroughly steeped in duplicity." She concluded that stupid things happen to smart people because of their "desperate loneliness" and willingness to believe in fantasy. What she does not talk about was her complicity—the pact she made with a perverse other with whom she nurtured a gratifying illusion for five years.

Another example of catfishing as a social perversion began in 2011 when Montreal-based Alyona Minkovski began Facebook communication with Amina Arraf, a lesbian Syrian-American blogger allegedly living in Syria (Brekke, 2015; Deraspe, 2015). Minkovski and Arraf developed a serious relationship, even though they never spoke by phone or in person. Minkovski was attracted to Arraf's nonconformist views and encouraged her to create a blog, which she did, naming it "A Gay Girl in Damascus." The blog presented Arraf as a young woman with close ties to the Assad regime and strong empathy for those oppressed by it. Her blog captured the world's attention and was viewed by Minkovski and other gay advocates as an act of courage in the light of Syria's persecution of the LGBT community. Matters intensified when Arraf reported that she had been kidnapped by Assad's police, an act that encouraged some gay activists in the Middle East to risk outing themselves to help search for her. Digital posters distributed across the Web in English and Arabic proclaimed, "Free Amina Arraf: Borders mean nothing when you have wings."

Arraf was eventually revealed to be Tom MacMaster, a married, white American male from Georgia, a graduate student in medieval studies at the University of Edinburgh. After finally disclosing his true identity, he professed, "I do not believe I harmed anyone" (Peralta & Carvin, 2011). An additional twist to this case is that Paula Brooks, editor of Lez Get Real, the original site on which MacMaster posted as Arraf, turned out to be former Air Force pilot, Bill Graber (Flock & Bell, 2011). During their correspondence, neither man realized the other was pretending to be lesbian. "Borders mean nothing when you have wings" seems an apt motto for Internet perversion.

Is catfishing illegal? It is hard to tell. Despite the chaotic trail of deception and harm he left, MacMaster was not prosecuted. These new Internet transgressions require new laws (perversion brings the law into being). Violators take advantage of the fact that law has not caught up with technology. States differ in prosecuting catfishing. Criminal impersonation is difficult to prosecute unless there is clear identity theft and proof of injury or loss to the victim. When prosecuted, catfish are usually charged with misdemeanors. Nineteen-year-old Andriy Mykhaylivskyy of Rutherford, New Jersey was given a 6-month jail sentence for luring a classmate into an online relationship by creating a fictitious Facebook account for Kate Fulton, a girl he later claimed had been kidnapped while vacationing in Bulgaria. He even asked people for the $50,000 ransom money (Sudol, 2014).

Sometimes misrepresentation can provide catfish with more information than they bargained for. Teen Marissa Williams invited men she met on the Internet to her home for sex. Her aunt, with whom she lived, tried to teach her a lesson by creating a fake online suitor, but the "joke" was on her. Marissa confessed to this fake suitor that she hated her aunt and wanted her dead. She asked him if he'd help kill her aunt. The aunt called the police and Williams was charged with solicitation of murder (Donnelly, 2014).

Romancing the mark: cyber swindling

One in five relationships begins online; one in ten Americans has used an online dating site or mobile dating app (Smith & Duggan, 2013). More than a third of new marriages begin online (Jayson, 2013). Sites like Match.com and eHarmony have made it possible for many adults to expand their dating possibilities beyond anything imaginable a couple of decades ago. The popular mobile dating app Tinder claims users make about one billion swipes per day. The bad news is that online sites have become settings for scam artists to swindle tens of millions of dollars each year. Many of those persuaded to empty their bank accounts are retired women over 50 who live alone (Olson, 2015). They are ideal targets because they usually own their own home, have savings, and are lonely, gullible, and hungry for romance. *The New York Times* claimed that in a 5-month period in 2014, 6,000 people registered complaints that they had been swindled out of $82.3 million (Olson, 2015). Despite the fact that online dating sites warn users not to send money to anyone who contacts them, this cautionary advice often goes unheeded.

Most cases begin with a man who alters and uses an inactive profile on a site like Match.com to contact a potential victim. Once interest is established, he quickly shifts to communicating on a private email or telephone. Contacting the woman with daily letters filled with amorous attention, he establishes trust and cultivates romance. Reading her profile carefully and making sure to match her search requirements, he convinces her he is Mr. Right, her Prince Charming and soulmate. There is one hitch: he is "temporarily" overseas on business. They make detailed plans to meet, keeping the fantasy of a shared future alive. After a few weeks or months, he suddenly reports he is in trouble: he's in the hospital; he needs to pay for work permits; he hasn't been paid; he's lost his credit card; he's been robbed—any reason to evoke sympathy and induce the woman to wire money. He promises to pay her back. This is repeated, for different reasons, for larger sums, until the woman has emptied her bank account or realized she has been defrauded (Olson, 2015).

When victims of romance fraud finally face the truth, they are overcome with shame and humiliation for having been played. Many are too embarrassed to confide in friends or families. Women are not the only victims. Al Cirelli (Wallace, 2010), a proud 68-year-old man, committed suicide after sending $50,000 of his own and his son's money to a woman in Ghana who called herself Aisha. The person whose seductive photos were used for the fraud claims hundreds have illegally appropriated her image. Aisha had promised to meet the retired businessman in Yonkers, New York, where he lived, to start a new life together. She assured him romance and money were on their way. On the day she was scheduled to arrive, Mr. Cirelli received an email stating that she had committed suicide—"blown her head off"—in Chicago. Realizing he had been duped and/or heartbroken, Cirelli took his life.

Psychoanalytic theories of imposture and deception

Impostors are nothing new. Kaplan (1987) claimed imposture was a rare male disorder that nonetheless flourished in the eighteenth-century British literary world. Statistics from the first three seasons of *Catfish* indicates the gender breakdown is 57 percent female, 42 percent male. Helene Deutsch

(1942, 1955) claimed, "The world is crowded with 'as if' personalities, and even more so with impostors and pretenders ... Ever since I became interested in the impostor, he pursues me everywhere. I find him among my friends and acquaintances, as well as myself" (p. 503). Discovering we can convincingly pretend to be someone else and, even when we don't, we still harbor an impostor, Deutsch coined the term "as if" personality to describe people who are good mimics and who adopt a persona without authenticity. Phyllis Greenacre (1958) wrote that the impostor was nearly always male, with exhibitionist tendencies and omnipotent fantasies: "Imposture appears to contain the hope of getting something material, or some other worldly advantage" (p. 93). She considered three factors present in the impostor: (a) disturbed sense of identity; (b) perceptiveness about certain aspects of reality and "brazenness or stupidity" about other aspects; (c) malformation of the superego, conscience, and ideals. Importantly, Greenacre mentioned that impostors can succeed only in social contexts in which there exists receptivity to trickery.

Face-to-face relationships pose challenges for impostors. The Internet, with its anonymity and accessibility, makes it easy for people to shed their skin and replace it with a virtual one—whether adopted from the real world or created from the imagination. In a famous *New Yorker* cartoon, a dog "speaks" to another, saying, "On the Internet, no one knows you're a dog" (Steiner, 1993). As we spend more time on the Internet, our lives become increasingly "virtual" and distanced from physical reality. The line between real and virtual becomes blurred, making it more difficult to distinguish these two domains which, after all, may not be as distinct as they appear at first blush. The cyberworld exists inside a machine (or "web" of machines) as an "as if" reality. The real world, too, is always within our experience, embodied and radically unfolding through the operations of the mind-body. Doesn't it seem "as if" the earth doesn't move and the full moon is the size of a quarter? Physicist David Deutsch (1997) effectively argues that the human brain is a "virtual reality generator" and that reality itself might be a simulation. Philosopher Marcus Arvan (2015) strongly contends that reality is a simulation. Historian Yuval Harari (2015), author of *Sapiens*, claims there are essentially two characteristics of humans: their biology and ability to invent fictions.

The self can be extended into places, things, and people around it, nested as it is in overlapping circles of family, friends, neighbors, state, and nation. The self embodies the world that both gives it being and reflects it. Because the self does not end at the boundary of its flesh but fills the surround with itself as it takes the surround within it, it easily finds itself at home in the virtual world where it may invent itself in numerous ways. Arguing that digital technology provides unprecedented possibilities for self-extension, Belk (2013) discussed five changes wrought by this technology: (a) dematerialization (of information and data); (b) reembodiment (as avatars, photos, videos, or catfish); (c) sharing (blogs, social media, photos, and videos); (d) co-construction of self (through digital gazing and communication/interaction); (e) distributed memory (through digital archiving).

There may come a time when virtual worlds, continually improved by technological advances, may be experienced as so real as to be nearly indistinguishable from "real" worlds. Adoption of virtual worlds for entertainment and social networking grows daily. Second Life, a three-dimensional virtual world in which users create representations (as many as they wish) of themselves called avatars, has become very popular. Avatars live in a virtual home, work at a virtual job, interact with other virtual beings, and even engage in virtual sexual acts they would not dare to perform in their "first" life. For many, virtual living already feels more real than the alternative: people spend twice as much time online as they did ten years ago—especially young adults who spend an average of 30 hours per week in virtual worlds (Cooper, 2015).

Psychoanalysts have traditionally positioned themselves as truth seekers who view deception as symptomatic of illness. Fromm (1959) described Freud's uncompromising search for truth. Yet in *The Project*, Freud (1950) claimed lying was a way children create private space allowing autonomy from parents. Weston (1996) similarly wrote about lying as developmentally useful because it attempts to control and protect access to one's inner thoughts. Livingstone Smith (2004), in his book *Why We Lie: The Evolutionary Roots of Deception and the Unconscious Mind*, claims humans are born liars, lying to ourselves and others. Deception and lying may have evolutionary advantages (e.g. animals that can turn the color of their surroundings to deceive predators into believing they are inanimate). Gediman and Lieberman (1996) emphasized the ubiquity of lying in everyday life, focusing on the narcissistic and sadistic elements in such acts. Winnicott (1965) argued for the need to be rid of the False Self to reach one's True Self. Extending Mervin Glasser's (1979) work on self-preservative and sadistic lying, Lemma (2005) identified the following motivations for lying: to hurt another person by trickery; to induce another's affection by transforming the present self into a more attractive (but untrue) version; to protect the self from a threatening "other." All these configurations involve distancing from current reality and active pursuit of a new reality, while seeking vengeance, a relationship, or safety.

Psychoanalytic theories are often developed without connecting to social and cultural realities (Cushman, 1995). We cannot afford to ignore these realities when considering catfishing. We live in a digital age. Much of life is lived online. We live in a postmodern world in which truth and objective reality are constantly being questioned and viewed through a skeptical, often disdainful, lens. Opposing the view that faking it is a universal human quality is that which argues our culture has become increasingly corrupted by fakes. Scruton (2012) argues that fakery has become a social activity in which people act together to draw a veil over unwanted realities and encourage each other in the exercise of illusory powers. He claims we have entered an era in which fakeness is endorsed by social norms and is eroding high culture. Holan (2016) addresses fakery through a political lens. She calls 2016 the year of fake news, with Donald Trump taking Lie of the Year honors by spinning untruths, like claiming Ted Cruz's father was involved in assassinating President Kennedy. The Oxford Dictionary selected "post-truth" as its word of the year: "Objective facts are less influential in shaping public opinion than appeals to emotion and public belief." Keyes (2004) claims we live in a post-truth era in which deception has become a routine part of life, eroding our code of ethics and foundation of trust. All observe that the Internet, led by Facebook and Google, facilitates the spread of lies. One need only consider the evolution of Finsta, a popular (especially among middle schoolers) fake instagram account, which Patterson (2016) calls "the Wild West of social media" due to its lack of rules that leads to immorality and cyberbullying.

Some psychoanalysts (e.g. Goldman, 2007) claim the idea of authenticity is a delusion and that pretense can be representative of healthy strivings. I believe human life exists between the two extremes of absolute authenticity and absolute deception. Trickery, sinister seduction, deception, betrayal, and perversion stand in reciprocal and necessary relationship with striving for authenticity, accountability, coherence, and transparency. There is no one true self and no one false self either. The idea of a core self is a belief rather than a fact, yet remains a powerful concept (Belk, 2013). There are selves in situation, selves that constellate around a historical center of gravity, and patterns of selfhood that issue from one's historical embodiment, that can encourage striving for authenticity or engagement in deception. Here, one thinks of the relational concept of multiple selves (Bromberg, 1999; Davies, 2004, 2005). The question remains as to whether peoples' online selves express a self-state—a unique, perhaps dissociated, part of the self—or something constructed and entirely different and separate from the self. This topic has already begun to be researched (Sung, Moon, Kang, & Lin, 2011; Belk, 2013)

Extreme cases of manipulation call to mind psychopaths and con men. It is generally agreed that such characters are the least analyzable and least likely to seek therapy (Becker, 2010), unless mandated by courts to do so. Deception evokes problematic countertransference. Distinctions must be acknowledged with regard to whether people believe their own lies (LaFarge, 1994), and whether the lie is in the service of sadism or self-preservation (Lemma, 2005). Some patients exploit others for their own needs and desires.

Patients can use analysts as fetishized objects (Renik, 1992) in a perverse transference (Etchegoyen, 1991; Bach, 1994). The analyst becomes audience, co-conspirator, and "corrupt container" (O'Shaughnessy, 1990) in a perverse pact (Stein, 2005). As patients involve therapists in their Internet escapades, some darker than others, it places us in their, at times, sadomasochistic, erotic world, confronting us with our own sexual desires and ethical challenges. Often trust is violated in the treatment alliance with the aim of reversing the power dynamics. A colleague told me she had Skyped with a patient for an entire year before discovering that a third person had been present during all their sessions. What she believed were private interactions turned out to be perverse, voyeuristic, and exhibitionistic enactments to which she had not consented.

Patients google us, and those with advanced computer skills can invade our privacy in deeply disturbing ways. When they share their dating behaviors, we may become involuntary voyeurs to fantasies and acts we sometimes find ethically reprehensible. Since many patients sharing Internet behaviors are much younger than their therapists, analysts may doubt themselves, questioning whether they are simply behind the times. "Everyone does it," I was told by a patient who lied about her age and posted old photographs on her online dating profile. Does everyone do it? I wondered. This type of perversion aims to get the analyst to accept lie as truth, to share in the illusion created to seduce the other, to boost the patient's self-esteem, and to enact revenge on harmful figures in the patient's history. The best-case scenario might be one in which the patient wishes to be caught.

Braving a new world

The Internet is now a primary source for information, communication, entertainment, and trade. This amazing tool has brought us closer together by transforming the world into a global village. A person can travel that village in an instant and expand his or her social network in previously unimaginable ways. The Internet has had major impacts on those in committed relationships, those looking for a relationship, and those seeking casual or unconventional sex. Social media, dating apps, hookup apps, affair websites, porn sites, and even matches made to commit heinous crimes are accessible with the click of a mouse. Cyber love potentially feeds people's fantasies. Fantasy loving is so much easier than loving in the real world. Along with the benefits of anonymity and accessibility, Internet relationships come with costs and risks. What begins as an online chat can end in addiction, deception, fraud, stalking, and death. The dangers inherent in novel applications of technology should not be underestimated by any of us, especially those in the mental health professions.

References

Arvan, M. (2015, January 30). The peer-to-peer hypothesis and a new theory of free will. *Scientia Salon*. Available from: www.scientiasalon/wordpress.com/2015/01/30/the-peer-to-peer-hyporthesis-of-free-will-a-brief-overview (accessed November 19, 2018).

Bach, S. (1994). *The Language of Perversion and the Language of Love*. Northvale, NJ: Aronson.

Becker, S. (2010, April 16). Therapy only furthers psychopaths' agenda. Science and technology. *Sott.net*. Available from: www.sott.net/article/206909-Therapy-only-furthers-psychopaths-agendas (accessed November 19, 2018).

Belk, R. (2013, October 1). Extended self in the digital world. *Journal of Consumer Research*. Available from: www.jcr.oxfordjournals.org/content/40/3/477 (accessed November 19, 2018).

Brekke, K. (2015, July 30). I was catfished by the poser behind 'A gay girl in Damascus.' *Huffpost Gay Voices*. Available from: www.huffingtonpost.com/entry/a-gay/girl/indamascus_55b6fe4b0a13f9d1b4165 (accessed November 19, 2018).

Bromberg, P. (1999). Playing with boundaries. *Contemporary Psychoanalysis, 35*(1): 54–66.

Cooper, A. (2015, Sept. 10). Being thirteen: Inside the secret world of teens [Web log post]. CNN. Available from: http://cnnpressroom.blogs.cnn.com/2015/09/10/cnnsanderson-cooper-360-breaks-news-about-teens-and-social-media-in-provocativetwo-year-long-investigation/ (accessed November 19, 2018).

Cushman, P. (1995). *Constructing the Self, Constructing America: A Cultural History of Psychotherapy*. New York: Da Capo Press.

Davies, J. M. (2004). Whose bad objects are we anyway?: Repetition and our elusive love affair with evil. *Psychoanalytic Dialogues, 14*: 711–732.

Davies, J. M. (2005). Transformations of desire and despair: Reflections on the termination process from a relational perspective. *Psychoanalytic Dialogues, 15*: 779–805.

Deraspe, S. (Producer/Director). (2015). *A Gay Girl in Damascus: The Amina profile* [Motion picture]. Canada: Esperamos Films/National Film Board of Canada.

Deutsch, D. (1997). *The Fabric of Reality*. New York: Viking Press.

Deutsch, H. (1942). Some forms of emotional disturbance and their relationship to schizophrenia. *Psychoanalytic Quarterly, 27*(3): 359–382.

Deutsch, H. (1955). The imposter: Contribution to ego psychology of a type of psychopath. In H. Deutsch, *Neuroses and Character Types*, pp. 318–338. New York: International Universities Press.

Donnelly, M.S. (2014, June 13). Some 'Catfish' tales are too dark for television. *MTV News*. Available from: www.mtv.com/news/1845419/catfish-dark-stories/ (accessed November 19, 2018).

Dosh, K. (2012, October 29). The 10 most common lies in online dating profiles. *Woman's Day*. Available from: www.womansday.com/relationships/dating-marriage/advice/a6759/online-dating-profile-lies/ (accessed November 19, 2018).

Etchegoyen, H. (1991). *The Fundamentals of Psychoanalytic Technique*. London: Karnac.

Flock, E., & Bell, M. (2011, June 13). 'Paula Brooks,' editor of 'Lez Get Real,' also a man. *The Washington Post* [Web log post]. Available from: www.washingtonpost.com/blogs/blogpost/paulabrooks-editor-of-lez-get-realalso-a-man/2011/06/13/AGld2ZTH_blog.html (accessed November 19, 2018).

Freud, S. (1950). Project for a scientific psychology. *The Standard Edition*, pp. 283–398. Vol. I. (Originally published in 1895.) London: Hogarth Press.

Fromm, E. (1959). *Sigmund Freud's Mission: An Analysis of His Personality and Influence*. New York: Harper.

Gediman, H., & Lieberman, J. (1996). *The Many Faces of Deceit: Omissions, Lies, and Disguise in Psychotherapy*. Northvale, NJ: Jason Aronson.

Glasser, M. (1979). Some aspects of the role of aggression in the perversions. In I. Rosen (ed.), *Sexual Deviations*. Oxford: Oxford University Press.

Goldman, D. (2007). Faking It. *Contemporary Psychoanalysis*, *43*(1): 17–36.

Greenacre, P. (1958). The Imposter. *Psychoanalytic Quarterly*, *27*(3): 359–382.

Harari, Y.N. (2015). *Sapiens: A Brief History of Humankind*. New York: Harper.

Hartley, D. (2011, September 29). Perfect stranger: How I fell victim to online 'romance fraud.' *The Huffington Post*. Available from: www.huffingtonpost.com/dori hartley/internet-romance-the-mons_b_981068.html (accessed November 19, 2018).

Holan, A.D. (2016, Dec. 13). 2016 Lie of the year: Fake news. Available from: www.politifact.com/truth-o-meter/article/2016/dec/13/2016-lie-year-fake-news/ (accessed November 19, 2018).

Jarecki, A., Schulman, A., Bishop, B., Metzler, D., Joost, H., Karshis, J., et al., (Producers). (2012–2015). *Catfish: The TV Show* [Television broadcast]. United States: Catfish Picture Company and Relativity Media.

Jarecki, A., Smerling, M., Joost, H., & Schulman, A. (Producers), & Joost, H., & Schulman, A. (Directors). (2010). *Catfish* [Motion picture]. United States: Relativity Media and Rogue Pictures.

Jayson, S. (2013, June 3). Study: More than a third of new marriages start online. USA Today. Available from: www.usatoday.com/story/news/nation/2013/06/03/online-dating-marriage/2377961/ (accessed November 19, 2018).

Kaplan, L. (1987). *The Family Romance of the Imposter Poet: Thomas Chatterton*. Berkeley, CA: University of California Press.

Keyes, R. (2004). *The Post-Truth Era: Dishonesty and Deception in Contemporary Life*. New York: St. Martin's Press.

LaFarge, L. (1994, October 4). Transference of deceit. Paper presented at the Association for Psychoanalytic Medicine, New York.

Lemma, A. (2005). The many faces of lying. *International Journal of Psychoanalysis*, *86*: 737–753.

Livingstone Smith, D. (2004). *Why We Lie: The Evolutionary Roots of Deception and the Unconscious Mind*. New York: St. Martin's Press.

Olson, E. (2015, July 17). Swindlers target older women on dating websites. *The New York Times*. Available from: www.nytimes.com/2015/07/18/your-money/swindlers-target-older-women-on-dating-websites.html (accessed November 19, 2018).

Patterson, D. (2016, Oct. 5). What the Finsta?! The darker world of teenagers and Instagram. *Huffington Post*. Available from: www.huffingtonpost.com/entry/what-the-finsta-the-darker-world-of-teenagers-and_us_57eb9e03e4b07f20daa0fefb (accessed November 19, 2018).

Peralta, E., & Carvin, A. (2011, June 12). 'Gay girl in Damascus' turns out to be an American man. *NPR, The Two-Way*. Available from: www.npr.org/sections/thetwo-way/2011/06/13/137139179/gay-girl-in-damascus-apologizes-reveals-she-was-an-american-man (accessed November 19, 2018).

O'Shaughnessy, E. (1990). Can a liar be psychoanalyzed? *International Journal of Psychoanalysis, 71*: 187–195.

Renik, O. (1992). Use of analyst as a fetish. *Psychoanalytic Quarterly, 61*(4): 542–563.

Rosenbloom, S. (2011, Nov. 12). Love, lies and what they learned. *The New York Times*. Available from: www.nytimes.com/2011/11/13/fashion/online-dating-as-scientific-research.html (accessed November 19, 2018).

Rudder, C. (2010, July 10). The big lies people tell in online dating. *OKTrends, Data Research from OKCupid*. Available from: http://blog.okcupid.com/index.php/the-biggest-lies-in-online-dating/ (accessed November 19, 2018).

Scruton, R. (2012, Dec. 19). High culture is being corrupted by a culture of fakes. *The Guardian*. Available from: www.theguardian.com/commentisfree/2012/dec/19/high-culture-fake (accessed November 19, 2018).

Smith, A., & Duggan, M. (2013, Oct. 21). Online dating and relationships. Pew Research Center, Internet & Technology. Available from: www.pewinternet.org/2013/10/21/online-dating-relationships/ (accessed November 19, 2018).

Stein, R. (2005). Why perversion? 'False love' and the perverse pact. *International Journal of Psychoanalysis, 86*(3): 775–799.

Steiner, P. (1993, July 5). On the Internet, no one knows you're a dog [Cartoon]. *New Yorker*.

Stoller, R. (1985). *Observing the Erotic Imagination*. New Haven, CT: Yale University Press.

Sudol, K. (2014, June 25). Rutherford teen in 'catfish' scam sentenced to 6 months in prison. *NorthJersey.com*. Available from: www.northjersey.com/news/rutherford-teen-in-catfish-scam-sentenced-to-6-months-in-prison-1.1041137 (accessed November 19, 2018).

Sung, Y., Moon, J. H., Kang, M., & Lin, J. S. (2011). Actual self vs. avatar self: The effect of online social situation on self-expression. *Journal of Virtual Worlds Research, 4*(1): 3–21.

Wallace, S. (2010, Aug. 18). Driven to suicide by a romance scam. Abc7ny.com. Available from http://abc7ny.com/archive/7617743/ (accessed November 19, 2018).

Weber, L., & Moses, J. (2013, August 14). 8 Types of catfish on *Catfish. Vulture, Devouring Culture*. Available from: www.vulture.com/2013/08/eight-types-of-catfish-the-tv-show.html (accessed November 19, 2018).

Weston, W.A. (1996). Pseudologia fantastica and pathological lying: A forensic issue. In L.B. Schlesinger (ed.), *Explorations in Criminal Psychopathology: Clinical Syndromes with Forensic Implications*, pp. 98–115. Springfield, IL: Charles C. Thomas Publisher.

Winnicott, D.W. (1965). Ego distortion in terms of true and false self. In D.W. Winnicott, *Maturational Processes and the Facilitating Environment*, pp. 140–152. (Original work published 1962.) London: Hogarth and the Institute for Psycho-Analysis.

Zeman, N. (2013, June). The boy who cried dead girlfriend. Available from: www.vanityfair.com/culture/2013/06/manti-teo-girlfriend-nfl-draft (accessed November 19, 2018).

The known analyst

Chapter 17

The therapist revealed
Who knows what, when?

Bruce Hammer

If, as many authors have pointed out, the therapeutic field is intersubjective, co-created by patient and therapist, then the enactments and explorations that define the course of a therapy are shaped not only by the patient's transference but also by the character of the analyst and its expression in the analyst's transference. Aron (1991) speaks of encouraging patients' exploration of their experience of the analyst's subjectivity, expressed in the therapist's character-driven participation, as being essential to the therapeutic process. Searles (1979) postulates that the patient strives to cure what impedes the other person, at first the parent, later the analyst, from providing a better, development-enhancing relationship for the patient. Sapountzis (2009) suggests that the analyst trapped in an impasse has to first understand that the impasse involves what the analyst does not understand about him or herself, discovering their blindness before they can move through the impasse they and their patient are co-creating. In this chapter, I am particularly interested in exploring impasses where the therapist is unable to grasp what the patient struggles to know about them and unable to see themselves as the patient experiences them—those instances where the process of discovery is on the therapist's part in response to work by the patient.

While walking up the stairs from the train track in New York City's Penn Station seven days after 9/11, I found myself recollecting a formative childhood experience: my daily walk past the house of my neighbor, Mr. Brill. An 80-foot fence separated me from his large, menacing, Doberman pinscher who would attack the fence viciously along the entire 80 feet, barking and growling, desperate to destroy me. Only once was the gate open. Only once did he knock me down and stick his snarling mouth inches from my face before he ran down the block, before I ran home trembling. From then on, every time I passed that house, I prepared for the open gate, just as I prepared for the explosion of a bomb as I turned each corner of Penn Station that day.

After 9/11 my childhood of many fears—of the dark, of being attacked by bullies, of my father having a final heart attack—seemed more present.

I became more in touch with the impact that this dynamic—my desire to flee what I feared and the counter need to stay and face my fear—had on my shaping material presented by patients and my participation in the work. Not until my patient, Steven, worked on getting me to see this did I fully understand.

I believe the therapist's character—by which I mean those enduring patterns that others recognize as the way we treat and react to people—influences the therapeutic interplay to a much greater degree than we and our patients would like to acknowledge. By influence I refer to the specific issues that routinely capture a therapist's attention, the struggles that tend to engage that particular therapist, and the choices that therapist repeatedly makes in organizing patient material. To get the work done, most patients, at least for some period of time, maintain an illusion that their therapist comes to the therapeutic relationship with no personal agenda, no predetermined propensity to focus on and resolve certain issues in certain predictable ways. While we strive to put the patient's goals ahead of our interpersonal needs and our desire to avoid anxiety, our understanding of defense and security operations predicts that we are much more limited in our ability to succeed at this task than we would like to admit. What can our patients expect from us in the service of their efforts to get to where they are going when they run into the places where we characteristically go for cover? Forced to face what we would rather not know about ourselves, we could be expected to attempt escape. Becoming defensive, we could attempt to recast issues as emerging from the patient's rather than our transferences, possibly like the patient's parents did. We could be vindictive in our interpretations, make amends, or simply cloud the picture—all reflexive attempts to hide because the patient has made us anxious by making something about us clearer than we would like.

I believe many patients avoid confronting therapists because they fear loss of the support and safety afforded them in the therapeutic alliance. Some patients may selectively in-attend or choose to avoid aspects of the therapist's influence, consciously deleting reference to it once they sense our resistance or inability to embrace their message to us. The deal they think they have struck is, "I'll protect you from anxiety and you'll protect me." They may take to heart the proverbial admonition: "Don't bite the hand that feeds you." Others express love, respect, and protection of their therapist by putting their exploration of us on the back burner.

Does the therapist's transferential influence play a critical role in every therapy to a degree that it has to be a focus in the work? I don't think so. But let us consider patients whose formative relationships were dominated by parental transference, whose voices were delegitimized as crazy, who were successfully intimidated into giving up their voices, who lacked power and were at the mercy of their parents' vision of them. The therapist's transferential power poses a very real threat to these patients who now find themselves at the mercy of their therapists' vision of them, however accurate or inaccurate it is. But, I suggest, the therapist's transference offers a path to work through the patient's previous powerlessness. When the patient discovers the therapist as self-serving, defensive, or subtly abusive in ways that are historically familiar to the patient, the therapist is faced with making the choice to own his personal actions and defensive maneuvers without attributing them to the patient's influence. For some patients, only after they perceive the therapist as capable of owning and working with their transferential selves can they trust the therapist and allow the focus to be on the patient's transference. Moments when the therapist is in the hands of the patient, when positions of knowing are reversed, and when the patient takes ownership of the therapy, can be critical to the therapeutic effort because they empower the patient.

The model that presents and maintains the "good" therapist acting unequivocally in the patient's interest may lack credibility for these patients and may lead to a déjà vu sense of powerlessness and alienation within the therapeutic relationship. Even if we are receptive to one-sided exploration of our participation by the patient, we may still subtly dissuade or cloud the patient's attempt to gain validation of their experience of us. We can imagine a patient who, after years of being unable to articulate what someone has done to them, or to get that person to acknowledge doing it, comes to a therapist who claims to be cut from a different cloth, and confronts the therapist—maybe at first way off the mark, or in a clumsy or overzealous manner—with their view of the therapist's participation. Does the therapist move towards, away, or against the patient's efforts to make their view of the therapist known? When the therapist maintains a boundary, is it maintained in the service of the patient's analysis or of the therapist's protection? Patients leave therapists all the time rather than address the therapist's issues, sometimes because they lack a willing partner.

Case vignette

Steven came to therapy shortly after his father died. Over the first year he communicated the facts of his life—in particular, memories of being tormented by his father and brother. Steven's father, a frustrated attorney unable to provide adequately for his family, enforced a doctrine of absolute authority within the home and was especially sadistic towards Steven. Steven was not allowed to complain about brutal mistreatment at the hands of his brother, protect his private possessions, turn away from scenes that scared him on television, cover his ears when a passing fire engine bothered him, protect himself, or fight back. He had been punched, punished, and ridiculed often for what his father called "resisting." He was the designated "little girl" in a family of real men. His mother saw no evil and identified Steven's sensitivity and fearfulness as the problem. At age 13, Steven developed what he called his "banging problem." He became unable to tolerate the sound of the slightest touch of objects, such as the sound a fork makes when lightly tapped on a plate, or the click of the door bolt. At these moments, his impulse was to smash the plate, but the urge was too dangerous to consider. He began to eat in his room on paper plates to avoid ridicule.

When we began working together, Steven was living at home, dedicated to avoiding all contact with his brother. He kept the door to his room locked and would only leave when his brother was out of the house. He planned his journeys out of what he called his "jail cell" with forethought, taking back with him what he would need in case he were trapped in his room by his brother's return. Over the years the "banging problem" mushroomed into extreme sensitivity to all tapping sounds. He experienced these noises in the night as physical violations, creating headaches, sleeplessness, and a sense of wanting to explode but being unable to. Steven believed his brother was actively engaged in violating his psychic integrity as he had in childhood, but now used more subtle actions to torment Steven, like tapping on the walls of Steven's room as he went by. At these moments Steven wished he were stronger and had the courage to kill his brother by beating his brains in with a baseball bat. What occupied his thoughts most was the desire to end his miserable life along with the shame and humiliation he felt for being powerless and crippled.

A year into therapy, Steven became extremely passive. He came to sessions empty-headed, not knowing what he should talk about, waiting for me to direct him. As time went on he found that nothing we addressed or investigated made any difference. He continually agonized that life was passing him by, but he lacked the energy to take steps to improve his lot. He was hopelessly trapped. He asked me often for concrete suggestions but was hesitant to take any action. After a long period of being stuck in this pattern, Steven started taking steps in life with great trepidation. I encouraged him to get computer programming training. He did. He got a job making $70,000 a year. I encouraged him to get out of his house and away from his brother. He moved into his own apartment. But his inner torment persisted. He longed for personal contact with friends and women, but was terrified of being humiliated and degraded. He developed a few acquaintances at work but spent weekends alone. He concluded that his life would always be empty.

Several years later, Steven discovered his voice in sessions. What he began to tell me for the first time, emphatically, was that I did not appreciate the fear he was raised to endure, or the impact of my suggestions on him. When he acted on them, he only became trapped in new situations that he experienced as abusive and humiliating. He said I had treated his resistance as if it were irrational while I ignored the fact that the so-called gains he had made were not appreciated by him. At first I was taken aback. I did not consider this an accurate reflection of what we had accomplished. My attempts to remind him how we had come to this point made him angry. My focusing on his participation in creating our relationship only made him angrier. I found myself remembering Mr. Brill's Doberman. I had been terrorized by that dog—but only once. The fence between me and that growling Doberman was very real to me, as was my fear, but in reality the probability of attack was very low. In my mind's eye I pictured Steven walking down the street every day. There was no fence between him and his father and brother. Unlike me, he would have to withstand constant terrorization by the dogs who would always be waiting for him. There was no place to run.

Steven grew bold. Often he waited as if taking in what I was saying, only to pounce on me out of nowhere, pointing out how with this word or that thought I was jumping to conclusions, twisting what he had said. Accuracy was extremely important to him. Did I care that his last job was torturous, or did I just want him to have any job? Who was I to decide for him what would be a step in the right direction? How respectful was I of his needs to avoid others? How determined was I to win my point? I just presumed that making contact with people was good, didn't I? I probably liked to tell people what to do, didn't I? Who had invited me to share my opinions in the first place? It was clear that he had studied me for years. It was tempting to see this as his transference, and it was, but I was captured by his accuracy. I had heard these things before: from my wife, my children, my friends—perhaps in muted form, perhaps from people who had the luxury to be amused, ignore me, or push back on me, but I had heard them.

I surrendered. I started to consider his vision of me. I wondered if his world was too frightening for me; if I was the one who needed to act to change things in his life; if I needed to have him escape his Doberman brother. I realized that I couldn't stand his passivity and that I had been saving myself through encouraging his actions. Steven became oppressive in his commitment to keeping me muzzled. I wondered where he got the trust in me that I wouldn't attack him with a baseball bat. I became sullen. I longed for a fence with a gate I could close. I found myself wanting to tell him, "Get out of here; leave me alone." I wondered why I didn't say that. Was this technique or fear? I decided to defend myself against his shutting me up, telling me what I meant, putting thoughts in my mouth and then attacking them. I felt abused. I accused him of trying to make me cower in the corner, of treating me as his father treated him. Steven liked those sessions. He was surprised and delighted that he could actually intimidate anyone.

We routinely became embroiled in arguments that would leave us both frustrated with how we each did not understand what the other thought they had clearly said. After each argument we would piece together our individual perceptions of these interactions. Often the focus was on how we each defended ourselves from what we perceived as the other's aggression. We both accepted these experiences of each other. I shared with Steven how my mother had also found everything I said to be stupid. Sometimes I remembered and shared examples from our long relationship that validated a point he was raising about me. He found this helpful.

I remember a breakthrough session. For weeks I had resisted leading Steven in any way, or offering him suggestions on the terrible traps he found himself in. I listened carefully for an invitation to touch his stuff and got none. Finally he asked where had I gone; why was I so quiet? I told him I was trying to keep out of his way. He asked me what I had been hearing from him. I told him I heard how terrible his life was, how hopeless he felt, how the job and the apartment and his associations at work meant nothing if he could not be free of his torment. How he would like to be dead. I had nothing more to say. I had thought this would be too depressing for him, too empty of hope. But I realized that I was the one that couldn't stand the despair. I couldn't just lie there on the ground and let the dog devour me. The amount of time he wasted in not living was unnerving to me. I was completely powerless and couldn't stand it. Everything about me wanted to jump up and shriek: Let me out of this experience! I shared what I had learned with Steven. He knew the experience well.

The next session he mentioned how satisfied he was that we had worked out something between us, that he had worked out anything with another person. I acknowledged his working so hard to get me to learn something. He wanted me to know that he felt hopeful about the therapy. I felt optimistic as well.

That optimism was short-lived. Triggers continued to go off routinely in our interactions, setting us off on our intertwined transferential paths, each of us experiencing extreme frustration in the other's resistance. Although we had come a long way, whenever we slid into feelings of being completely misunderstood and stymied in our attempts to communicate, we both felt that nothing had or ever would be different between us.

A few things became clear to me during this phase. Steven was not going to take in anything I was saying, any perspective I was offering, any way I had of understanding him. I had somehow signaled that I was not to be trusted. He was going to shut me up as soon as I spoke, because—as he reported—I was changing his words, shifting his meaning in subtle ways, attributing meaning to statements that he hadn't intended. He rejected what he perceived as my suggestion that his participation in his life was shaped by his psychology, and that he was an active agent with a perspective. He was committed to seeing his participation as predictable, unavoidable responses determined by the nature of whatever situation he found himself in. He held firmly to the conviction that he held no power as an active agent in his life.

As he struggled to break out of these impasses, he explained that semantics and the use of language were very important to him. He experienced his parents as having been united in their dedication to subtly induce him to see himself as crazy and themselves as loving, creating a reality that did not reflect his sense of himself and the family he lived in. They did this by substituting his words with their words, claiming they were quoting him, and wrongly attributing intentions to him. In short, he had been gaslighted by them, and he was not going to allow himself to be gaslighted by me. He grew agitated while pointing to inaccuracies in what I was saying. He was enraged when I pursued my vision of things after he had negated it. My attempts to reframe and use metaphors to better understand him in the context of his life appeared to traumatize him. I was just another father seeking to violate his psychic space.

During this period, I experienced Steven as driven to have me see things through his eyes by obliterating my view rather than shaping it. His message was that my perspective had everything to do with how I wanted to see him and nothing to do with how things really were for him. He wanted me to own up to my transference. Steven had been unable to influence how his father experienced him. He believed that his father's transference had been toxic and that his mother had blindly supported her husband's vision. He referred to their mutual "psychotic" commitment to convincing him he was crazy and destroying his self integrity. Steven was not going to have another man figure out what made him tick, at his expense.

In the midst of one of these breakdowns between us, while trying to be extra careful in my choice of words, I remembered how important it had been for me as a young adolescent to have my parents understand my experience of them and our lives together; how my father and mother on any number of occasions could not make sense of what I was saying; and how crazy it made me feel. I recalled feeling completely exasperated as they would shake their heads in unison and validate each other's opinion that I was confused. I recalled how I grew enraged and sunk into despair when I very much needed them to "get" me. I spontaneously decided to share with Steven several of these memories just as they occurred to me. I connected these to how Steven's ridicule and complete dismissal of what I had to say had led me, without my realizing it, to double down in my attempt to be understood; and that sometimes I couldn't change course because I was locked into getting him—who I experienced at these moments as being *my* father—to tell me that I was making complete sense. In that moment I realized that I had been using the working through of our breakdowns to achieve something that made sense in the repetition of my own life. Steven was amazed by this realization, and we both spontaneously started laughing at the realities that brought us to this psychoanalytic crossroads.

In the months that followed, Steven often referred to my transference themes whenever they fit the situation to better understand what was transpiring between us and to maintain better contact with me as his therapist, as if he were reminding himself that I was not really his psychotic father even though he experienced me as such. I experienced a newfound freedom to make clear just what was bothering me about how he was treating me. I questioned whether I had done the right thing by sharing my transference information and worried about its ongoing impact, but it was too late to erase my intervention. I found myself recalling a statement made by Warren Wilner, one of my supervisors circa 1986, that "sometimes the therapist has to go first." I wondered if this gave me permission to have crossed what I believed was a line.

Over the next few months, Steven began to tolerate my drawing connections between his reactions in the present and themes of his family life in the past. He sometimes joined in, drawing connections himself. Was this in response to showing him how my participation in our therapy was shaped and driven by forces from my interpersonal past, showing him that I too operated from a transferential place; that I, too, was shaped by my past experience; that I, too, drank from the same fountain that I was inviting him to drink from?

When I look back, I wonder if Steven's ability to let me touch him was made possible by my going first and letting him see how my reactions to his touching me were driven by the way I organize experience in the present based on interpersonal experiences in my past. As the therapy progressed, there were times when he and I could discuss, fine tune, debate, even change each other's minds as if we trusted that the other's intent was to improve understanding of ourselves. He seemed to allow that he had added to the difficulty in our relationship; that he was subject to the forces of being raised by his parents and, more important, that those forces shaped the way he reacted and experienced situations in the here and now. Eventually he came out of the psychoanalytic closet and allowed himself to take ownership of the damage that had been done to him and acknowledge how that damage was reflected in his obsessiveness, paranoia, vigilance, overreactions to perceived threats, and his rage, acknowledging that it now resided in him and shaped his interactions with the world.

It has been a long time since we slipped so far down the slope that we couldn't use our shared memories to pull ourselves out of the transferential hole.

Reflections

I have chosen to refer to the therapist's transference as opposed to calling it countertransference because I believe that we tend to conceptualize and experience countertransference as having to do primarily with the impact of the patient on us, regardless of how we define it. While I recognize the importance of the patient's impact on our experience as a phenomenon and critical tool, I am speaking to another very important phenomenon—the impact of the therapist's transference on the experience of the patient—and suggesting that it also can serve as a critical tool. More specifically, I am focusing on the sudden discovery by the therapist that the therapist's transference has created a significant impasse. The patient's participation can then be understood to be in part a countertransferential reaction to the therapist. I believe this occurs to a much greater degree than we would like to acknowledge.

If therapists' transferences play a major role, the question remains: how do we use them to the patient's advantage? Under what circumstances should therapists share the discovery of their transference? When is this constructive, perhaps even required, to work through resistance and impasse? If I believe making my transference visible is appropriate with certain patients, how do I determine which patient characteristics allow for engagement of this type? Does the intensity, duration, and impact of my transference determine if and when I should divulge? Does my comfort level and adeptness at working with my transference issues—either ones that are rediscovered or ones that are first discovered—determine whether I should or am able to bring them into the therapeutic process? When does this inclusion hijack using the patient's therapy as a place to work on "my stuff"?

I conceptualize Steven's use of me as a corrective emotional experience. I unknowingly brought into his therapy something that resembled a destructive early life experience with his parents, and then unwittingly afforded him an opportunity to influence a different outcome. Steven played a critical therapeutic role in illuminating what I was unconscious of and thus improved my ability to be a better therapeutic partner. I believe that Steven, for the first time in his life, experienced himself as having interpersonal power. That experience offset the message he had received from his parents—that his voice, the essence of who he was, offered nothing of value to their development as people. For my part, I thought my acknowledgement that I had received something of value to my development from Steven's therapy was akin to a teacher thanking a student for furthering their understanding of academic material that had eluded them, or a parent thanking a child for providing the parent with a cherished life experience. Healthy children feel valued for influencing their parents becoming better parenting partners, internalized by these children as confidence that they add value to relationships.

Concluding remarks

As therapists, we have the power to set the rules of play and legitimize investigations. We can chose to move towards rather than away from engaging the patient who brings the experience of being with us into the dialogue. If patients have the courage to say whatever comes to their mind, they will inevitably turn their attention to the therapeutic relationship, and often to the most problematic aspects of that relationship for the patient—the therapist's transference. It is a testament to the power of our resistance that we believe that whatever transpires with our partners, children, and friends won't happen in the therapeutic relationship. The fact is, we are likely to burden patients with our unconscious. Most of the people our patients attempt to have relationships with will do the same. The therapeutic relationship affords patients a tremendous developmental opportunity to tackle relationship issues and course correct how they participate in relationships by addressing problematic aspects of their relationship with us, specifically, how we interfere with or impede their development. If we are open to the existence and exploration of our transference, we can help patients succeed at disentangling and clarifying at least one problematic relationship in their lives. That could be a very valuable experience for both patient and therapist. If we are not open to the exploration of our transference by the patient, then ironically we may turn it into an impediment.

References

Aron, L. (1991). The patient's experience of the analyst's subjectivity. *Psychoanalytic Dialogues, 1*: 29–51.

Sapountzis, I. (2009). Revisiting Searles's paper "The Patient as a Therapist to the Therapist": The analyst's personal in the interpersonal. *Psychoanalytic Review, 96*: 665–84.

Searles, H.F. (1979). *Countertransference and Related Subjects: Selected Papers.* Madison, CT: International University Press.

Chapter 18

Dialectics of desire
Longing and fear of being "known" in the injured analyst

Marsha Aileen Hewitt

Clinical prologue

It is often the case that the most profound insights with the most enduring impact on one's life may be conveyed via a seemingly incidental remark whose obvious truth is so glaringly apparent one is left wondering, "Why didn't I see that?" Many years ago, early in my analytic training, I presented a clinical vignette to my supervisor who I was certain would disapprove of my "disclosing" a personal detail to a patient. In our first session, this patient described difficulties relating to his wife and teenaged daughters. She threatened to leave with the girls if he didn't "get help." In the midst of his distressed and anxious account, he startled me with the sudden question: "Are you a parent?" There was something desperate in his tone and searching look. The moment was affectively charged with shared anxiety. Where did *this* come from, I wondered? What should I do? I tend to be reserved with people generally about my private life, especially in the professional contexts of my university teaching and psychoanalytic practice. My analytic training taught that disclosure of personal information by the analyst could dangerously approach "wild analysis." Even worse, personal disclosure was considered by some of my teachers as "non-analytic." I felt miserably trapped by my patient's question. My inclination was to answer. Why not? But—what would my supervisor think? If I answered the question, which seemed perfectly reasonable, did that mean I would be committing a boundary violation?

I felt strongly that this man deserved an honest answer. After all, he did not ask how many children I have, their names, ages, or the schools they attended. I did not think he was after details of my personal life. I had encountered that kind of inquiry from patients before, and I had no trouble responding appropriately. This situation *felt* different. What I heard him asking in his tone and look was simply: "Are you a parent, like me? Can you possibly understand what I am going through? Do we have a shared life experience that will give me the confidence to embark upon this terrifying journey with you?" This is what I "heard" in his pain and fear. Still, I hesitated. If I answered, would I be foreclosing exploration of important analytic material? I didn't think so. Finally, I answered: "Yes." This clear, firmly articulated single word emerged from a partially conscious but very strong intuition that disclosures *may* be simply "a function of being together intersubjectively" (Pizer, 2006, p. 43). That is how it felt in that moment. The patient relaxed, then continued. The tension between us lifted. He felt reassured and I was able to refocus my analytic concentration. From there we embarked upon a mutually satisfying therapeutic relationship that lasted four years.

When I told my supervisor about this, I was by no means confident that I had done the right thing *psychoanalytically*. I feared he would tell me I had violated a sacred rule: anonymity. As I related this vignette, I was aware of feeling apologetic, and somewhat confused. Why did I need to apologize? For a violation of professional conduct? A boundary transgression? Underneath my sense of needing to apologize lay a deeper sense of conviction that I had done the right thing. It did not *feel* as if I had acted unprofessionally. Things were proceeding well between the patient and me. Nevertheless, I expected criticism along the lines of having breached the definition of "psychoanalysis," which I told my supervisor. He listened carefully and thoughtfully, as he always did, then asked very gently: "If you were on the subway, and struck up a conversation with a total stranger, and the person asked you if you had kids, what would you say?" Puzzled by this apparently unrelated query, I said "well, yes." He leaned forward in his chair, looked at me and said, "Then why on earth would you deny your patient a simple human courtesy that you would extend to a total stranger?"

Of all my rich and invaluable experiences as a supervisee while in analytic training, this very simple question remains one of the most important guiding influences on my work as an analyst. In that supervisory session I learned something about the challenge we face to "continually integrate our real life experiences with our professional knowledge" and work (Gurtman, 1990, p. 613). I believe that if I had retreated to the safety of an imagined and illusory psychoanalytic fortress of anonymity in order to wall myself off from my patient's desperate and frightened need to establish a human connection with me, I would have never seen him again. Withholding a basic courtesy I would extend unhesitatingly to a complete stranger would have left him feeling "diminished, shut out, unimportant, treated like a child who 'shouldn't know such things,' abandoned and betrayed" (Rosner, 1986, p. 361). The experience with this patient, along with my supervisor's supportive response to my work with him, has proved to be an abiding, profound source of strength and guidance that sustained and helped me navigate the multidimensional reverberations on my analytic practice caused by a life-threatening crisis.

The fall

One glorious autumn day, I was rushing back to my office after squeezing in a flu shot during my lunch break. It had been a hectic clinical day fuelled mostly by coffee. I had afternoon patients, so I needed to hurry, no time for lunch. Rushing along a busy downtown street, I fainted. The ensuing head injury landed me in hospital for two harrowing weeks. Several days passed before the doctors could make a prognosis. The attending doctor told me and my husband that it would be several days before it could be known for certain whether I had suffered brain damage, would need brain surgery, or die. Although none of that occurred and I made a full recovery, I could not return to teaching or clinical work for two and a half months. There were nine more months of numerous medical tests to determine what caused the faint. All this was to come. My first, most urgent thought when I regained consciousness in the hospital emergency room was that I needed to inform my patients, some of whom were at that moment waiting at my office.

There is a small, but growing literature (within a much wider literature on the controversial subject of self-disclosure) exploring the various ways of informing patients of interruptions in treatment due to the analyst's illness. Most of it addresses what happens when the analyst is diagnosed with a condition that requires a planned absence for medical treatment such as surgery or chemotherapy. There is very little written about how to handle sudden medical emergencies involving the analyst, when clinical work is interrupted in a "state of unknowness, confusion, and turmoil, when there is no preparation, and when the analyst's very life may be at risk" (Rosner, p. 358). It is important to note that in cases of sudden, life-threatening disruption, the analyst *does not have the luxury of choosing how patients should be notified of cancellations and by whom*" (p. 359, italics added). My first of what would turn out to be many "disclosures" was "introducing" my husband to those patients left wondering where I was that day when he called from the emergency room to tell them I was in hospital. I was unable to use a phone, since the nature and severity of my injuries were such that I was unable to see for nearly two weeks. My husband called everyone, informing them briefly that there had been a medical emergency, I was in hospital, and that I'd get in touch with them as soon as I could. I decided they should know the basic facts: I had suffered injuries due to a fall; I was fine (alive); I could not say exactly when I would return to work, but that I would keep them posted.

I heard later from every single patient (I did not lose any) that they appreciated my husband's honesty and calm assurances. I felt at the time, and still do, that my patients deserved the *respect* and *courtesy* of knowing why their therapy had been so suddenly disrupted. As Anna Freud rightly observed, it is important to remember that "the analyst and patient are also two real people, of equal adult status, in a real personal relationship to each other" (in Rosner, 1986, p. 369). Despite the grim circumstances, my disclosure was as deliberate and mindful as possible. My central priority in navigating this difficult, entirely new situation was the therapeutic goal of the best interests of my patients. I agree with Stuart Pizer (2006) that "to *not* disclose may be as mystifying in the analysis, and as compelling toward collusive dissociations, as it can be in family life" (p. 41). It was my view at the time, and remains so to this day, that my professional responsibility required that I treat my patients with courtesy and respect by informing them, with only as much detail as necessary, about this unexpected situation with as much calm and clarity as possible.

Disclosures: what, when, how, and how much?

Paul Dewald (1982), in his widely quoted, yet surprisingly often misunderstood paper (Morrison, 1997; Plopa, 2013) discusses the "reality experience of the separation and its impact" (p. 360) on the patient, especially those sudden, unforeseen disruptions due to the analyst's illness. In his own case, he carefully titrated the details and nature of information he gave each patient based upon his assessment of their particular needs. (I followed a similar procedure.) Dewald rightly maintains that the meanings and effects of the analyst's illness "vary widely from patient to patient" (p. 355). In cases where the severity of the analyst's illness or injury is unavoidably apparent in his appearance (as it was in Dewald's and mine) it is far more difficult to find a balance between spontaneous, even narcissistically driven self-revelation and carefully thought-out, therapeutically grounded self-disclosure that is genuinely motivated by its benefits to the patient. (See Meissner 2002 for a carefully nuanced exploration of this distinction.) When I returned to work, most patients were shocked by and remarked upon my extreme paleness and dramatic weight loss in ways that ranged from concerned curiosity to guilt-laden anxiety. With patients generally belonging to the first group, I thanked them for their concern and said I probably looked worse than I actually was. We were then able to resume our task. With patients who were anxious and/or fearful that they had either somehow caused my accident or would hurt me by overburdening me with "their problems," I tended to explain in greater, yet restrained detail, the nature of my condition. I might say something like, "Yes, I suffered a serious concussion due to my fall, and this kind of thing often leaves one feeling more tired than usual. I can understand, and appreciate how distressing it is for you to see me this way. But I *am* well on my way to full recovery." (In retrospect, I am not sure how much conviction my assurance carried for them or me with this last statement.) Like Dewald, I had to constantly assess and reassess how much information was necessary for them to feel safe and comfortable enough to proceed with our work.

There were unpredictable, maddening and humiliating ways that my medical situation intruded upon my work with patients.[1] I had little control over the scheduling of numerous tests, such as CT scans, EEGs, and MRIs. This entailed frequent, often sudden cancelations and rescheduling sessions. I told my patients these unforeseen disruptions were due to medical tests, also explaining that their scheduling was beyond my control. Given their own experiences with the medical system, everyone fully understood that appointments for specialized medical procedures are almost impossible to negotiate. Usually, I was able to reschedule my patients, who were extremely cooperative. Every one of them reacted with compassion and understanding, including those who also experienced feelings of abandonment, anxiety, and anger. *Mostly*, I was able to work with these situations well enough.

In her posthumously published paper, Amy Morrison (1997) described her compromised sense of professional and personal identity as she struggled to work through her cancer treatment: "From strong and healthy to vulnerable and ill; from caregiver to caregetter. For some, there are powerful feelings of shame in this loss and transformation," often resulting in the analyst's defensive attempts to "hide and be secretive" about his or her condition (p. 238). I thought I had found a balance between disclosures that would be helpful to my patients and my own need for privacy. In retrospect, I realize that some of my efforts to reassure my patients about my recovery were at times exaggerated, inflected with dissociated denial. It was difficult to admit to myself how seriously injured I had been. More than that, my resassurances to my patients were in part an expression of my own dissociated terror that I was possibly permanently damaged, not only by my physical injury, but also by the emotional trauma that accompanied it.

One day shortly after my return to work, a university colleague who had visited me in hospital articulated one of my worst fears when he asked quite abruptly if I had suffered any "cognitive deficits." A number of well-meaning colleagues eagerly shared horror stories with me about people (unsettlingly, all much younger than I!) they had known whose concussions kept them confined in darkened rooms for years; whose personalities changed; who didn't regain their full cognitive abilities; who forgot where they lived. Listening to these stories with as much politeness as I could muster as I fought to contain my panic, I assured everyone I was fine, I just needed rest. When I returned to my university teaching, the Dean looked at me and said I looked "frail." The remark stung me with shame. I immediately remembered detective novels from the 1930s where the derogatory slang for a woman was "the frail." "Frail" is not a word I would ever have dreamed of as describing myself. Morrison writes that another troubling ramification for the analyst is in the "effect of knowledge of one's illness on the attitudes of colleagues, and the loss of control over rumor and misconception" (p. 238). In her case a colleague advised one of her patients to terminate treatment so that the patient could assert "control" over the experience of loss when Morrison died. Other colleagues gossiped that she was dying. In my own fear of being misportrayed as "frail," or worse, being cognitively damaged, I refused to accept that I needed more time than I allowed myself for rest and recovery.

Transgression, compassion, forgiveness

One day, during a session with a patient who was in the early phase of struggling with unresolved, accumulated childhood traumas around sudden losses and deaths at the time of my accident, I noted that our time was up. We had been discussing the ways in which these traumas were compounded and intensified by my (life-threatening, but I never told her this) injuries and sudden disappearance. She became quite flustered (not how she usually was at the end of a session) and muttered something about being surprised as she gathered her things. Then it hit me that our session was *not* over. We had fifteen minutes remaining! Appalled at what I had done, I quickly told her I made a mistake and suggested we carry on. As she tearfully continued to head for the door I asked her as calmly as I could to sit down so that we could figure out together what had just happened. Thankfully, she did.

In that sickening moment of combined embarrassment and distress at how I had hurt my patient, I connected with my dissociated terror that maybe I *had* suffered some undetected brain damage, or some hideous cognitive impairment; that I was either losing my mind or my intellectual capacity; that dementia was right around the corner. My doctors had continued to assure me there was no medical basis for these fears. I knew that I had experienced significant emotional trauma, some of which was unconscious although deeply felt. Shortly after my release from hospital but before resuming clinical work, I returned to analysis. I was concerned to protect my patients from precisely the kind of dissociated enactment that occurred with this patient. Despite my best efforts, my most careful work with my analyst, I had shamed my patient and myself. This clinical moment forced me to confront a far deeper, unacknowledged shame arising out of an unbearable fear that I was somehow permanently mentally impaired from my injury. I had returned to work sooner than I should have in part—only in part—because I needed to shore up my battered sense of self. I felt an unconscious urgency to reclaim my identity and usual self-experience as strong, healthy, and professionally competent. Despite my most careful efforts, for some time I remained unaware of a dissociated grandiosity generated by a narcissistic need to remain in my therapeutic role as care *giver*, not care *getter*.

I decided in that moment of shocking emotional clarity to acknowledge my own dissociated anxiety with my patient which I fully realized only then. Holding back would only have humiliated her more deeply. I apologized for my lapse and the pain it was causing her. I explained that I was probably not as fully recovered as I thought. As I told her this, I became aware of another feeling that was powerfully emerging, a feeling of profound gratitude that arose with such force I decided I should, that I *needed*, to share it with her. The gratitude I was feeling was accompanied by an equally powerful awareness that she and all my patients had been helping me through the long, restorative healing process simply by continuing our analytic work. They *stayed with me*, allowing me to work with them in our usual way, despite my obvious weakened condition and frequent need to reschedule appointments. I began to understand that they had been caring for me as I was caring for them.

In that moment it was clear that she (and they) trusted me and my professional ability enough to accompany me through this difficult time in my life. In allowing me to resume my analytic work, she (and they) were helping me through the healing process. As she cried quietly, I gently explained this to her. I told her that I hoped she could bear with me through the unpredictable ups and downs of my recovery process, of which my most recent lapse was an example. She relaxed considerably as I explained this to her, and thanked me for sharing my experience. She understood and accepted that I was neither trying to get rid of her nor couldn't stand working with her. Still deeply hurt by what had just happened, she also was able to feel respected as a co-creator and equal participant in our analytic process. More than that, she experienced a more deeply felt compassion for my situation that allowed her to forgive my transgression and put it in its proper perspective. We were both able to acknowledge that *she* had been helping *me* in my recovery. This led to the further realization that psychoanalysis is always a two-way, bi-directional, mutually healing process between two people who become more of who they can be, becoming who they potentially are, together. Freud (1917) was thus only half right when he wrote that through psychoanalysis, the patient becomes who "he might have become at best under the most favourable conditions" (p. 435).

A few sessions later, she told me that she thought that she had caused my accident. We had met earlier that day. In that session, I had expressed my concern that she was riding her bike on busy city streets without wearing a helmet. Her mother was an overbearing woman who used fear as a weapon of control, harassing her with dire threats in a world where safety lay in an obedient, confined, confining relation to her. As long as she did what her mother told her and viewed the world through mother's eyes, she would be safe, according to her mother. Not surprisingly, my patient irritably dismissed my concern. Her father had succumbed to head injuries when she was a child. In that same session, we explored her associations to the dangers of head injuries, which came sickeningly close to home later that day. Her anger that I was 'telling her what to do' later turned to agonizing guilt that she had somehow caused my accident, which stirred unbearable anxiety within her that she was forced to hold for two and a half agonizing months, until I returned to work. During that time, I was able to talk to her briefly on the phone and update her on my progress, which helped in maintaining her sense of contact with me. Over time, we were able to talk about her anger at me on the day of my accident, and her guilt and terror that she had 'caused' my injury. This led to deeper exploration of her ambivalent feelings of relief that I had not died, along with her rage at my suddenly abandoning her at a time when she felt vulnerable and dependent upon me. She was then slowly able to connect with deeply painful feelings of shame, weakness and terror that often accompany her experience of helpless vulnerability in intimate relationships. I believe that this, and the analytic exploration of other frightening, painful and disassociated aspects of my patient's internal world was facilitated by my disclosing to her my own feelings of shame and vulnerability in the session I prematurely ended. After having survived the shock of that moment in which I temporarily "lost" my analytic mind and "dismissed" my patient too early, we were able to explore many of her previously dissociated, sequestered, transference feelings. That work is still going on.

Can (should) there be a "one-size-fits-all" theory of analytic disclosure?

Sander Abend (1995) describes the "compelling reasons" (p. 208) he had for disclosing aspects of his own illness to patients, thereby reversing a previous decision against it. Instead, he decided to make "clinical judgments" in accordance with the particular needs of each patient, saturated as he knew they most certainly would be with "countertransference considerations" that have little to do with ideals of "objectivity and selflessness" (p. 209). When the analytic work is suddenly disrupted by unexpected illness, it is useless and counterproductive, he writes, to retreat to pre-established theories concerning disclosure. Sometimes theories, no matter how important and generally helpful they are, offer inadequate insight or guidance. Bearing this in mind, Abend advises that we should not feel compelled to construct theoretical justifications for allowing our own natures and needs to affect the way we work, since we have no choice in the matter; after all, we can only reasonably aspire to do the best we can for our patients. *Let us not convert that limitation into some form of institutionalized rationalization to the effect that we act as we do only because it's better for our patients that way, but concentrate instead on trying to make it turn out to be better for them* to the best of our ability, because of (and despite) our "reflexive" ways of responding to them in the clinical encounter.

(p. 211, italics added)

Abend's statement should not be interpreted as giving free license to indulge in 'wild' psychoanalysis that privileges the analyst's narcissistic gratification by disregarding what is in the patient's best therapeutic interest. Not everyone, however, agrees with Abend's view. Meissner (2002), for example, wants to establish a firm "guiding principle" that will determine when self-disclosure of any kind is "therapeutically indicated" (p. 829). I agree with his concern that the therapeutic needs of patients being protected no matter what difficulties and challenges are going on in the analyst's life. In Meissner's view there is a tension between "disciplined" and "spontaneous" disclosures that encapsulate (p. 828) and may even threaten due consideration of the important questions of what to disclose, when and how to disclose, or even whether to disclose at all (p. 827). He believes in the importance of analytic neutrality, the preservation of which is crucial to the analyst's ability to stay the therapeutic course in the interests of his patient. He cautions against "burdening" (p. 839) the patient with the analyst's problems, and he is right to be concerned about this as a real possibility, however unintended. Based upon my experience, I find it hard to imagine that any analyst would be oblivious to this precise danger. Yet there are times when, for the sake of the patient, the analyst must at least be prepared to take this risk while closely monitoring and assessing her own countertransference feelings along with the patient's responses.

Meissner's focus on the great importance of preserving analytic neutrality, along with the many excellent questions he raises with regard to it, radically weaken in the context of sudden, life-threatening medical emergencies faced by the analyst. Meissner criticizes Barbara Pizer with the chiding observation that she "tries to make the case that disclosure of a life-threatening illness in the analyst is inescapable ... Disclosure may be inescapable for the analyst, but not necessarily for the patient. Even serious illness does not escape the governing perspective of neutrality" (p. 835). How then, and in what way, should an analyst who has a sudden heart attack, or a life-threatening accident on the way to the office, inform her patients that she will interrupt their therapeutic relationship, say for an indefinite period, or perhaps even permanently? How to avoid mystification? What about the retraumatizing impact of mystification on patients whose traumatic pasts were loaded with mystifications that undermined their sense of reality? What about patients whose sense that something terrible has happened mismatches what they are being told as the official story? Patients who have suffered traumatic abuse struggle with their sense of reality as it is. How much worse and potentially more traumatizing might it be for patients who unconsciously pick up something closer to the severity of what has really happened to the analyst yet who are left to struggle with their dark fantasies of something possibly worse than what actually happened. Leaving patients in these kinds of situations strikes me as cruel.

Here I must return to emphasize the values of human courtesy and respect that must inform every analytic relationship that I discussed previously. I have no doubt that Meissner lived by those values in his clinical work. However, his remarks on analytic neutrality as expressed in his criticism of Barbara Pizer reveal the way he tends to privilege what he sees as the integrity of theory over basic human need. In a very telling remark, he admits that he often finds himself "attuned to my own subjective experience (at times identifiably affective *but for the most part cognitive*)" (p. 836, italics added). It is precisely at this point that Meissner diminishes the common humanity that contains and connects analyst with patient in favor of a theoretical fortress which provides a psychic retreat from the experience of too much affect on the part of the analyst in the therapeutic session.

Earlier in his article, as if anticipating a relationally-oriented criticism, Meissner objects that "the portrait of the classical analyst painted by (relational and intersubjective theorists) as withdrawn, uncommunicative, uninvolved, and somehow isolated from interaction with the patient is patently a caricature—not one adhered to by a preponderance of practicing analysts" (p. 832). There may well be a great deal of truth in these words. Yet as quoted in the paragraph above, Meissner clearly values the analyst's cognitive capacity over that of feeling. Recalling and extending Abend's observation quoted earlier, it would be misleading to pose the clinical complexities surrounding the question of disclosure in terms of competing theories, be they classical, relational or intersubjective. The very difficult, unpredictable and painful issues pertaining to how and when to disclose information to patients in the event of a sudden serious crisis in the analyst's life transcend any theoretical school, because they belong to *all* theoretical schools. This is because such unforeseen events can happen to any human being at any time. In such cases, we are thrown back not on our theories, but our basic humanity.

In closing, perhaps I may invoke Freud (1917) once again. His deceptively simple definition of the goal of psychoanalysis echoes this basic reality: that through the analytic experience, our patients become who they "might have become at best under the most favourable conditions" (p. 435). The enhanced, expanded humanity of both analyst and patient, which both carries and promotes therapeutic action (Loewald, 2000) must take precedence over what can only be described as a defensive pseudo-loyalty to analytic theories and principles. Without question, we need psychoanalytic theories. However, we must hold our theories lightly, constantly evaluating and re-evaluating them in the light of the human reality before us. To do otherwise is to risk lapsing into deadened ideologies. Life is full of surprises, and some of them leave us stranded in strange territories without any maps. Philip Bromberg (2011), although writing in another context, nonetheless provides analytic wisdom that applies to the questions considered here: "It is the analyst's ongoing and often personally painful effort to struggle with the unpredictable process of sharing his shifting self-state experience that is his greatest contribution to the patient's (and his own) growth" (p. 136). This is what Laing means when he writes that the therapeutic process is a mutual struggle to reclaim—and perhaps redeem—our shared humanity. After all, and in the end, "Psychotherapy must remain *an obstinate attempt of two people to recover the wholeness of being human through the relationship between them*" (Laing, 1968, p. 45).

Note

1 See Stuart Pizer's (2009) account of the impact of his temporary colostomy bag on his patients, and his decision to address it directly.

References

Abend, S. (1995). Discussion of Jay Greenberg's paper on self-disclosure. *Contemporary Psychoanalysis*, 31: 207–211.

Bromberg, P.M. (2011). *The Shadow of the Tsunami and the Growth of the Relational Mind*. New York: Routledge.

Dewald, P.A. (1982). Serious illness in the analyst: Transference, countertransference, and reality responses. *Journal of the American Psychoanalytic Association*. 30: 347–363.

Freud, S. (1917). Transference. *The Standard Edition of the Complete Psychological Works of Sigmund Freud*, Vol. 16, pp. 431–447. J. Strachey (trans). London: Vintage/Hogarth Press.

Gurtman, J.H. (1990). The impact of the psychoanalyst's serious illness on psychoanalytic work. *Journal of the American Academy of Psychoanalysis and Dynamic Psychiatry*, 18: 613–625.

Laing, R.D. (1968). *The Politics of Experience and the Bird of Paradise.* Harmondsworth, UK: Penguin Books.

Loewald, H. (2000). On the therapeutic action of psychoanalysis. In H. Loewald, *The Essential Loewald: Collected Papers and Monographs.* Hagerstown, MD: University Publishing Group.

Meissner, W.W. (2002). The problem of self-disclosure in psychoanalysis. *Journal of the American Psychoanalytic Association,* 50: 827–867.

Morrison, A.L. (1997). Ten years of doing psychotherapy while living with a life-threatening Illness: Self-disclosure and other ramifications. *Psychoanalytic Dialogues,* 7: 225–241.

Pizer, S. (2006). 'Aerial kiss attack': Affect communication, demystification, and analytic self-disclosure: Discussion of Barbara Pizer. *Contemporary Psychoanalysis,* 42: 41–45.

Pizer, S. (2009). Inside out: The state of the analyst and the state of the patient. *Psychoanalytic Dialogues,* 19: 49–62.

Plopa, P. (2013). Being a cancer patient in analysis while continuing to work as an analyst. In N. Straker (ed.), *Facing Cancer and the Fear of Death: A Psychoanalytic Perspective on Treatment.* Lanham, MD: Rowman & Littlefield.

Rosner, S. (1986). The seriously ill or dying analyst and the limits of neutrality. *Psychoanalytic Psychology,* 3: 357–371.

No longer known

Chapter 19

The altered brain and the illusion of knowing

J. Gail White and Michelle Flax

"Knowing" the other has always been central to psychoanalysts. Indeed, Psychoanalysis can be defined as the science of how subjects construct meaning. Massive brain changes from dementia or brain damage can lead to major personality changes. What happens when the known other is irretrievably altered? Psychoanalysts are deeply familiar with these calamities of the human condition. We know that our well-being, which depends on our intact minds, cannot be taken for granted, as uncertain as we are of so much in this existence.

What is it like to relate to those who have undergone such catastrophic changes? They are "gone" *as we knew them*. We have lost *how they knew us*. And yet, they are still present and active in our lives. The dilemma we face is how to keep their identity in mind when they cannot keep ours. How do we hold an allegiance to them despite the wrenching pain of losing them and the world we lived in together? How do we learn to know them in a new way? Are the traces that remain enough to build a new kind of knowing?

Both authors are currently dealing with changes in loved ones, a sister and a daughter respectively, due to brain tumours. Both of us lost our fathers to brain tumours as well. We have long struggled on this journey of loss and grief. As analysts, both of us have worked with people who have suffered catastrophic brain changes, as well as with those who love them.

We found aspects of four conceptual models helpful: (a) current neuropsychological thinking; (b) psychoanalytic mourning theories; (c) philosophical ideas of aporia and presence; (d) Klein (1935) and Bion's (1962) concepts of shifting anxiety positions and affective links.

Damasio's (1999) neuropsychological viewpoint helps in understanding what it means to lose the knowing of someone. He describes various selves related to consciousness, one of which is the autobiographical self or the conscious and unconscious organized record of past and present experience of the person. We all require an ability to learn and retain records of our various experiences and to reactivate those records in order to have a sense of self-knowing and being known. Brain injuries often result in the loss of ability to build an autobiographical self, complicating both how we might know the altered other and how they might know others and themselves.

To know the other is not only to know their conscious aspects—their qualities and behaviours. It also involves the implicit and unconscious dimensions we pick up by tuning in with "the third ear" (Reik, 1948), our unconscious receptor. Knowing is always relational. In catastrophic change, we lose *shared* experience, inevitably altering our internalized object relations. Our wishes and illusions of the altered other often have to be abandoned in light of the new reality.

Freud (1915, 1917) writes eloquently about the nature of loss. He draws our attention to our tendency to idealize lost loved ones, thereby avoiding the ambivalence of our loving and hostile feelings. When we lose someone to disability, we often idealize them as we knew them which complicates our mourning process.

André Green (1986) writes about an internalized deadness often experienced when there has been a psychic loss. It is like the other as we knew them has been buried alive. Mourning this loss is vital, yet often feels staggering and unfathomable as the other is still very much alive. In death, there is concrete evidence that the other is gone. Where there has been overwhelming brain change, the afflicted person may look or act in familiar ways but something essential has been lost. In the absence of funereal ritual and ceremony which allows us to externalize our grief and share it, psychic loss is unlikely to be fully recognized or fully symbolized. The former self of the other continues to exist for us psychically. When we are unable to mourn, our energy is absorbed (Volkan, 1981), constraining our ability to build a new relationship. The fact that the other is still here allows for hope that they will be magically returned to us. Thus our psychic loss is continually re-experienced. Korff-Sausse (2017) writes that the task is to be able to go through the mourning process for the disabled other even as we continually invest in that other.

The concept of aporia—a Greek word meaning "without passage"—refers to a philosophical puzzle or a seemingly insoluble impasse. While it is a state of being at a loss, faced with a conundrum, an aporic event has the potential to set a creative force in motion.

The philosophy of "presence" (Ghosh & Kleinberg, 2013) helps us grapple with the discontinuity we face when the past is not contiguous with the present. Freud theorized that the past is both present and absent at once in the transference, dreams, unconscious utterances, and enactments. "The past is never dead; it is not even past" William Faulkner (1951, p. 229) wrote. This cannot be said with such certainty with brain-altered persons. Even if past memories are intact, the question is whether the person can build a present sense of who they are. The philosophy of presence reminds us not to explain discontinuity away but to give it its due. The task is to honour the past, even as the bridge between past and present is broken. We do this by being present with the absent other, as well as with the person who is now before us.

This is seldom easy. Brain injuries deliver catastrophic threats to the self. Melanie Klein (1948) poignantly expresses how people struggling with threats to the self are persecuted by terrors of annihilation. Brain-altered persons are shocked, often remaining psychically frozen, sometimes attacking loved ones, especially those who care most for them. These patients are usually unaware of the damage wrought in their primal projected rage. Most often, they cannot anchor themselves in the depressive position (Klein, 1935) where they would be able to take responsibility for their actions. How do we hold fast to the depressive position within *ourselves* so as not to destroy the internalized relationship?

Bion (1962), a close colleague of Melanie Klein, describes three internal emotional ties to objects: **L** refers to attachment and care; **H** refers to antipathy; **K** denotes curiosity and the desire to know the object. Brain alterations deeply affect a sense of being known and knowing the other—both for the person suffering the brain change and for those who love and care for them—fraying emotional links. How do we maintain our wish to know the other (a **K** state of mind)? How do we prevent the intrusions of our loving and hating emotions (**L** and **H**) from interfering with our curiosity and our impulse to "know" (Bion,1962; Fisher, 2006)?

What we have found useful is to hold on to the golden threads of the relationship as it once was, a relationship that held our projections, illusions, attachment needs, hopes, and dreams. The challenge is to find new ways of living with the presence of history, not as a haunting presence, but as an essential and constitutive element in the present. In the face of many discontinuities, the struggle is to retain continuity with the person we knew and with whom we had a shared world. In so doing, we forge creative ways to relate to the altered other.

To illustrate these questions and our struggle with them, we highlight two case studies. The first is a patient who developed dementia during her analysis. The second is a patient whose loved one has dementia.

My (J.G. White) 96-six-year-old patient, Elizabeth, has developed a growing and deepening dementia. On the horizon, she and I could see this aporic event coming as dementia set in. As with all aporic events, we were at a loss. For some time, I was awash in the strangeness of it all. We struggled to maintain the ongoing cohesion of our sessions as self and other became unsettled categories. Often, I would have to review our last session to help her with continuity.

We still meet three times a week—at her home now for her convenience. The routines of our sessions seem helpful in holding her anxiety at bay. This anxiety marauder arrived with the onset of dementia. We have lost the free association so essential to the analytic process. We are often marooned in painful silences where I actively work to find her again and to help her find "me with her" again. The absence of what we were is very much present and manifests in me as an urgent need for meaning and knowing.

There are continuities in our work—her need to see me, comfort in sharing tea, our eye line capturing the new bouquet of roses that her husband, in his allegiance to what she once was, arranges for her. We sit in the same chairs, drink from the same teacups, and meet at the same times as always. But the discontinuities of memory, relatedness, and experience grow weekly. The present is filled with discontinuities for Elizabeth—fragments unlinked, unlinkable, and unintegrated into her larger personality. The present is lost and forgotten in seconds. These interruptions—gaps in the sequencing of time—interfere with the building and holding of her memory. These gaps plague us.

In the analytic dyad, as in friendship, one must go before the other. One must take stock of the lost one, grieve, and then go on to be the bearer of the relationship as we *knew* it. Only one of us—me—will enact the work of mourning the loss of our relationship. I know that her forgetfulness will lead to my eventual exile from her memory, this "seamstress" (Woolf, 1975, p. 55) that threads our lives together. Will I carry the knowledge of her carefully and maintain fidelity to our relationship?

I struggle to hold the mutually constructed meaning of our relationship alone. Is it bad faith to bemoan the loss of a relationship that has been interrupted in order to take pity upon oneself? And yet I do. I feel so sad as the meaning we have constructed over the years begins unraveling. To know, by definition, is to have memory. How do I hold onto knowing her? Luis Bunuel (1984) wrote: "You have to begin to lose your memory, if only in bits and pieces, to realize that no memory is no life at all ... Our memory is our coherence, our reason, our feeling, our action" (p. 4). Those with a deeply altered mind can no longer respond to us in the same way, can no longer offer a correction to our shared story. I already miss her.

I have found three ways of connecting with Elizabeth that allow us to move from a discontinuous state into continuity again. The feeling of "us as we were" is then revived. Talk of the long ago past proves to be an adhesive place where we can dwell temporarily while at the same time finding comfort in the present.

Another way we connect is in being playful. We play with words, words that she still highly values. The most common words she uses to describe how she feels are "discombobulated" and "disheartened." When I utter the word "discombobulated" now, it serves as a brief splendid anodyne for her anxiety. There is still some momentary satisfaction she receives in the naming of her feeling with me.

Then there is the poetry—our particular way of knowing each other. Poetry functions as guy wires—structuring, stabilizing cables—linking the present to her long-term memory. My father and Elizabeth were born in the same year—1921. This period with Elizabeth harkens me back to his brain tumour that left him unable to know me. My slow losing of Elizabeth reminds me of similarly losing the knowing of him. The way I could reach him was by reciting poems to him—poems he encouraged me to memorize throughout my growing up years. By his bedside, at the end, I would say the first lines of a poem—"One thing is certain and the rest is lies." He would finish: "The flower that once has blown forever dies" (Khayyam, 1859, p. 55). He would be calmed. The poem was a way, in his annihilated state, to find "us" again. He always told me as I was growing up that poetry would be useful. "It makes hard things bearable in life and it heightens the joys," he said. And it has.

This stumbled upon technique allowed me to find Elizabeth. Several years ago when we were confronting the spectre of her impending death when she was 86, we found our way through reading poetry about death and endings (White & Flax, 2014). Now in her "discombobulated" state, I lead her to poetry and she and I find continuity again. She calms and steadies herself automatically as I begin a line of a poem and she completes it and corrects me as we go along—the way my father and I did in his last hours. When she recites, she smiles warmly. She is back in continuity. The gap is bridged, fleetingly. Caught in this dialectic of presence and absence, poetry serves as an essential link affirming our knowing of each other.

The second case study concerns a man whose wife of 37 years has Alzheimer's dementia. She was placed in a home two years ago as he could no longer care for her.

"It feels like a never-ending Shiva," Allan said sadly. While his wife, Sandra, recognizes him, her ability to stay with a conversation varies. The essence of his wife was her family. Now she sometimes cannot recognize her children and grandchildren. While she was an agreeable and sweet-natured person most of her life, now she is feisty, easily frustrated, and shows unexpected meanness to those tending her. Allan is often taken by surprise by this turn in her personality. It is a moot point whether this "meanness" is a sign of a previously disavowed state, now uninhibited. Perhaps, but brain changes muddy the personality water too much for us to know.

I (M. Flax) feel deep empathy for Allan as he describes how he is now on tenterhooks when he engages with his wife who can berate him unexpectedly. His feeling resonates with me. While my daughter's brain condition following her brain tumour has now greatly improved, over the past decade I never knew which daughter I would encounter: my charming, empathic, loving daughter, or the frustrated, angry, depressed daughter who emerged through the massive trauma of dealing with a brain tumour and its sequelae. In this concordant countertransference (Racker, 1957), I imagine I know something of what Allan is going through. I wonder if this is a mistake—assuming knowledge can prevent the exploration that would help me know Allan's layered experience. In my countertransference, I also feel lucky that my daughter is improving in memory, demeanor, and cognitive capacity while Sandra's condition will likely deteriorate until her death.

"How can I be committed to two women at once?" Allan agonizes. He has recently struck up a relationship with another woman, but is deeply troubled about the idea of moving forward in that relationship. It is this that he has come to see me about. Can he live *with* himself if he makes a new relationship? Can he live *by* himself if he does not? He is lonely and depressed since his wife's dementia began interfering with their lives. He feels simultaneously guilty and justified, sad and excited by the new relationship. He considers my question: has he begun this new relationship to help him avoid facing the massive loss? He is in an ongoing grieving state that he can hardly bear. His wife is still present, sometimes achingly so, he says. He longs for those times when they can reconnect, albeit briefly. He laments for what might have been, for the wonderful retirement that they dreamed about and saved for, for being grandparents. Yet "we are still grandparents together," he says, confused.

Does Allan still "know" his wife? She is much the same physically, but she carries herself differently than she did even six months before. He can no longer predict how she will react at dinner with the family, or even in response just to him. What does he still know of her, he wonders? This heightens his dilemma. He is legally married to her, but which "her"? If they no longer know each other as they used to, is it so bad for him to have another relationship? He justifies his new love interest this way.

As we explore his history, it becomes clear that there is unexpected repetition in the story. Allan remarks that he visits his wife daily at 6pm. I ask if there is particular significance to that time. He suddenly remembers that his father visited his mother around the same time. She was diagnosed with Alzheimer's near the time he was marrying Sandra, and died 7 years after diagnosis. His father was attentive to his mother but began a relationship with a new partner a few years before her death. Allan was outraged that his father was making a relationship with another woman while still married. He saw no nuances in those days, he admits. Allan maintained his outrage until his father's death, remaining loyal to his mother's memory. He now finds himself in the position his father was in when his mother was put into a care facility.

His present conflicted state is complicated by his prior outrage, by the idea that he is no better than his disloyal father.

As we work together Allan begins to come to terms with the lost loyalty to his mother that kept him tethered to an old idea of himself. His loyalty to his wife is now freely given. "She isn't who she used to be, but she's still mine," he notes. He has come to forgive his father. In so doing, he can forgive himself. In forgiving himself, Allan can mourn more fully what he has lost. What "might have been" can be acknowledged *and* left behind in the face of the new reality.

Allan describes a situation with his wife near the end of our work: he wants to take her to his granddaughter's seventh birthday party. A highly accomplished woman, Sandra was previously always very mindful of her appearance. Allan booked an appointment at her hairdresser. He has gentleness in his eyes as he recounts this. I find myself tearing at this kindness. "It is who she was. She would have hated not looking her best," he says. I wonder if my tears are for myself, Sandra, my daughter, or for him. It is his allegiance to Sandra's former self with which I am struck–his paying homage to who she is, who she was, and who she might have been, even if the present Sandra is so altered from the wife he knew and loved.

In the end, we are left with the paradox of knowing *and* not knowing the other. Since the unconscious is timeless, we must remember that the past will always be with us. "Actual time ... does not pass, which is why events and people apparently bygone, are still actively intervening" (Scarfone, 2016, p.514). At the same time, our idealized view of the person as we knew them complicates our knowing in the present. Past pleasures are remembered fondly, while present difficulties are highlighted in comparison. The illusion of knowing points to the paradox within which we cannot know the altered other without holding on to our previous experience of them, yet if we hold on too tightly to our previous experience, we cannot fully know the present, altered person. This is the tension we learn to live with. Emotional situations and the attendant strong feelings of love and hate, loss and regret can threaten to destroy our basic curiosity to know the person. It is incumbent upon us to know the present as we walk with the past. A holding attitude in the interest of knowing the other is the best we can do.

Death and psychic loss take from us not only some particular life within the world but also someone through whom the world opened up to us in a unique way. If we keep the notion of "knowing the other" supple and open-ended, we can think of knowing as an ongoing process, even as it is susceptible to biopsychosocial insult. "Knowing" is not a fixed state. Rather, "knowing" another is a complicated psychic function that includes not only the "realistic" aspects of the other as we perceive them now, but also the unconscious ongoing knowing of the other as we have always known them. Overwhelming brain change forces a paradigm shift in relatedness. To "know" an altered other is to allow for changes in our internal self and object relations so that we might know them more fully as they *were* to us, as they currently *are* to us and also, importantly, what they *might have been* for us.

References

Bion, W. (1962). *Learning from Experience*. London: Karnac Books.

Bunuel, L. (1984). *My Last Sigh*. London: Jonathan Cape.

Damasio, A. (1999). *The Feeling of What Happens: Body and Emotion in the Making of Consciousness*. New York: Harcourt Brace.

Faulkner, W. (1951). *Requiem for a Nun*. New York: Random House.

Fisher, J.V. (2006). The emotional experience of K. *International Journal of Psychoanalysis*, 87: 1221–1237.

Freud, S. (1915). On transience. *The Standard Edition of the Complete Psychological Works of Sigmund Freud*, 14: 305–308.

Freud, S. (1917). Mourning and Melancholia. *The Standard Edition of the Complete Psychological Works of Sigmund Freud*, 14: 237–258.

Ghosh, R., & Kleinberg, E. (eds.) (2013). *Presence: Philosophy, History and Cultural Theory for the 21st Century*. Ithaca, NY and London: Cornell University Press.

Green, A. (1986) *On Private Madness*, pp. 142–173. London: Hogarth Press.

Khayyam, O. (1859). *The Rubaiyat of Omar Khayyam*. Translated by E. Fitzgerald (first edition). London and Glasgow: Collins.

Klein, M. (1935). A contribution to the psychogenesis of manic-depressive states. *International Journal of Psychoanalysis*, 16: 145–174.

Klein, M., (1948). A contribution to the theory of anxiety and guilt. *International Journal of Psychoanalysis*, 29: 114–123.

Korff-Sausse, S. (2017). The psychoanalytical approach to disability. In S. Korff-Sausse & R. Scelles (eds.), *The Clinic of Disability*, pp. 83–105. London: Karnac Books.

Racker, H. (1957). The meanings and usage of countertransference. *Psychoanalytic Quarterly*, 26: 303–357.

Reik, T. (1948). *Listening With the Third Year: The Inner Experience of a Psychoanalyst*. New York: Farrar, Straus, & Giroux.

Scarfone, D. (2016). The time before us (The unpast in W.S. Merwin, W. Benjamin, and V. Woolf). *Psychoanalytic Dialogues*, 26(5): 513–520.

Volkan, V.D. (1981). *Linking Objects and Linking Phenomena: A Study of the Forms, Symptoms, Metapsychology, and Therapy of Complicated Mourning*. New York: International Universities Press.

White, J.G., & Flax, M. (2014). Failure of the body: Perseverance of the spirit. In B. Willock, R.C. Curtis, & L.C. Bohm (eds.), *Understanding and Coping with Failure: Psychoanalytic Perspectives*, pp. 164–171. London and New York: Routledge.

Woolf, V. (1975). *Orlando*. Harmondsworth: Penguin.

Chapter 20

The unrecognized analyst

Jeffrey Sacks

Introduction

In the oedipal myth, the reward of the riddle knower or seer is the Kingdom, but a blind knower, another seer, offers insight to observers of which the unknowing King is deprived. This literature-influenced model offers us two "blind" figures, one tragic, the other wise. Freud's pioneering exploration of this myth offered our field an opposition between seeing, knowing, or recognizing versus blindness, not knowing, or misrecognizing, the Oedipus complex. This opposition of knowing and unknowing forms an early cornerstone of the psychoanalytic world.

Within that paradigm, psychoanalytic theory of psychopathology is often concerned with complex mental states of not knowing and misrecognition. The amnesiac does not know her own history. The hysteric misrecognizes her body. Traumatized subjects, in their dissociation, do not see internal reality and misrecognize external actuality.

In the ever-changing therapeutic arena, focus shifts from misrecognition and not knowing to recognition and knowing. The knower/helper's recognition facilitates healing for the unknowing patient. This intersubjective process of seeing and healing is based upon a therapeutic alliance, an interdependent process involving mutual recognition. Transient utopian intersubjective visibility is embedded within the recognition/misrecognition process between two unique others. Contemporary clinical praxis' evolves from the tragedy of blindness and misrecognition to the relief of seeing recognition.

Combining elements of literature, philosophy and psychoanalysis can enrich the therapeutic alliance. The resulting hermeneutic model embraces unknowable, never-ending meaning. It offers an interaction between lightness and dark, seeing and blindness, recognition and misrecognition. This dialectic suggests the possibility of an unknown creative synthesis, offering blindness as a paradoxical type of vision or wisdom.

Contemporary psychoanalytic treatment offers opportunities for healing moments of transient mutual recognition embedded in even more bewildering states of recognition and misrecognition of self to self and self to the other—bewildering in the sense that blindness or obliteration may represent interpersonal recognition as well as misrecognition.

Transient moments of mutual recognition between patient and analyst can be thought of as an ideal space where the dyad collaborates in the exploration of complex, dissonance-burdened intersubjectivity. Clinical theory has developed toward collaborative exploration of moments of misrecognition based on a therapeutic platform of transference and defense. No longer is the clinical world embedded in opposition-bound blindness versus seeing. Clinical work moves towards a new, hopeful, unknown synthesis and liberation.

What transpires within the healing mutual and self-recognition processes when a patient dissociates, completely failing to recognize the analyst? What transpires when linguistic metaphors move into actuality? In this chapter I will discuss the interplay between recognition and misrecognition in the context of a patient who ceased to recognize (or negated) her therapist. This period of non-recognition challenged the therapeutic dyad yet, paradoxically, served as a bridge to unknown or unrecognized experiences essential for the healing process.

This case suggests that dramatic blindness toward another can open the psychic space to renewed recognition of oneself. This recognition/nonrecognition interaction between self and another, as well as self to self, suggests blendings between vision and blindness (like the Oedipus myth) and self-development and the relationship with the other. Moments of nonrecognition might be viewed as both tragic and hopeful.

This unusual clinical experience stimulates many challenging questions related to philosopher Paul Ricoeur's orienting concepts of mutual recognition, vulnerability, and gratitude. Transient utopian healing moments of mutual recognition float in a sea of inevitable misrecognition. These shifts in invisible currents precipitate vulnerability and helplessness within in the other dependent clinician. Ironically, vulnerability (a type of blindness or helplessness) can be thought of as the new, hopeful state for contemporary clinicians.

Ricoeur's interdisciplinary platform blends philosophy, literature and psychoanalysis. Emphasizing mutual recognition, misrecognition, and vulnerability, it helps illustrate the nearly impossible necessity for some patients to allow themselves to both know and be known by a helping other. Under these circumstances the clinician is challenged by a contradictory mirror image of absence and inevitable vulnerability.

This clinical example of enhanced potential self-recognition in the presence of other non-recognition offers a new possibility of hope within the clinical situation, in spite of the clinician's unknowing helplessness and vulnerability—hope in a sense that blindness offers a type of vision. The bewildering duality of recognition and misrecognition are helplessly encountered, lost, and regained in the relationship between patient and analyst. The embrace of this unfamiliar situation moves clinical theory and the clinician towards acceptance of the state of unknowing vulnerability.

Gratitude, itself a paradoxical state of tolerating and enduring this vulnerability, is another Ricoeurian articulation of a new orientation embedded within contemporary analytic work. Acceptance of the role of vulnerable participant alters the knowing vision of the helper and shifts the core therapeutic alliance toward one of mutual recognition.

Ironically, the capable person within the intersubjective area now is a vulnerable one. Agency, even for the clinician, is now a two-party process. Healing and development are also conceptualized as two-party processes. For Ricoeur, we are alive as one, but need another to be truly human. We are all dependent on another to be human and to make sense of our lives. We need partners in our search for agency, affirmation, and mutual recognition, but reside in a world of dissonance, misrecognition, and vulnerability.

When misrecognition has dominated the self, the other is seen through the eyes of misrecognition, violence, and annihilation. In other words, not seen. This state that I call primary misrecognition and its misguided attempts towards affirmation, affects the self as well as the other, leaving clinicians and patients challenged and at times overwhelmed.

"Negative hallucination ... the reverse side of hallucinatory wish fulfillment ... [is] indispensible to the constitution of psychic space (p. 13) [and] is a disinvestment ... so as to be able to encounter oneself at the price of murdering the other person" (André Green, 1999, p. 185).How to proceed during this challenging but essential phase of misrecognition or obliteration will be explored through this clinical vignette.

Clinical

Nancy, a long-term patient with a history of self-mutilation and dissociative states, misses her appointment, without calling. This was very unusual. She has struggled with changes in my schedule in the past with despair and rage. She feels her appointment time is literally her time that needs to be maintained as an anchor, even a body part. I waited awhile, then texted her. She responded, "You must have the wrong number." She had no knowledge of me, our appointment, or any previous sessions. "Who am I?" she asks. I gently responded with some information about her life, our work, and her suffering. She desperately calls her husband for confirmation of my existence.

She agrees to come to her next session if I tell her where and when it is. She reports being unaware of my office address that she has been visiting for many years.

In the past, Nancy has experienced intense longing for relief and death. Now the analyst and suffering patient dyad were obliterated, psychically absent or dead. As I pondered the experience, considering how her attacks on her body had been attempts to resurrect something dead inside, I wondered if my own disappearance from her psychic landscape was her attempt to "privilege" me, and protect or resurrect me back to life.

I was bewildered and curious. Considering her affiliation with death and mutilation, I felt both "privileged" and uneasy about this new terrain of obliteration. What had I done to provoke my/our obliteration? What misrecognition could have activated this assault? Was it an assault by me that she experienced? Was the obliteration of me an obliteration of her, the patient I was working with?

How could I continue our work? Had Nancy left the process due to being unable to tolerate the connection, the recognition in the midst of potential separation and loss? I was gone, but in reality I was the same as ever, sitting in my office thinking about a patient, aware of her history. She destroyed me in her mind and in doing so destroyed her own past. The link between past and present, history and identity, had been severed.

Nancy had begun to own her feelings of connection to the work. Suddenly the gradual realization that her youthful life at home must have been one of violence and neglect was gone. The absenting of the injured self who could see her family in the morning, after a night of some physical torment, without agony, that suffering self was annihilated in her amnesia of me and our work together. Her new knowing narrative and my existence were gone.

Previously we had speculated about her suffering self through the reconstruction of memories of physical abuse by her older brother. Now that horror was lost. A threatened loss, a new type of assault, a new bit of neglect and abandonment, surfaced. This new challenge overwhelmed both her narrative history and the patient/helper dyad. Her husband's considering a position in another city was overwhelming to the ongoing treatment. I wondered if she felt I was killing her by not moving with her, not protecting her from the literal disconnection.

In reaction to these complex currents, Nancy lost her memory of our work together. I was gone, but she felt neither mourning nor loss. Rather, I simply never was. I knew nothing about her. There was no loss, nothing to mourn. Our connection, our mutual recognition, never occurred. Like a trick in a magician's routine, the audience is bewildered, amused, and disturbed. What had I seen? Did the elephant truly disappear? Did I really no longer exist for Nancy?

As we talked about the possibility of Nancy relocating to another city, I recalled how frequently she accused me of wanting to be rid of her and her agonies. Now on the verge of that wished/feared fantasy, she obliterated our work and me. She moved from mutilating herself to mutilating our relationship and obliterating me. Somehow she took the decisive step of deleting our work and my imprint on her mind.

Gradually I realized the opportunity to vanish was a bridge to her suffering, a chance to be present in my absence. I accepted this negation as a privileged affirmation. Hopefully I thought this non-recognition was embedded in a blend of recognition, meeting of self and other, and opportunity for moments of renewed mutual recognition.

Of course I was uneasy, unsteady, and uncertain in this dramatic territory. I had to accept that I was experienced as a poetic figure, an unrecognized helper. I had moments of relief when remembering Nancy's frequent accusations of my human fallibilities. In spite of her desperate demands that I be perfect, I was helpless and vulnerable. I surrendered to the bewildering experience of obliteration with faith in our work and hope in the affirmation of the negation. I would recognize her without reciprocity. I had no choice. I was learning about gratitude.

Nancy returned to treatment at her husband's urging, still unaware of her analyst's existence. The "new" patient tested my knowledge of her life. I shared what I knew about her as a person who had suffered overwhelming, recurrent childhood trauma. I shared my thought that her work as an obliterator of her abuse at breakfast as a child was in the name of maintaining and protecting her childhood family. Her self-deception was her "cure" as a child. Now she needed that "cure" of her loss of the treatment—obliterating me and her pain.

Self-deception is a magical cure for the experience of the horrific, a temporary relief that causes the myriad pathologies associated with trauma. It seemed up to me to continue our meetings in spite of Nancy's timid suggestion that all her painful memories might now be gone. During this phase, she recalled a new childhood horror in which an ambulance was called and a hospital visit occurred. She had been abused to the point of needing hospitalization. This had never been spoken of, or thought about, until now. Through the fog of dissociation she asked, "How could that happen? How could a trip to the hospital be lost by the entire family?"

Nancy's dissociation of me offered me a privileged seat at her childhood family breakfast table. Despite frustration, I tried to experience the amnesia with gratitude as a new opportunity. I felt grateful that she had metaphorically killed me. I strove to live inside the metaphor, walking across a bridge that did not exist, feeling comfortable that more would develop. I was hopeful and learning about delay and/or postponement as a form of affirmation.

As Nancy cautiously resurrected my existence, she became in danger of losing her own. She called after a session asking for help in getting home. She could not remember her address. She was not hopeful or grateful, but I continued to be. I recognized her by sharing information I knew about her life and her address. I talked about her children and some recent worries about them, their caretaker, their school, her job and husband. I guided her home. We agreed to talk on the phone for her next session.

Gradually, Nancy was reconstructing me—my phone number, age, face, fragments of my life that I had shared, my children, my wife's death. She was recognizing me, affirming my existence, in spite of a long held belief that I disliked her and would be glad to be rid of her and her troubles.

In developing her image of me, Nancy allowed herself to redevelop parts of herself, filling in the past with a new eye to new memories. She recalled several episodes of forced near drowning inflicted on her by her older sibling. I thought of waterboarding and was horrified. How could she keep that a secret, and why? Had she truly been unaware of these faux drownings, faux deaths? Resurrected me observed her connection or reconnection to the ambulance trip to the hospital after the faux drowning got too real.

I tried to imagine Nancy's life with her family and wondered what prevented her from asking for help. I began to see her as a protector of her brother and his envious rage. She was protecting her parents from knowing the unknown. In some sense she knew about negation as an affirmation. In her internal drama, she was the hero, the protector, the invincible one, and now so was I.

I had survived not a destructive force in the struggle for recognition, but a type of obliteration or drowning. Now I knew more about her. Perhaps we could continue working toward healing mutual recognition. This recognition turned out to be both more and less mutual than I bargained for.

The resurrected clinician realized that, later in life, Nancy injured herself when overwhelmed by life's challenges. Negation, injury, and invincibility was her model, surely not fallible man and certainly not gratitude. Death was her metaphoric solution. Real death was her psychic hope. This negation of her life—her death and mine—was her blended solution to bewildering paradoxical life events.

How to help her evolve and tolerate life with its inevitable vulnerability? At least I was back and we had learned much about her past. What would help reconfigure that past? How to evolve from invincibility to vulnerability? How to explore our mutuality? Perhaps our mutual recognition could be organized around our mutual obliteration.

The first moment I shared my existence with Nancy on the phone, she seemed terrified or perhaps horrified that she did not recognize someone claiming to be her analyst. Now she was recognizing me. I was a privileged member of the unknown known. A place that I had read about, thought about, yet never truly experienced as dramatically. Looking back, I was frightened as well. What were the rules in this place? This was vulnerability that I claimed to know about, but obliteration is not easily embraced. This case points to the complex demands on the new capable clinician as vulnerable. Accepting the absence, yet continuing to recognize the other and her narrative, is an unfamiliar, bewildering state.

Conclusion

This case provokes many challenging questions, some familiar, many not. Familiar ones such as, "Why now?" can be addressed. Nancy was massively anxious both at the looming separation from me as well as remembering her unbearable, dissociated childhood abuse. She called upon a familiar mental mechanism: obliteration of the traumatizing object, in this case me. I was leaving her.

Nancy believed I, like her brother, wanted her metaphorically dead. I, like he, would be relieved by her absence. In this familiar state of stress and death, she called upon a familiar process. This process of continuity (separation and loss) brought her to a familiar state of discontinuity and obliteration of challenging events. She could partially exist in a world of loss and aggression, but only on her own.

I was a transference object: the murdering (separating) brother. Ironically, obliteration offered her a type of peace at the family breakfast table. No disturbing events, no family disruption. She was the hero of continuity and stability through discontinuity. In her current life, attachment to her therapist and its threatened loss was the new trauma. Again, obliteration was an elegant solution. She would leave treatment as if it had never occurred.

This brings us to the unfamiliar: how to proceed when the patient, after a period of recognition and relating, calls upon the inevitable nonrecognition? The unfamiliar in this case is the opportunity to embrace the metaphoric assault and death with gratitude and without knowing interpretation. To speak or know seems desperate and false within her current or recurrent drama. I accepted the obliteration with unfamiliar gratitude.

I accepted her metaphor as a gift. I was metaphorically within her family in which recognition of attachment comes with dangers of betrayal, loss, and inevitable misrecognition. Paradoxically, this metaphoric recognition contains elements of misrecognition as well. With my acceptance and gratitude of my obliteration, I retained the WE, the paradoxically imperfect, therapeutic, mutual recognition.

Perhaps I was her mother/brother in the sense that we had formed a working relationship and shared life's currents. I was her mother in the sense of loss and absence of the upcoming separation. I was her brother in the sense that I would be relieved if her frequent suicidality was gone. I would be relieved if her agitated state when I needed to change my schedule was gone. Obviously I also was not her brother/mother or the hateful object. My respect for her struggle, intelligence, and other strengths and talents was obliterated. She was alone without me. This aloneness was the continuity of her obliterating mentation.

This complex state of mind or analytic attitude was offered to me through reading Ricoeur. His "The Course of Recognition" (2005) ends with a cautionary note: "when praise of mutual recognition leads us to forget the originary asymmetry in the relation between the self and others, which even the experience of peaceful states does not abolish. Forgetting this asymmetry would constitute the ultimate misrecognition at the very heart of actual experience of recognition" (p. 261). As his warning suggests, I had felt surprised at my obliteration. His caution helped me accept the helplessness of this situation.

Passivity for the helping clinician seems unfamiliar and paradoxical, yet essential for this challenging situation. My tolerance of my helplessness ironically offered a road into Nancy's life.

Nancy was dependent on her parents' recognition of her abuse, but no recognition came. Misrecognition of the facts was the organizing principle of this family's stability. In treatment, our stability was dependent on the opposite: Nancy's recognition of me as her ally, not her murderous rival or abandoning mother.

The concept of gratitude offers on unfamiliar state of acceptance, even embrace of helplessness. I offered my existence by continuing to meet and reminding Nancy of our work. My ongoing recognition of her and us as well as me offered a platform of recognition in spite of the misrecognition.

As we returned to the mutuality of our work, Nancy remembered her own sense of self during her delivery of her child. Recently when she was emotionally paralyzed and unable to prepare herself for a medical procedure, I helplessly asked, "What can I do to help"? She shared at the next session the power of her realization that I could not help her do the preparation. She was alone with herself and knew that fact, perhaps for the first time. Somehow that realization was disturbing as well as empowering. There was no need to struggle with me for recognition. She recognized herself. She focused on her doing, her existence, and her action. She later shared her thoughts about the doing: "I tried to get myself to childbirth. No turning back. Just do it." A birth, indeed, of a stronger budding self, as well as a birth of the other.

This budding self was a moment of self-recognition. It grew out of our mutual recognition as well as her nonrecognition. Nancy would "survive" her medical procedure as I had survived her anesthetization of my existence inside her self. This clinical experience of negation was a privileged affirmation for both of us.

For Ricoeur, the course of recognition is the "passage from mastering meaning, to self-recognition, and onto mutual recognition where we place ourselves under the tutelage of a relationship of reciprocity ... that modulates one's ability to act, one's agency" (2005, p.248). This recognition implies "the dialogical constitution of the self" (2000, p.xiii) and the dyadic development of agency.

I hope you will be left: wondering how visible or invisible you are in each clinical setting; pondering this odd state of gratitude and nonrecognition; reflecting on clarifying the impediments to mutual recognition as the therapeutic process and the therapeutic action—the new praxis for contemporary psychoanalysis.

References

Green, A. (1999). *The Work of the Negative*. London: Free Association Books.
Ricœur, P. (2000). *The Just*. Chicago, IL: University of Chicago Press.
Ricœur, P. (2005). *The Course of Recognition*. Cambridge, MA: Harvard University Press.

Concluding thoughts

Ionas Sapountzis

The twenty chapters in this volume all dealt with different aspects of knowing and not knowing. They explored issues related to social events, cultural trends, and the knowing patients and therapists can create in the course of treatment. Authors examined the knowing therapists can themselves gain as they reflect on the experiences of their clients and on the conflicts and complications that have emerged in the virtual realities created by recent technological advances that have altered the way individuals access the world and connect with others. Other contributors focused on uncanny or unspoken knowing, the kind of knowledge patients and therapists can intuitively reach about each other that points to a level of identification and even a level of attunement of which they are often unaware. Present in all contributions was a recognition of the courage that is required in the search to know, and the faith one needs to have in what can emerge and what can be found.

The wide variety of topics addressed attest to how infinite and ongoing the effort to make sense of emotions and experiences is, and how our level of awareness shifts and expands as we face different issues in our work and in our private lives. This incessant search for meaning is particularly felt in therapeutic work as we delve into many different, yet interrelated spheres of knowing, from the personal and interpersonal to the contextual and cultural. What makes the task of knowing more difficult and uncertain is that we are not seeking factual knowledge, the kind sought in natural sciences that contributes to a preexisting fund of knowledge and relies on an understanding of what is known and what remains unknown. The knowledge we seek with our patients is more fluid, transient, context-bound, tied to realities and dynamics we cannot foresee that often influence how we perceive events and respond to others. Adding to the complexity and fluidity of our task is the fact that our knowledge and our capacity to tolerate and make sense are not simply elements that steadily increase as we come to know more over the years and accumulate experiences. Instead, they are subject to changes and shifts as we and the world around us change, and what was is no more and what we could not imagine as possible before is now present and has altered the way we experience ourselves and others. In other words, our knowledge, however incomplete or partial, is always unfolding and shifting, sometimes making a mockery out of what we thought we knew a little while ago and had little reason to question.

The transient and context-based nature of knowing has long been recognized and acknowledged in the field of psychoanalysis. Different theories that have been proposed over the years and have been the subjects of heated arguments, point not only to different sensitivities and ways of conceptualizing clinical phenomena, but also to different foci that more often than not are associated with different eras and worldviews. The transient nature of what we know is also evident in how analysts experience their role in treatment. Unlike earlier analytic eras that were characterized by asymmetrical, rather hierarchical relations and by a more authoritarian, therapist-based kind of knowing, an increasing number of analysts today are mindful and more tolerant of different perspectives and points of view. Psychoanalysts once had an unshakeable belief in what the work could uncover. Today they hold a more temperate view as they have come to realize the limitations of what can be known, and the extent to which what is shared in the course of treatment and what becomes available for exploration and understanding— Bion's (1962) selected facts—are determined by what patients can tolerate and are willing to share. Adding to the growing skepticism in our field is the increasing realization that developments in science and technology that have increased opportunities for access and communication have failed to lessen the passions and primitive emotions that influence how individuals respond to others and how receptive they are to what a treatment can offer to them.

Like the protagonists in Saramago's (1997) novel, *The Blindness*, who came to realize how ignorant and blind they had been in their lives, we have come to realize over the years how ignorant or—better—how constricting we can be when we insist on specific theories and are dismissive of other possibilities and points of view. Contrary to what we had initially believed, the metapsychological theories we have relied on to understand our patients and formulate treatment hypotheses reflect, as Levenson (1988) argued, not so much the soundness or veracity of the ideas that are formulated by these theoretical models as the influence of former supervisors and mentors and the formative role they have had in the way we practice.

Levenson's observation points to how linked our understanding is to the presence of colleagues, mentors, parental figures, and others whose voices and perspectives have shaped the way we think and experience ourselves. One can see that even in Saramago's dystopian tale. The awareness the main characters reach over the course of their ordeal would not have been possible without the support and anchoring they experienced from each other. This raises a very simple but crucial question: Can we ever know without the other? Or, to put it differently, is there a knowledge that is independent of the other? Perhaps, one can argue, this is the case when one is engaged in understanding phenomena in physics, chemistry, geology, and mathematics. But even in these areas one can discern, if one looks for it, the shadow of the other, the encouraging, approving, often facilitating gaze of a parent, spouse, or mentor.

In our field, we have been aware for quite some time of how intertwined our knowledge is with what our patients evoke in us and sometimes make possible for us. Therapy is an interpersonal event and, therefore, that which emerges and becomes known is never exclusively an aspect of the patient's or analyst's experience but something created in the interaction between them in the confluence of past histories and current expectations. Of course one can argue that therapy is a deeply personal event, one that is experienced at a deeply personal level. After all, our sense of "I," the understanding we reach and the knowledge we develop about ourselves, is an experience that involves the singular and unique. But it is a singular and unique experience that emerges in the context of subject-object dualisms and is made possible by the presence and influence of the other. However personal and seemingly disconnected from the input of the other the knowing we reach may feel, the fact is that what we come to know is created in the context of our interaction with the other. This of course applies to both patients and analysts. As one can find in every chapter in this volume, the knowledge we reach with our patients does not leave us unchanged. The perspectives that are realized in every treatment and the different realities that are identified and explored change not only our patients' understanding of themselves and of their relationships, but also our own experiences as therapists and fellow participants in the treatment.

Perhaps more unsettling than the influence others have on what we come to understand and know is the realization of how limited the understanding we reach can be, how the theme of our life, as Grotstein (2000) observed, the essence of who we are, as Winnicott (1963) put it, and the essence of what is all around us, will remain somewhat unknown to us. A look at the political and social discourse of our times and the almost manic insistence on evidence-based practices, even though the reported evidence is incomplete and at best indicates how uncomfortable we are with these limitations, even though we like to think otherwise. Why is that? Why is the idea of not knowing so anxiety-provoking to many of us? One plausible hypothesis may be that if we accept the view that our knowledge is limited, we deprive ourselves of the certitude that comes from adhering to one model of thinking and the sense of safety that can be found in that. Another plausible answer may have to do with the difficulties we experience in tolerating our uncertainties, especially the idea that we go on in life without fully knowing ourselves and without having the level of knowledge we thought we had.

There is, however, something liberating in that view, in the realization that we cannot fully define ourselves and that our knowledge and what we come to know are forever unfolding. It is the liberation that comes from the realization that the knowledge we seek is not a finite entity but one that changes as the world around us changes and as we are presented with realities that have not been, until that moment, part of our reality. Our capacity to grow as analysts or laypeople depends not just on what we have come to understand and the knowledge base we have created, but also on our capacity to tolerate our doubts and the injury of not knowing. What we offer to our patients is not a fixed understanding of what happened and what is happening, what was and, therefore, what is, but our desire to listen, to take in and render meaningful what often is ineffable and unknown to them. Interestingly, in our quest to know the other and to understand his or her world, we find ourselves becoming more appreciative and understanding of other realities and possibilities and, surprisingly, more known to ourselves. If in every analysis there ought to be two frightened people in the room, as Bion (2014) famously stated, then there also ought to be two people transformed by the journey and what they come to know as a result.

An interesting paradox in the quest to know is the fact that the more one seeks to know and the more one knows, the more one realizes how little one knows. Referring to the vastness of what is to be known and the limitations of what can be known, Socrates reportedly said to his students that the only thing he knew with certainty was that he knew nothing. Socrates was not a cynic and not dismissive of the quest to know. But he was keenly aware of the multiple vistas that become apparent as one seeks to know and opens oneself to what can be found. Looking back, one can argue that, like Socrates, one fact we have come to know with certainty over the years, or better, one illusion we do not feel the need to hold onto, is that we can never offer or reach the kind of insight that would fully define a person. Although all analysts have many moments when a statement, an observation, and even an interpretation had a deep and palpably moving effect, the actual effect and the lasting impact of that statement or interpretation came not so much from the analyst's capacity to know the patient fully as from the ability to make the patient feel known and to value what the patient has been able to share. A skeptic may say that seeking to know is a futile effort because so much remains unknown. But the passion to know—the desire to know—is not an elusive quest to reach some finite knowledge, although many may aspire to just that. It is a search for something more personal and meaningful. Embedded in the quest to know is the desire to know and also the wish to become a better person, one who is more aware of him or herself and more present in the world.

This volume is the result of our continuous efforts to know and learn and the growth that comes from that desire. It is an endless quest that requires not just passionate curiosity about the nature of the elements around us, as Einstein reportedly said, but also passionate belief in the value of searching and the awe and sense of discovery that come from what we find and what we come to realize. This book, and the passionate discussions from which it arose, attests to the nature, value, productivity, and possibilities of that drive to know.

References

Bion, W.R. (1962). *Learning from Experience*. New York: Basic Books.

Bion, W.R. (2014). Brazilian Lectures. In W.R. Bion, C. Mawson, & F. Bion (eds.), *The Complete Works of W.R. Bion*, Volume VII. London: Karnac.

Grotstein, J.S. (2000). The ineffable nature of the dreamer. In J.S. Grotstein, *Who is the Dreamer Who Dreams the Dream? A Study of Psychic Presences*, pp. 1–36. Hillsdale, NJ: Analytic Press.

Levenson, E.A. (1988). Real frogs in imaginary gardens: Facts or fantasies in psychoanalysis. *Psychoanalytic Inquiry*, 8(4): 552–567.

Saramago, J. (1997). *The Blindness*. Orlando, FL: Harcourt.

Winnicott, D.W. (1963). Communicating and not communicating leading to a study of certain opposites. In D.W. Winnicott, *The Maturational Process and the Facilitating Environment*, 1965, pp. 179–192. Madison, CT: International Universities Press.

Subject index

adulthood, emerging 30, 38
AFCARS (Adoption and Foster Care Analysis and Reporting System) 144
aporia 201–202
ASRM (American Society for Reproductive Medicine) 145
association 40, 55, 182, 194; free 204

catfishing 8, 161–174
chaos 5, 15–16, 71, 74, 123; external 16; internal 16
consciousness 1, 8, 35, 38, 61–62, 76, 89–90, 96, 118, 122–123, 158, 163–164, 178, 180, 189, 201–202; superconsciousness 120, 122; universal 122
countertransference 7, 16, 65, 83, 96, 102, 104, 106–108, 110–111, 138–139, 142, 170, 185, 194–195, 206

dementia 192, 201, 203–206
depression 22, 28, 82, 103, 106
Depressive Position 44–46, 203
development 101–102
dissociation 33, 53, 56, 80, 102, 119, 190, 209, 213
dreams 2–4, 11, 15–21, 24, 27, 33, 35–36, 38, 42, 47, 59, 61, 75, 110, 202–203; life crisis 3, 22, 27

eating disorders 4, 51–57
ego 44, 102, 108, 123
emotion, central 16
environment 19, 81, 101–102, 107, 122, 146, 156

hermeneutics 92, 94

id 101, 108, 161
illuminations 110, 113, 115
immigration, invisible 9, 11, 142–153
implicit process 89, 96
impostor 161, 167, 168
inattention, selective 158
intelligence, contemplative 123
interpersonal 18, 76, 83, 102, 125, 148, 178, 184, 185, 210, 218, 220

loss 54, 57, 59, 65, 75, 83, 121, 138, 159, 166, 178, 190–192, 201–204, 206–207, 212–213, 215, 216; psychic 202, 207

meritocracy 134, 136

neuroscience 89, 91

Oedipal triangle 162, 164
Oedipus complex 149, 209

Paranoid-Schizoid Position 44
privatization 134
psychoanalysis 1, 9, 11–12, 15, 20–21, 24, 46–47, 57–59, 66, 79, 85, 96, 99–100, 108–109, 116, 126, 127, 133–134, 136, 142–143, 148–150, 153, 188, 193; analytic process 6, 17, 18, 21, 96, 121, 139, 193, 204; interpersonal theory 102, 153; psychoanalytic theories 90, 167, 169, 197; relational process 15; relational psychoanalytic model 125

224 Subject index

representation 19, 89, 102, 158
revelations 36

self 8, 15–16, 18, 20–21, 24, 28–30, 35, 45; false self 7, 101–102, 104, 106–108, 121, 127, 169, 170, 174; knowing 12–19, 21–22, 24–28, 32–33, 40–41, 44, 51–53, 57, 74, 89–92, 96, 110, 114–115, 118, 120, 122–123, 142, 147–148, 155, 157–159, 179–180, 189, 201–202, 204–205; self-conscious 161; self-defeating 3, 28, 32–33, 37, 38, 106; self-direction 28; self-esteem 51, 65, 171; self-examination 35; self-healing 37, 38; self-protection 8; self-states 7, 80, 84, 102, 118, 122, 124–125; self-systems 20; true self 24, 101, 104, 106–109

self-object 43, 45, 65, 92–95, 164
spiritual knowing 7, 117–119, 122–125
suicidality 95, 216
superego 102, 108
surrender 7, 11, 83, 118, 120–121, 123–125

therapeutic dyad 125, 210; analytic dyad 16, 89, 125, 204
Third, the 118, 208
transference 6, 210, 215; transferential blindness 287

unconscious 15, 17, 33, 35, 47, 56, 63, 67, 70, 101, 106, 156, 163, 169, 185–186, 192, 201–202; *see also* implicit process

Author index

Abend, S. 194–196
Akeret, R.U. 3, 11, 22–27
Alpert, J. 132
Altman, N. 134
Applegarth, L.A. 148
Arnett, J. 30, 32
Aron, L. 124, 134, 177
Arvan, M. 168

Bacal, H. 41, 90, 97–98
Bach, S. 171
Balint, M. 42, 45, 91
Becker, S. 170
Belk, R. 168, 170
Bennett, J. 31
Berger, R. 148
Berry, D. 6, 80–85
Bion, W.R. 41, 72, 77–78, 91–92, 123, 203, 221
Bleiberg, E. 1
Blos, P. 29, 35
Bohart, A. 37
Bollas, C. 18–19, 149
Borg, M.B. 6, 11, 80–85
Bourgeault, C. 123
Brekke, K. 165
Brenner, G.H. 6, 80–85
Brodzinsky, D. 144–146
Bromberg, P. 20, 54, 57, 84, 102, 124, 170, 197

Cahn, N. 146, 148
Carey, N. 147
Cerfolio, N.E. 7, 11, 117–127
Cohen, Y. 91

Cooper, A. 169
Crawshaw, M. 146
Cresci, M. 7, 11, 101–109
Curtis, R.C. 1–12
Cushman, P. 169

Damasio, A. 201
Daniluk, J.C. 144
Davies, J. 170
Davis, F. 59
Deraspe, S. 165
Dewald, P. 190–191
Deutsch, D. 168
Deutsch, H. 167, 168
Diez, C. 8, 12, 154–160
Dimen, M. 135
Doctors, S. 95
Donnelly, M. S. 166
Dosh, K. 163

Ekstein, R. 70
Ehrensaft, D. 149–150
Etchegoyen, H. 171
Evers, J.L.H. 148

Fairbairn, W.R.D. 18, 91
Faulkner, W. 202
Feast, J. 146
Ferenczi, S. 42, 91
Ferro, A. 75
Fink, B. 53
Fisher, A.P. 147
Fisher, J.V. 203
Flax, M. 10, 11, 201–208
Flock, E. 166

226 Author index

Fosshage, J. 20, 90, 91
Frankel, E. 125
Freud, S. 134–136, 142, 169, 193, 197
Freundlich, M. 146
Fromm, E. 22, 133, 169
Fulcher, M. 146

Gabbard, G. 91, 96
Gediman, H. 169
Geist, R. 92, 94, 98
Gentile, K. 147
Ghent, E. 120, 124
Ghosh, R. 202
Goldman, D. 170
Golombok, S. 146
Gosden, R. 146
Graybow, S. 134
Green, A. 46, 202, 211
Greenacre, P. 168
Grotstein, J.S. 220
Gurdon, J.B.G. 144
Gurtman, J.H. 188

Hammer, B. 9, 11, 177–186
Harari, Y.N. 168
Hard, A. 145
Hartley, D. 165
Hayashi, K. 144
Henig, R.M. 29, 30
Hertz, R. 148
Hewitt, M.A. 9, 12, 187–198
Hirsch, I. 102
Hoffman, I.Z. 108
Holan, A.D. 170
Hyman, S. 3, 11, 28–39
Hoppenwasser, K. 56
Howe, D. 146

Inhorn, M.C. 145
Isaksson, S. 148

Jarecki, A. 163, 164
Jones, S. 147
Jørstad, J. 64
Josephs-Sohan, M. 148
Juffer, F. 146
Jung, C.G. 125

Kaley, H. 7, 11, 110–116
Kaplan, D. 114, 167
Katz, A. 5, 11, 59–66
Keyes, R. 170
Khan, M. 44
Khayyam, O. 205
Kirk, H.D. 205
Klein, M. 201, 203
Knafo, D. 8, 11, 161–174
Kohut, H. 45, 91, 97, 98
Korff-Sausse, S. 202
Kramer, W. 145, 146, 148
Krimendahl, E.K. 73

Lacan, Jacques 47
LaFarge, L. 170
Laing, R.D. 197
Langs, R. 40, 44
Layton, L. 134
Lemma, A. 169, 170
Levenson, E.A. 16, 83, 115, 219
Livingstone, S.D. 169
Loewald, H. 91, 197

Malavé, A.F. 9, 11, 142–153
Malberg, N. 31
Mamo, L. 144
Marks-Tarlow, T. 90
Mayer, E.L. 123
McWilliams, N. 33, 106
Meissner, W.W. 190, 195, 196
Miller, T. 37, 145
Mitchell, S. 2, 17–18, 20, 144
Morrison, A.L. 154, 190–192

Nacht, S. 91
Nordqvist, P. 143, 146, 147, 148, 150
Norton, M. 132, 137
Novick, J. 91

Ogden, T. 92
Orange, D. 90
O'Leary, J. 7–8, 12, 131–141
O'Shaughnessy, E. 70, 171

Palacios. J. 144, 146, 147
Panksepp, J. 115

Paul, M. 148
Patterson, D. 170
Peralta, E. 166
Perlitz, D. 6, 11, 89–100
Petrucelli, J. 4, 11, 15, 51–58
Piketty, T. 132
Pizer, S. 188, 190
Phillips, A. 53
Plopa, P. 190

Quinodoz, D. 3, 75

Racker, H. 206
Reeves, R. 135–136
Renik, O. 171
Richards, A. 64, 134
Ricoeur, P. 10, 210–211, 216, 217
Rose, J. 148
Rosenbloom, S. 163
Rosner, S. 188–190
Rudder, C. 162
Ryan, J. 136

Sacks, J. 10–11, 209–217
Sapountzis, I. 1–12, 28, 69–79, 177, 218–222
Scarfone, D. 207
Scruton, R. 170
Searles, H. 60, 81, 177
Selman, P. 153
Shaw, D. 91
Siegel, D.H. 144
Slade, A. 31, 74

Slavin, J. 92
Spar, D. 147
Spock, B. 30–31
Stacey, J. 146
Stein, R. 171
Steiner, P. 72, 168
Steptoe, P.C. 145
Stern, D. 2, 149, 158
Stoller, R. 162
Strozier, C.B. 45
Sudol, K. 166
Sullivan, H. S. 80, 133, 150, 158
Sung, Y. 170

Tallman, K. 37
Tolpin, M. 92
Truckle, B. 71

Vaughn, S.C. 145
Volkan, V.D. 202
Volkman, T.A. 148

Watson, R.I 3, 11, 15–21
Weber, L. 165
White, J.G. 10, 11, 201–208
Willock, B. 4, 11, 40–47, 70, 74
Winnicott, D.W. 1, 5, 41, 47, 71, 72, 74, 77, 90, 101, 107–108, 121, 169, 220
Woolf, V. 204
Weston, W.A. 169

Zeman, N. 163

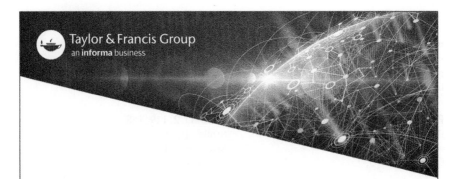